SHRM Prep 2023-2024

CP and SCP Study Guide + 536 Test Questions and Detailed Answer Explanations (4 Full-Length Exams)

Printed in the United States

Table of Contents

Chapter 1: Introduction 7

Chapter 2: Business Acumen and Communication in HR 9

Chapter 3: Consultation and Critical Evaluation 16

Chapter 4: Ethical Practice and Cultural Effectiveness 22

Chapter 5: Leadership 27

Chapter 6: Relationship Management 38

Chapter 7: Talent Acquisition 45

Chapter 8: Retention and Motivation 55

Chapter 9: HR Strategic Planning 61

Chapter 10: Structure of the HR Function 69

Chapter 11: Employee and Labor Relations 76

Chapter 12: Organizational Effectiveness and Development (OE&D) 84

Chapter 13: Technology Management 92

Chapter 14: Workforce Management 99

Chapter 15: Corporate Social Responsibility 106

Chapter 16: Diversity and Inclusion 113

Chapter 17: Conflict Resolution 120

Chapter 18: HR in the Global Context 128

Chapter 19: Risk Management 135

Chapter 20: Total Rewards **141**

SHRM-CP Test 1 .... **148**

SHRM-CP Test 1: Answers and Explanations **203**

SHRM-CP Test 2 .... **238**

SHRM-CP Test 2: Answers and Explanations **289**

SHRM-SCP Test 3 .... **325**

SHRM-SCP Test 3: Answers and Explanations **382**

SHRM-SCP Test 4 .... **420**

SHRM-SCP Test 4: Answers and Explanations **477**

Note:

A link to the downloadable materials is on the last page.

Chapter 1: Introduction

The Society of Human Resource Management (SHRM) is committed to bringing innovation to human resource (HR) management. The corporate landscape is constantly evolving. Therefore, to keep pace with the changing market trends and requirements, it is important to increase learning excellence.

The role of SHRM is to support HR partners all across the world by offering certifications. This society is responsible for developing programs and in-house courses to serve both public and private customers. It also makes various networks, products, and services available to members of SHRM forums.

For more than 70 years, SHRM has been providing practical tools to those who want to build a career in HR. This society aims to help HR practitioners better engage with the organizations they work for and make desirable outcomes a reality. It also helps HR professionals advance their careers by learning actively from the latest HR market trends. The two behavioral competency certificates produced by SHRM are the SHRM-CP and the SHRM-SCP.

SHRM-CP or SHRM-SCP Exam

Before pursuing the SHRM certification, you need to decide whether you want to apply for the SHRM-CP or the SHRM-SCP exam. You need to determine your eligibility before deciding which credential suits your capabilities best. To gauge your eligibility level, look at your formal education and the years of work experience you have in HR-related environments. Study the eligibility criteria section on the SHRM website for more information.

The SHRM-CP is the ideal certification for HR practitioners involved in operational roles, policy implementation, and development of staff contracts.

The SHRM-SCP certification, in contrast, is for those who want to take up senior-level roles. If you are going to take on strategic roles involving policy development, HR operation supervision, performance metrics analyses, and HR strategy alignment, this advanced-level certification is ideal for you.

International students should keep the policies and criteria of their home countries in mind when choosing either the SHRM-SCP or SHRM-CP exam.

The Society for Human Resource Management Exam

The Society for Human Resource Management Exam has been developed for HR professionals who have either started their careers already or want to pursue HR management. This exam caters to those individuals who want to study business. It provides students with a detailed overview of the functions involved in HR management. Passing this exam gives HR practitioners who are in the early stages of their careers an opportunity to become more knowledgeable about their chosen field. It also makes it easy for them to transition into their new roles.

Chapter 2: Business Acumen and Communication in HR

The success of an organization depends on its HR department, which is responsible for connecting the business with the right individuals and resolving problems employees face on a day-to-day basis. It is also responsible for creating an environment that motivates employees to perform their best.

However, times are changing, so the practices followed by HR departments must change with them. Today, HR departments need to evolve into something more than just reactive or transactional entities; they need to move on to developing, planning, and implementing the appropriate practices within a business. The key to success for any business is the development of business acumen.

What Does *Business Acumen* Mean?

Business acumen is the quickest way an organization decides to deal with a business situation to drive the best outcomes.

Business acumen requires:

- Knowledge of the most profitable aspects of the business
- Understanding of cash flow and the current market situation
- Thorough understanding of the respective business niche

The Significance of Business Acumen

The success of an organization depends on the specialist management skills possessed by management and its HR business partners. Having business acumen adds to the potential of the HR department and brings more value to the company.

Senior management looks for partners rather than employees when selecting HR professionals. With the help of business acumen, HR partners can reassure management that they can understand and deal with the challenges the business faces. Business acumen helps HR professionals demonstrate to managers that a company can create an environment that boosts productivity while keeping employees satisfied and treating them as fellow businesspersons.

A company's decision-making power improves when HR professionals are treated as business partners. They help a company with its big decisions—contributions that are deemed valuable beyond measure.

Today, every company needs a professional HR partner. A company's success depends on how well it treats not only its customers but its employees. By having an HR partner by its side, an organization can make better strategic decisions.

HR professionals are trained to augment a business with valuable and unique insights. Their role is to bridge the gap between senior management and the workforce, effectively communicating messages to employees.

Understanding the business to the core is very important for all HR professionals. This allows them to create long-term strategies that align with a business's goals and objectives. It also helps them hire the right people with relevant skills to bring rewarding outcomes for the business in the future.

Developing Business Acumen

Every business is different and requires strategies that align with its specific objectives. While developing business acumen, HR professionals should keep in mind the needs, environment, and challenges the business faces.

The following are some suggestions that help in the development of business acumen.

Understanding Finances

Developing business acumen requires HR professionals to be familiar with the financial standing of a business, including financial statements, cash flow, balance sheets, and more. They should also be able to read profit-and-loss statements and reports in order to make strategic decisions for the company. Information acquired from these statements should be used to make the decision-making process easier and more streamlined.

Getting Familiar with the Current Business Strategy

Understanding the current business strategy is important for developing business acumen in an organization. Doing this makes it easier for HR professionals to make strategic decisions that benefit both management and employees.

Understanding the Business Environment

To develop business acumen, HR professionals need to understand the business environment. The majority of established businesses periodically rotate managers to help the managers become familiar with all aspects of a business; however, that is not the case with start-ups or small-scale businesses.

HR professionals must understand finances, how a business operates, customers' expectations, and more.

HR professionals should be familiar with both the external and internal environments of a business. They should keep a close eye on the market by keeping up with news, social media, industry publications, and business competitors. Staying in touch with business leaders also helps HR professionals understand the external business environment.

Improving HR Communication

HR communication is defined as the way a business chooses to engage with its HR department. For an organization to succeed, it must bridge the communication gap between management and employees. Improving HR communication allows organizations to get more from their workforce.

Communication plays a crucial role in helping an organization thrive. The success of an organization depends on the satisfaction of its employees. Therefore, the role of the HR partner is to keep management and the workforce on the same page. The HR department serves as a communication channel between the two. Effective HR communication boosts employee morale and helps employees be more productive and committed to their jobs. Effective HR communication could be anything from training staff to providing them with necessary information about wages, salaries, benefits, company news, and more.

Relaying useful information to staff is crucial for success. However, ineffective communication can cause the bridge between leadership and employees to break. According to research, 74% of employees believe they do not have access to important company information, and around 72% of employees are not familiar with important company strategies that affect their day-to-day work lives.

Research has proven that employees work better when they are familiar with a company's objectives and strategies. It is the HR department's responsibility to create a strong communication loop between leadership and employees.

The HR department can improve communication in the following ways:

1. Effectively Plan Internal Communication

Improving communication requires the HR department to create long-term strategies. The focus of these strategies should be increasing productivity and improving communication within an organization. Before creating these strategies, you must figure out the gaps in the current plan. Once you have identified the areas that need improvement, you can figure out how to fix them.

Companies without a long-term strategy to manage internal communication lag behind their competition. It does not matter how big or small the organization is—having a long-term internal communication plan is crucial to survival.

You can create an effective internal communication strategy by following these steps:

- Understand the way your company operates. Learn what employees expect from management.
- Keep employees informed by setting clear and achievable goals. This step will improve engagement and make employees' roles more interesting for them.
- Put effective channels in place to streamline communication between leadership and the workforce. This could be anything from an intranet to apps for employee engagement.
- Carefully plan the extent to which information will be shared internally.

2. Implement an All-Inclusive Communication System

Having an all-in-one and secure HR platform is important for streamlining business operations. This platform should contain all the necessary information regarding the workforce, including important documents, salaries, contract details, employment history, personal information, and more.

An all-in-one HR platform can benefit both leadership and employees by making it convenient for all personnel to access important documents, such as forms, standard templates, and information on procedures, policies, etc.

3. Create an Environment That Encourages Face-to-Face Communication

A dispute within an organization cannot be resolved without face-to-face communication. Most organizations rely on emails for both internal and external communication. Personalizing an email takes time that most companies lack. In this case, the best option is to create the right environment that encourages face-to-face communication because facial expressions and tone of voice play an important role in communication.

Replacing emails with face-to-face communication is crucial for building trust within a company. To develop trust and confidence with employees, companies should switch from emails to video calls if face-to-face conversations are not possible. Verbal communication can improve the environment within a company; it creates a friendly environment for both the company and its employees to thrive in.

Integrating employee communication apps into the system improves a company's HR strategy and makes it more practical for employees to interact with a company's content.

4. Plan Your Strategies While Focusing on the Company's Culture

Having a common goal to achieve makes it easier for employees and leadership to communicate. A shared culture keeps both parties closely connected. An effective HR strategy aligns employees' goals with the company's goals. An HR professional needs to improve consistency and create a friendly work environment that boosts productivity.

5. Creating an Effective Plan to Welcome New Employees on Board

It always takes new employees some time to become familiar with a company's practices. It is the responsibility of HR professionals to help new employees take specific steps to become valuable assets to a company.

All new employees should be provided with the information they need to excel in their roles, tools that will make them more comfortable with the environment they have just entered, and the confidence to use their creativity to produce outstanding results for the organization.

New employees should always feel welcome in their new workspace. They should be made to feel comfortable enough to connect and interact with their team members from day one. A dedicated HR platform should have training programs in place to make it easier for new employees to adjust to their new office environment.

Chapter 3: Consultation and Critical Evaluation

Sometimes a company needs to outsource its HR management responsibilities to an external service provider. A hired individual or team of professionals handles HR and associated issues for the company, including client management and development, as well as contracts.

A vast majority of independent HR consultants look for smaller companies to work with. This provides independent HR consultants with an opportunity to form long-term relationships by effectively utilizing their skills to help these companies grow and become successful.

Various large organizations are now resorting to outsourcing HR services, which in turn creates an excellent opportunity for independent HR consultants to grow their careers.

How Does HR Consultation Work?

An independent HR consultant should possess the same characteristics a business owner possesses, including:

- Business management skills
- Ability to work independently
- Ability to manage the office, customers, and business finances
- Ability to market the business

Independent HR professionals can choose a specific area to practice in or offer a broader range of expertise. When outsourcing HR consultation, clients consider a person's background and experience.

What Do Clients Look for in an HR Consultant?

Potential clients want to hire professionals who have worked with several organizations. They want professionals who can boost productivity by fully utilizing the capabilities of the in-house staff. Companies look for experts who are neutral in their stance, as it is important to resolve issues within a company rather than exacerbating them.

The global market has evolved immensely over time. Patterns and practices that were relevant in the past are now deemed redundant. To excel in the market, HR professionals need to stay current with the latest market trends. The best way to do so is to work with professional organizations that keep employees informed about the changes in the market. Working in an organization allows HR professionals to learn from their colleagues through the exchange of ideas.

Another great way to stay aware of market trends is to read material available online. Being aware of which particular publications play a vital role in keeping professionals informed about what is happening in the market is a must.

Business Management

As mentioned earlier, independent HR consultants should possess some of the qualities of a business owner. They should be able to use their time effectively to improve business operations for their clients. To effectively manage a business, HR consultants must be adept in:

Choosing Areas of Expertise

This choice depends on HR consultants' personal preferences. They can choose whether they want to focus on a specialized aspect of HR services or offer all-inclusive HR services.

Market Segments to Target

HR consultants must be familiar with the different market segments that they need to target through their services. They should be comfortable working with the audience they have chosen to serve. Otherwise, they can work with a specific industry, region, and more.

Legal Aspects

If HR professionals want to create their own business, they should become familiar with the legal structure of HR companies. They must also be aware of the legal issues they might have to face as owners of a corporate entity.

Working Independently or with Teams

HR professionals must decide whether they want to work independently or with a team. This aspect depends upon the needs and types of specific clients that HR professionals plan on working with.

Numbers

Whether HR professionals work independently or as consultants for an organization, each option comes with its own expenses. When deciding to work as an HR consultant, an individual must be familiar with these expenses and have the budget to meet them.

Administrative Functions

Effective management is important for the success of a business. Administration handles matters such as tax collection, invoice management, and legal or financial issues.

Licensing Requirements

Before starting any business, HR professionals should become familiar with licensing requirements. When it comes to HR consultancy licensing, different states have different requirements. Before starting a consultancy in a specific area, the HR consultant should be familiar with the laws and regulations.

Potential Areas of Focus

Independent HR consultants can offer a wide range of expertise or focus on a specific niche. However, selecting a specific niche narrows down the competition and makes it easier to market the business. Niche-specific HR consultancy services attract a wider range of clients.

Apart from external HR services, independent HR service providers can also offer day-to-day assistance to businesses in need.

The Work Environment

You do not need a traditional office to work as an independent HR consultant; you can work from home. However, you need to learn to balance your personal and professional life. Working from home is a convenient and cost-effective way to start your consulting business.

Marketing Consultation Services

Before pursuing a consulting career, you should try to network and make as many contacts as possible. Word-of-mouth referrals are very effective.

Having a website is another great way to spread the word about your business. You can use the website as your online portfolio and refer your clients to it. You can use social media to attract interested clients and rely on referral partners to promote your business.

Documentation

Agreements and contracts should all be documented for future reference. They come in handy when the partners or people within the contract change or want to walk away.

An agreement should *always* include the following:

- Detailed services to be performed by the HR professional
- Deadline for the completion of services
- Fee charged by the HR consultant for services provided

The Purpose of Critical Evaluation

Critical evaluation is a great tool for HR professionals because it allows them to perform their regular HR-related roles easily and helps them evaluate wider topics deeply.

In the previous chapter, we learned how HR practitioners are required to develop and define a business's goals, values, and mission while effectively communicating these across the workforce. HR professionals should also develop and implement strategies that make it easier to align practices with business goals.

In the HR world, critical evaluation is considered a key player in developing and implementing consultative solutions.

Assessing the Bigger Picture

HR professionals should always assess the bigger picture before starting the process of critical evaluation. Critical evaluation allows HR practitioners to observe the pros and cons of each of the available options.

The critical evaluation process should start from scratch so that the HR professional can identify problems, ask the right questions, and answer them accordingly.

Approach to Problem-Solving

Critical evaluation increases HR professionals' confidence in their problem-solving approach, making decision-making easier.

Evaluating Decision Quality

Critical evaluations allow HR professionals to evaluate the quality of their decisions. To manage this, HR professionals should narrow down their choices and compare each choice with the other. They should assess which options work best for a company. They should also rule out any assumptions and biases that may be affecting their decisions.

Implementing a Critical Evaluation When Necessary

A critical evaluation does not have to be implemented in every situation. According to the experts, sometimes you have to be spontaneous to derive success from the available possibilities. Overcoming biases requires you to stay curious and accept different possibilities. You just need to collect the right data to make effective decisions.

However, do not overanalyze the situation. Set a deadline to find a solution to a problem. Divide your time into different slots. Set some time aside to evaluate the situation and make your decision accordingly.

Chapter 4: Ethical Practice and Cultural Effectiveness

What Is Ethical Practice?

Ethical practice describes the act of seamlessly integrating common moral values into everyday business practices. Everyday business practices include all activities from the top of the hierarchy to the bottom, such as recruitment practices, account managing, sales procedures, etc.

A firm that integrates ethical practices into all its business practices trains employees to weigh matters in the light of established moral principles. These decisions include interactions not just between employees and management but between customers and employees too. A firm can have a large impact on the environment; therefore, this must also be an aspect considered for ethical practice.

All sectors of a business are set on a sliding scale of good to bad. Employees in the managerial staff must be aware of the different outcomes of their actions and the various parties that certain decisions may affect.

Ethical practices have now become the cornerstone of every good business. For example, according to a recent report, "79 percent of American workers said they would not accept a job with a higher salary from a company that has failed to take action in sexual harassment cases."

A good business requires customers, of course. Today's general population has become much kinder and more empathetic. Consequently, it has become necessary for every firm to show who they empathize with. The outcome of this decision paints two contrasting images: one, a firm gets shot down when it does not announce its allegiance, and two, a firm becomes successful when it *does* announce its allegiance. It seems a better picture can be attained only through good ethical decision-making skills.

What Is Cultural Effectiveness?

Cultural effectiveness is the ability to value and consider the perspectives and backgrounds of all parties.

The Importance of Ethical Practice Through Cultural Effectiveness

Incorporating ethical practices into a business is indispensable because it is the right thing to do. The Institute of Business Ethics' research firmly supports this stance.

The benefits of this are manifold. Some of these are benefits listed below:

1. **Acceptance of All Cultures, Religions, and Beliefs:** Ethical practice calls for the acceptance of all cultures, beliefs, and religions under a firm's roof. This increases the efficiency of the firm by keeping up employee morale. The feeling of acceptance causes employees to become more loyal to the company.

2. **Better and More Successful Customer Interaction:** Customer interaction is an important aspect of business that incorporates ethical practice. If the sales department constantly espouses good and humble behavior when interacting with difficult customers, the outcome can only be positive.

3. **An Honest and Reliable Company Image:** When a firm follows rules and regulations, it shows that its practice is fair and trustworthy. This not only makes current investors loyal but also works as a marketing strategy to attract new investors.

4. **Environmental Protection:** Lastly, protecting the environment also falls under the term of ethical practice. A company that invests in eco-friendly projects is largely popular in today's market. This creates

traction not only in the customer pool, but also in the supplier pool. Companies that supply materials to their sellers are selective about the image of the receiver firm, which is why an eco-friendly image is always a good image.

Tips on Ethical Practice

Keep Records Confidential

The HR department is in charge of a firm's files. To be in line with ethical practices, the HR department must be discreet about the information it maintains. This information can include personnel records, salary slips, complaint files, etc.

Highlight Consequences of Actions

Employees should be aware of the penalty for any misconduct. Providing a platform for filing anonymous complaints is helpful.

Stay Up to Date with Rules and Regulations

To make an ethical decision, an individual needs to know company policies and any overarching laws regulating business behavior.

Be Selective About Managerial Positions

Recruiting agencies should look for candidates who are well qualified and have core values that are in line with a company's ethos. These qualities make such individuals into both leaders and mentors to their subordinates, starting the chain of ethical practice.

Highlight Diversity and Inclusion

Diversity and inclusion (explained in full later in this book) are important [illegible]pects of ethical business practices. All employees should feel equally [illegible]ed by the company they work for. Training programs and seminars are [illegible]l in this respect.

Tips on Cultural Effectiveness

Appreciating Differences

A workforce needs to be aware of the different cultures that are represented within an organization. Awareness is not enough; these differences need to be celebrated too. Celebrating such differences can have many lucrative effects. For example, when all employees feel included and appreciated, they work harder. Additionally, differences can be used to make collaborative efforts in the form of hybrid marketing. This is useful, as it allows a company to target a wider audience instead of just niche demographics.

Encouraging Personal Growth

Companies should set up workshops and training programs for employees to overcome shortcomings in any areas they personally require practice in (these can include qualities like humility and self-awareness).

Reducing the Generational Gap

Age should be only a number in the workplace. There should be targeted projects that allow the mixing of different generations in an office. This can lead to innovative ideas in all aspects of business and give equal importance to employees of all ages.

Assigning Cultural Educators

The role of a cultural educator is not a specialized role per se but can be assigned to anyone who has the right core values and an abundance of exposure to different cultures (a well-traveled person). This person can act as a mentor to subordinates and teach them skills required for interacting efficiently with different communities. This task is especially important when a team is engaged in an out-of-country project.

Encouraging Adaptability

Adaptability refers to the acceptance of change and the ability to work around it lucratively in business. The ethos of a firm should be adaptable not just in the larger decisions, but also in the everyday work between colleagues.

Chapter 5: Leadership

What Is Leadership?

In a group environment, leadership is generally characterized as a social (interpersonal) impact link between two or more people who rely on one other to achieve common goals. By focusing on the group's maintenance requirements (the need for people to be accepted and strive to work together) and task needs (the need for the team to manage advancement toward achieving the goal that led to the formation of the group), strong leadership helps individuals and organizations accomplish their goals.

The Emergence of a Leader

There are two types of leaders in organizations: formal and informal. A formal leader is a person who is acknowledged as the group's official leader by those outside the group. Frequently, the organization appoints the formal leader to act as an agent of the organization in a formal role. As part of their appointed position, almost all managers operate as formal leaders. Members of a group can also choose the person who will act as their team leader.

Informal leaders, on the other hand, are not chosen by an organization. Athletic teams frequently feature unofficial leaders—persons who have significant influence over team members despite not holding a recognized leadership position.

Almost every workgroup has at least one unofficial leader. Informal leaders, like formal ones, can help or hurt an organization based on whether or not their influence pushes members of the group to behave in accordance with the organization's aims.

Motivational Theories

1. Goal-Set Theory

According to goal-set theory, people will perform much better at work if they have demanding, defined, and agreed-upon performance goals or targets.

Goal-set theory's first and most basic tenet is that people try to achieve the objectives they set for themselves. People who have goals are more driven. Because they are personally invested, their motivation is more intense and they have a more focused approach.

The second fundamental principle of goal-set theory is that challenging goals produce greater results than easy goals. This is not to say that challenging goals are always accomplished, but people tend to do better when they set out to do something harder.

In addition to recognizing a goal, goal-set theory suggests that people must also adhere to that goal. The degree to which people devote themselves to achieving a goal is referred to as goal commitment. Setting priorities is an important part of goal commitment.

When people are permitted to engage in the goal-setting process, they are more likely to stick to their goals. This relates to the concept of ownership. People who participate in the process are more likely to include characteristics that they believe will make the goal more intriguing, challenging, and reachable. As a result, it is a good idea to include people in the goal-setting process. This is because when you impose goals on people from the outside, you usually get less commitment.

2. Expectancy Theory

Expectancy theory argues that people choose the more appealing goal when presented with two or more options. Furthermore, the more appealing the chosen alternative is, the more motivated people will be to pursue it. People are motivated to maximize desirable results (a boost in salary) while minimizing undesirable consequences (a pay cut).

According to expectancy theory, people are also rational in their decisions concerning alternatives. They choose the option with the highest benefits and the fewest drawbacks.

3. Attribution Theory

Attribution theory describes the cognitive process through which people perceive the reasons or causes for their actions. Attribution theory is defined as "the process by which a person perceives events as being generated by a specific component of a generally stable environment."

Attribution theory is primarily based on Fritz Heider's work. Heider claims that conduct is illustrated by a blend of internal (e.g., aptitude or effort) and external forces (e.g., task complexity or luck).

4. Self-Determination Theory

The goal of self-determination theory (SDT) explains not just what motivates people but also how extrinsic rewards influence intrinsic motivation. In SDT, extrinsic motivation refers to doing something for the sake of achieving the desired result, whereas intrinsic motivation refers to doing something for the sake of the activity itself.

When an activity is intrinsically motivating, SDT determines whether or not it is inherently motivating. Numerous studies have shown that jobs are inherently motivating when they meet at least one of the three higher-order needs: expertise, independence, or affiliation.

Situational Leadership

The qualities, attributes and talents required in a leader are dictated to a significant measure by the demands of the circumstances in which individuals are expected to perform as leaders. Two key leadership traits—initiating structure and considering others—do not always result in beneficial outcomes. There are instances when instituting structure leads to increased performance and happiness, while at other times, the opposite occurs.

It is widely acknowledged that a leader's success depends on a person's followers. If leaders teach their team the proper ways to deal with problems, the team will be more successful in the long term.

There is a time and a place for every type of leadership. Employees in the early stages of development are seen as being extremely committed yet less competent in tackling tasks. In this case, leaders should be more directive than encouraging.

As employees' competence grows, leaders should use additional coaching techniques. Once employees have reached a moderate to high degree of competence, helpful behaviors are indicated.

Finally, delegating is the best strategy for leaders dealing with highly devoted and very talented individuals.

Directing

Directing is the most fundamental level of leadership style in the Situational Leadership Theory model. This is a leader-driven stage. Almost all new employees require a more direct leadership style. With little or no experience in their new positions, these individuals are marked by poor competence and intense commitment, reluctance to cooperate, and potential feelings of discomfort during the formative stage.

As leaders, we must focus on tasks rather than an immediate report's relationship because that relationship does not exist yet.

Coaching

Coaching is for individuals who have enhanced their dedication as well as their competence. Individuals are not completely sure about their abilities yet, but they are improving.

Leaders must still concentrate on tasks, which can take a significant amount of time. But their attention can now shift to the growing relationship with employees, drawing on the trust that has already been established and the support that has been displayed. Again, leaders must devote significant time to listening and providing guidance to their followers.

The idea is to keep employees interested so they can move on to the next level.

Supporting

Supporting is for employees who have become proficient at their professions but are still inconsistent and not entirely dedicated. They have advanced to a higher level of competence but are still unsure of their abilities or are not entirely devoted to doing their best and excelling.

Leaders must encourage such individuals. While explicit directions or frequent follow-ups are no longer necessary, leaders must continue to check in to ensure that tasks are being completed to the required standards.

Delegating

Delegating is the end objective: to develop employees who feel fully energized and are capable of taking the ball and running with it with minimum monitoring. Such employees are extremely capable, dedicated, driven, and empowered.

As a leader, you may delegate duties to such trusted employees with minimum follow-up, confident that acceptable, if not great, results will be delivered on time. Although continuing praise for great achievements must be provided as necessary, there is no longer the need to applaud individuals for every completed assignment at this stage.

Leadership Path-Goal Theory

The expectation theory of motivation is the foundation of Robert House's path-goal theory of leadership. The expectation theory of motivation suggests that employees are driven when they believe that their efforts will result in a great outcome, their sincere efforts will be recognized, or the rewards they will receive will be useful to them. According to the path-goal theory of leadership, a leader's primary responsibility is to ensure that all three of these conditions are met.

As a result, leaders produce contented and high-performing employees by ensuring that employee efforts lead to satisfaction and performance is rewarded with the desired benefits.

There are four types of leadership styles.

1. Directive

Leaders that are directive give explicit instructions to their subordinates. They guide employees by explaining role requirements, establishing schedules, and ensuring that staff are aware of their responsibilities on any given workday. When employees face role obscurity on the job (meaning they are confused about their job descriptions and responsibilities), the path-goal theory suggests that the directive leadership style functions well.

If people are unsure how to accomplish their tasks, giving them explicit guidelines will encourage them to start working. On the other hand, giving employees direction is ineffective if they already know their roles and are performing monotonous, repetitive, and highly regimented tasks. In fact, it could harm them by fostering a more confining atmosphere.

2. Supportive

Employees receive emotional support from supportive bosses. These bosses treat their employees well, show that they care about them personally, and encourage them.

When employees are under a lot of stress or have to do monotonous, repetitive jobs, compassionate leadership is more effective. Supportive leadership may also be more effective when people know exactly how to perform their responsibilities but find them disagreeable.

3. Participative

Participative leadership is a means of indirectly directing strategic choices for workers with a high internal locus of control (those who believe they influence their own fate), which is likely to be valued. When employees have high skill levels and the choices they make in the workplace are personally important, participative leadership may be more successful.

4. Achievement Oriented

Leaders who are achievement oriented set goals for their personnel and encourage them to achieve these goals. Employees are challenged by their leader's manner, which focuses their minds on work-related goals. When employees have both elevated amounts of talent and high motivation levels, this method is very likely to be successful.

Transformative vs. Transactional

In addition to the four main types of leaders, two more exist: transformative and transactional. Transformational leaders align their goals with those of employees. As a result, workers who work with transformational leaders begin to focus on the company's success rather than personal success. On the other hand, transactional leaders guarantee that employees will exhibit appropriate behaviors and deliver resources in exchange for their benefit.

Transformational leaders have four tools at their disposal to influence employees and build dedication to the company's objectives:

1. **Charisma** – This refers to a leader's ability to inspire trust and dedication in employees.
2. **Vision –** Transformational leaders have a vision that inspires others.
3. **Intellectual stimulation** – This involves challenging corporate standards and the status quo and encouraging people to think imaginatively and work harder.
4. **Individualized consideration** – This involves leaders showing personal respect and compassion for their employees' well-being.

Transactional leaders employ three different strategies to change and inspire their organizations, whereas transformational leaders rely on their charisma, genuineness, and personal appeal to do the same. Employees are rewarded based on their achievements, known as contingent rewards. Active management allows employees to execute their jobs without intervention while also anticipating potential issues and avoiding them. Passive management involves a manager who waits until something bad happens before intervening.

Performance Calibration

Performance calibration is a process through which managers (usually from the same department or function) assess job performance and individual performance rankings. Performance calibration includes taking steps to ensure that managers use a consistent set of criteria when evaluating employees.

One of the key purposes of this performance assessment process is to efficiently reward top achievers. Managers' performance ratings on goals, competencies, and other criteria are critical data points in HR and leadership decision-making. Performance evaluations are used to determine salaries and make decisions about promotions, strategic planning, and the deployment of developmental resources. Thus, companies can benefit from performance calibration in a variety of ways.

Talent Calibration

It is important to distinguish between talent and performance calibration. Performance calibration is concerned with a specific period's efficiency and is usually tied to reparations of some kind. Talent calibration is future-oriented to measure the general robustness of an organization's talent pool. It considers many elements (e.g., potential, competencies, and future organizational talent demands). Talent calibration is built on the foundation of performance calibration.

Ranking Requirements

It is also important to distinguish between performance calibration and forced ranking. Managers are asked to rate employee productivity, then "push" employees into a bell curve with particular percentages associated with forced ranking. While forced ranking has been used successfully in many firms to generate productivity, it might lead to employees believing that the performance evaluation process is rigged or otherwise unjust.

The Process of Performance Calibration

There are three steps to the performance calibration process.

1. **Appraisal**

The process starts with a performance evaluation. At the start of a project, managers evaluate a team, the performance criteria, and model specifications. The rating scale definitions that will be utilized to create appraisals should be carefully scrutinized. Managers provide performance appraisal scores when training is complete. Technology solutions frequently include online information that prominently highlights the scale benchmarks so that management is reminded of them.

2. **Calibration**

The finalized appraisals are sent to the senior leadership/HR team for higher-level assessment once the appraisal is done. HR can coordinate calibration meetings with managers and other senior officials at this point. Both an executive overview and analysis of overall organizational and departmental statistics and a discussion of personal performance should be included in calibration conversations.

3. **Feedback**

Managers should have a thorough awareness of an organization's quality standards and how the members of their team fare in comparison to others inside and outside the team.

What Is Influence and How Does It Work?

Rational Approach

The use of facts, evidence, and logical arguments to persuade people that your point of view is the best option is termed *rational persuasion*. This is the most widely used influencing technique. Presenting actual facts that are clear, explicit, relevant, and timely is an important part of effective logical persuasion.

Personal Appeal

Personal appeals require rapport and communication between a leader and the people who are being persuaded. The leader asks for a special favor with a personal appeal, such as carrying out a request or supporting a plan out of respect before revealing what it is.

Charm and physical attractiveness play a big role in how personally appealing someone is.

Forming Coalitions

Coalition tactics relate to a group of people working together to achieve a single goal. Unions that threaten to strike if their expectations are not met are a prevalent example of internal coalitions. Coalitions also use peer pressure to achieve a goal. Marketers and businesses that use client lists to sell their goods and services also employ this strategy. The fact that a customer purchased something from the company is a silent endorsement.

Leaders give people ethical clues. As a result, employees' ethical conduct is influenced by leadership attributes and style. Being viewed as a good leader is linked to being moral, and an effective leader creates a more pleasing workforce. More modern approaches to leadership, such as servant leadership and authentic leadership, emphasize the significance of ethics for strong leadership.

Some characteristics of leadership appear to be ubiquitous. However, cultural factors influence attributes, such as how strong leaders should be and whether they should devote themselves to the welfare of their workforce.

Chapter 6: Relationship Management

Relationship Management

The practice of managing relationships in a business is known as employee relationship management (ERM). These connections can be made between a company and its employees and between coworkers on the same level.

Employees need a work atmosphere that allows them to be creative. Employees' performance and productivity improve when they have a relaxed relationship with their coworkers. If such a relationship develops, they will have stronger communication, collaboration, and cooperation with each other.

Why Conflict Has Both a Good and Bad Side

People frequently believe that all disagreements are negative and should be avoided as much as possible. On the contrary, there are some situations where a small degree of stress is beneficial. Conflict, for example, can lead to the quest for new ideas and techniques to solve organizational issues. Conflict can spark innovation and change. It can also help motivate employees in situations where they feel compelled to succeed and, as a consequence, push themselves to fulfill performance goals.

However, when individuals and organizations concentrate their resources away from performance and goal fulfillment toward resolving a dispute, conflict can have severe implications. Continual confrontation can have a negative impact on people's mental health. Conflict has a significant impact on stress and its psychophysical repercussions. Finally, unresolved conflict can wreak havoc on a group's social climate and undermine group cohesion.

Types of Conflict

To understand the origins of a conflict, we must first determine the type of conflict that exists. There are at least four different types of conflict:

1. **Goal Conflict**

When one person or group desires a different conclusion than the others, goal conflict can arise. This is essentially a battle over what objectives will be pursued.

2. **Cognitive Conflict**

When one individual or a group of people has ideas or attitudes that are incompatible with those of others, cognitive conflict can arise. In political arguments, this is a common type of conflict.

3. **Affective Conflict**

Affective conflict occurs when two people are unable to communicate or come to an agreement with one another. When one person's or group's thoughts and feelings (attitudes) are inconsistent with those of others, this form of conflict arises.

4. **Behavioral Conflict**

When one individual or group does something (i.e., acts in a certain way) that is undesirable to others, behavioral conflict arises. Using vulgar language or dressing for work in a way that upsets others are examples of behavioral conflict.

Each of these types of conflict is usually provoked by a different set of circumstances, and each can result in a wide range of responses from an individual or group.

Levels of Conflict

There are numerous levels of conflict. The number of people involved in a fight is referred to as the level. Is the dispute between an individual, two people, two or more groups, or two or more organizations? The origins of a conflict and the most efficient methods for resolving it can be influenced by the level.

Intrapersonal Conflict

Intrapersonal conflict occurs when people are at odds with themselves. People experiencing an approach-avoidance dilemma are both drawn to and repulsed by the same thing.

In the same vein, a person can be enticed by two similarly attractive options, such as two great job opportunities (approach-approach conflict), or repulsed by two equally horrible options, such as the threat of being fired if one fails to address a coworker who has broken company rules (approach-approach conflict or avoidance-avoidance conflict).

Interpersonal Conflict

Interpersonal conflict is a type of conflict in which two people disagree with each other over something. You can, for example, disagree with a coworker on a topic of shared significance. Since there are just two parties engaged and each person represents the opposite side in the conflict, such confrontations frequently become deeply personal.

Intergroup Conflict

Intergroup conflict usually occurs when two opposing groups disagree over goals or resource sharing. For example, we frequently observe competition between the marketing and manufacturing sections within a firm as each competes for more resources to achieve its goals.

Intergroup conflict is the most difficult type of conflict to resolve due to the large number of people involved. During this conflict, within and between groups, coalitions form, and an "us versus them" mindset emerges.

Interorganizational Conflict

Interorganizational conflict is a common occurrence. We can witness interorganizational conflict in disagreements involving two firms in the same sector, two organizations in separate industries or economic sectors, or even two or more countries. In each situation, both parties' pursuit of their objectives is impeded.

Styles of Conflict

Those who have received sufficient conflict resolution training know how to moderate a situation and reach a satisfactory arrangement for all involved. Recognizing the various forms of conflict is the first step in conflict resolution.

The following are the five types of conflicts:

1. Keeping the Conflict at Bay

Pretending nothing is wrong, backpedaling, or entirely shutting down are all symptoms of avoidance or disengagement. By avoiding the dispute, you effectively pretend that it never occurred or that it does not exist.

2. Conceding

It takes a lot of cooperation and little fortitude to give in or accommodate the other party. In essence, you agree to assist the other party by acknowledging and respecting their point of view or proposal. This approach could be interpreted as allowing the other party to have their way. While this approach can help you reach an agreement and move forward, it can also make the accommodator feel resentful toward the other side.

3. **Defending Yourself**

It takes courage to take a stand, but it may also be insensitive. By standing your ground, you are effectively competing with the opposing side; you will go to any length to win the war. While a competitive attitude may yield short-term benefits, the long-term consequences of a prolonged conflict might be disastrous to an organization.

4. **Compromising**

Compromising is a huge step in resolving a problem. When both parties are looking for common ground, they use both boldness and thoughtfulness to come to terms with each other. They agree to focus on the bigger issues and let the lesser ones go; this approach speeds up the resolution process. Be aware that individuals who are compromising may employ passive-aggressive tactics to deceive the other party.

5. **Collaborating**

Collaboration is crucial in conflict resolution, but it necessitates a great deal of courage and thought. Listening to the other side, addressing common ground and goals and ensuring that all parties understand each other are all part of the collaborative process. Collaboration is a fusion of innovative problem-solving that is rigorous and does not make excuses. Collaborators are often valued in the organizations they work for.

The Five Conflict Resolution Techniques

Most people have one or more favored conflict resolution tactics that they employ on a regular basis. It is feasible to quantify an individual's proclivity for certain conflict resolution tactics using scientific methods.

The Thomas-Kilmann Model identifies five dispute resolution options. These strategies include:

1. **Staying Away**

Someone who employs an "avoiding" method tries to ignore or dodge a problem, hoping that it will resolve on its own or disappear.

2. **Accommodating**

Using the "accommodating" conflict resolution method means taking steps to address the other party's fears or requirements at the price of one's own wants or aspirations.

3. **Making Concessions**

Finding an acceptable settlement that will somewhat, but not completely, satisfy all parties' interests is the goal of the "compromise" technique.

4. **Competing**

When people utilize the "competing" conflict resolution technique, they are attempting to meet their own goals at the expense of the other party.

5. **Working Together**

"Collaborating" means coming up with a solution that addresses the concerns of all the parties involved.

When it comes to adopting a conflict resolution technique, the Thomas-Kilmann Model specifies two dimensions: assertiveness and teamwork. Assertiveness entails acting to meet one's own needs, whereas cooperativeness entails acting to meet the needs of others.

Each of the aforementioned conflict resolution tactics requires varying levels of aggressiveness and cooperation. Competing, for example, has a low degree of cooperativeness and a greater degree of assertiveness, whereas accommodating has a high degree of agreeableness and a low degree of boldness.

Choosing the Best Method for Resolving a Conflict

Even if one of the conflict resolution tactics listed above appeals to you more than the others, remember that all of them can be helpful in specific situations.

If a problem is insignificant and will not have long-term effects, it may be better to appease the other party rather than meet your own requirements. If the problem is more serious and will affect a large number of individuals, a more proactive solution may be preferable.

You must examine various variables when deciding on the appropriate strategy for resolving a conflict in any specific situation, including:

- The consequences for you or others if your desires are not met
- The ramifications of deciding to be more forceful
- Whether or not there is a joint or cooperative solution

Adapting management structure to avoid built-in friction, rotating team members, creating a shared "enemy," adopting democratic voting on issues, and effective problem-solving are all approaches to conflict management.

Accommodating others, avoiding confrontation, partnering, competing, and compromising are all methods of conflict resolution. Sometimes, conflict can lead to the brainstorming of new ideas. However, most of the time, it can be a cause for organizational dispute and disarray.

Chapter 7: Talent Acquisition

Recruitment

The hiring process is a crucial aspect of human resource (HR) management. It cannot be done without a well-thought-out strategy. Recruitment is a procedure that provides businesses with a pool of competent job candidates to choose from. Companies must first develop adequate staffing strategies and projections to identify how many personnel they will require before recruiting.

The estimate of how many people a company is willing to hire is based on an organization's annual budget as well as its short- and long-term intentions, such as the prospects of expansion and diversification and whether a company has any plans of dissolving anytime soon. In addition to this, the corporate life cycle also is a consideration.

Internal and external factors are used to forecast the changes that will be needed later on in a company or occurrences that will happen over time.

Internal Factors

The following are some internal organizational considerations to consider:

1. Financial restrictions
2. Employee unions
3. Levels of production
4. Increases or decreases in sales
5. Plans for global expansion

External Factors

Organizational external factors might include the following:

1. Rapid technological advances
2. Amendments in legislation
3. Unemployment rates
4. A change in the population
5. A change in the distribution of population
6. Competition

Once the predictive data has been obtained and reviewed, the HR specialist may identify gaps and begin recruiting people with the appropriate skills, education, and backgrounds.

Recruitment Strategy

Finding the appropriate talent at the right time and in the right location requires expertise and practice as well as an effective recruitment strategy. Understanding the labor market and the factors that influence the relevant components of the labor market is essential for making smart decisions in recruitment efforts.

The following are some of the elements to consider while creating a recruitment strategy:

1. Make use of a staffing plan.
2. Use questionnaires to confirm that the job analysis is correct.
3. Write the job description and requirements.

4. Establish a bidding system for recruiting and evaluating internal candidates for possible promotions.
5. Determine the most effective recruitment methods for the post.
6. Create a recruitment strategy.

The acknowledgment of a job vacancy is the first step in the recruitment process; the manager or the HR professional figures out the specifications for the job opening at this point. If the breakdown of responsibilities and job description is complete, an organization may focus on internal candidates only.

Internal applicants are those applicants whom the firm already employs. If an internal candidate matches the job requirements, they may be encouraged to apply for the position and the job opportunity may not be publicly advertised.

Many firms have formal job advertising protocols and bidding mechanisms in place for internal candidates. Job posts, for example, can be published through a listserv or another method so that all employees can see them. The benefit of advertising open positions to everyone inside and outside the company, on the other hand, is that it ensures that an organization has a diverse set of candidates.

After the job description and analysis are done, optimal recruitment tactics are then established. To acquire the best employees, most businesses will employ a variety of strategies. For example, it may be necessary to appoint an outside head-hunting firm to fill a high-level executive role. Conversely, advertising on social networks for an entry-level career may be the best method to acquire unique talent.

Another factor to consider is how the recruiting process will be managed under time constraints, such as a tight deadline or a small number of applicants. Furthermore, developing a protocol for the processing of applications and résumés will save time in the future. Some HR specialists, for example, may use tools such as Microsoft Excel to convey the hiring process timeline to key management.

Once you have completed these activities, you should have a diverse group of people to interview (this is called the selection process). However, further information is required to guarantee that the correct candidates are hired.

Job Analysis and Job Descriptions

A job analysis is a formal system for determining what tasks people undertake at work. It is used to ensure that a job and an employee are a good fit and determine how employee performance is measured.

Research is an important aspect of job analysis, including assessing current employees' job obligations, studying job descriptions for comparable roles with competitors, and analyzing any additional responsibilities that an individual could fulfill in the role.

According to studies, before starting any work redesign, a company should conduct a job diagnostic survey to identify job characteristics. Both the job specifications and the job description are developed using the information acquired from the job analysis. A job description is a list of tasks, duties, and objectives that the job requires. On the 0ther hand, job specifications explain the skills and talents that a person must possess to perform a particular job. Job descriptions are frequently written to incorporate job specifications; therefore, the two are linked.

We must first conduct a job analysis, then develop the job description and criteria based on that information.

Task-Based or Skills-Based Analysis

A task-based analysis and a competency- or skills-based analysis can be undertaken when ascertaining job requirements. In contrast to a competency-based analysis, which concentrates on the precise skills and understanding a person must have to execute a job, a task-based analysis focuses on job obligations.

A task-based analysis might comprise the following steps:

1. Provide performance appraisals for employees.
2. Prepare reports.
3. Respond to incoming phone calls.
4. Assist customers with product questions.
5. Cold-call three customers a day.

With a task-based analysis, the specific tasks are listed and each step is clear.

A competency-based analysis is less clear and more objective. A competency-based analysis might be more appropriate for specific, high-level positions.

For example, a competency-based analysis might include:

1. Able to utilize data analysis tools
2. Able to work with teams
3. Adaptable
4. Innovative

Recruitment Strategies

Now that you have constructed a job analysis, created a job description, and determined job specifications and the regulations governing the recruitment process, you can begin the hiring process. This strategy might be informal, but it should include information on where and when you plan to recruit.

Recruiters

Some companies hire personnel who are entirely responsible for the HR recruiting role. Recruiters use professional groups, websites, and other approaches covered in this chapter to find potential employees.

Recruiters maintain a steady pipeline of potential applicants in case a position that might be a good fit for them arises.

Executive Search Firm

Recruiting for executive positions, such as management roles, is the emphasis of these firms. They usually charge 10 to 20% of the appointed employee's first-year wages, which makes these firms fairly costly. They do, however, complete a lot of the legwork up front and provide individuals who fulfill the job requirements.

Provisional Staffing

Let's say your assistant is going on sick leave and you need to replace him, but you do not need to hire someone long term. As a solution, you can hire a temporary staffing business to send you competent applicants who are willing to work for short periods.

Typically, a company pays the employee's wage and the company pays the recruitment firm, so you will not have to add this person to your payroll. If the individual performs well, you may be able to offer full-time, permanent employment.

Corporate Recruiter

Corporate recruiters work for the firm they are recruiting for. This kind of employer may specialize in a certain field, such as information technology.

Dependent recruiters are paid only once they begin working, which is common in temporary recruitment and staffing organizations. Retained recruiters are paid in advance (either in full or in part) to conduct a specific search for a company.

While HR professionals may not be accountable for the minutiae of managing the hiring process when using recruiters, they are still in charge of the process and the recruiters. There is further work to be done on the job analysis, position description, job specifications, and interviewing of candidates.

Campus Recruiting

Colleges and universities can be great places to find new employees, especially for entry-level employment positions. Technical colleges offering courses in culinary arts, automotive technology, or cosmetology can be excellent resources for finding persons who have specialized knowledge in a certain field. Universities can give people formal training in a specific profession but no genuine experience, which is why many companies use campus recruiting programs to groom new employees who will eventually become managers.

To succeed, this type of recruitment program necessitates the development of relationships with university communities, such as college career services departments. It may also necessitate time to attend events on campus, such as career fairs.

Websites

There are numerous website choices for placing an HR ad, most of which are affordable. The disadvantage of this strategy is that you may obtain an overly large number of candidates' résumés from these websites, all of which may or may not be qualified. To counter this, many firms use software that looks for key words in résumés.

Social Media

Facebook, Twitter, LinkedIn and YouTube are all great locations to establish a media presence to recruit a wide range of employees.

The purpose of using social media as a recruiting tool is to generate interest in your company, share tales about successful employees, and promote a unique culture. Smaller businesses might take advantage of this technology by posting job vacancies as status updates.

Special/Specific Interest Groups (SIGs)

Individuals may be required to join special/specific interest groups (SIGs) that focus on certain themes for members. SIGs frequently offer job posting areas or a variety of discussion boards where job postings can be made.

Referrals

When recruiting new employees, a company may ask current employees if they know someone who might fit the job. Because most people will not suggest someone they think cannot do the job, the caliber of referred applicants is usually good. Emailing current employees about a job opening and offering incentives for referring a friend might be a quick approach to acquire candidates.

Since most official recommendation programs are successful, it is recommended that one such program be included in the overarching HR strategic policy and approach to hiring.

However, be mindful of relying solely on referrals for hiring, as this might lead to nepotism and a lack of workplace diversity. Nepotism refers to a preference for recruiting relatives of present employees, which can lead to a lack of diversity in the workplace and greater management concerns.

Events

Many companies, including Microsoft, conduct annual events to allow employees to network and learn about new technologies. Thousands of web developers and other professionals attend Microsoft's Professional Developer Conference (PDC), normally held in July, to update their skills and meet different people.

Some organizations, such as Choice Career Fairs, conduct job fairs across the country; attending one of these events can be a great opportunity to meet a wide range of prospective employers and employees.

Testing and Selecting

Aside from an interview, there are a few additional factors that can help predict employment success. If any test is to be used as a criterion for evaluating a candidate, it should be made clear to everyone who is interviewing. Criteria should be set based on specific test scores and expectations before the interviewing and testing process begins.

Testing

Following a successful interview, a number of exams may be administered. The following are some of the most common types of tests:

1. Cognitive ability
2. Personality
3. Physical ability
4. Job knowledge
5. Work samples

A cognitive ability test can assess reasoning, numeracy, and language abilities. An aptitude test measures a person's ability to learn new things, but the person's current knowledge is measured by an achievement exam. Depending on the job, one or both may be appropriate.

Some firms employ various methods of evaluating candidates after the interview process is completed. Work samples, for example, are a great way to understand how someone might perform at a firm.

It is possible to administer an aptitude or accomplishment exam to potential employees if they have applied for a technical job. An aptitude test assesses a person's potential ability to perform a task, whereas an achievement test assesses what a candidate already knows.

Some organizations also conduct drug tests before hiring. If the work requires it, a physical test may also be included. Honesty tests may also be conducted to assess a candidate's sense of confidence. These tests, however, may not be reliable because the "correct" answer can be easily guessed.

Chapter 8: Retention and Motivation

As an HR consultant, you will often have to analyze HR strategic plans and systems for small- to medium-sized businesses before advising a company on how to enhance them. Most of the businesses individual HR managers have to work with do not have huge HR departments, so hiring you as an HR consultant is less expensive than hiring a full-time employee.

Retention

Employee retention refers to empowering staff to stay with a company. Employee retention is influenced by a variety of factors, including compensation. The following are the reasons why 90% of employees leave a company:

1. Problems with the job they are doing
2. Problems with the boss
3. Incompatibility with the company's culture
4. Unhealthy working conditions

Despite evidence to the contrary, 90% of managers believe that employees leave because of money. As a result, managers frequently try to adjust compensation packages to keep employees from leaving, even if compensation is not the primary reason for their departure.

Development and Training

We want to make sure that once we have taken the effort to hire new staff, they are trained to do the job and reminded to keep honing their skill sets. This ensures that a company's productivity keeps increasing.

Proper training also aids employee motivation. Employees who believe their abilities are being developed are more satisfied in their positions, which leads to higher employee retention. The following are some examples of training programs:

- Job-related skills training, such as learning how to use a specific computer program
- Communication training
- Activities that promote teamwork
- Legal and policy instruction, such as sexual misconduct and ethics training

Awareness of External Factors

In addition to managing internal elements, HR managers must consider external forces that may impact a company. External forces, often known as external variables, are things over which a company has no direct influence. These factors could, however, have a beneficial or detrimental impact on HR.

The following are some examples of external factors:

- Offshoring and globalization
- Health-care costs
- Changes in employment legislation
- Expectations of employees
- The workforce's diversity
- The workforce's changing composition
- Downsizing and layoffs

External forces that have influenced HR include the current trend of flexible working hours (allowing employees to work when and where they want) and telecommuting (allowing employees to work from home or a remote location for a specific length of time, such as one day per week).

The HR department must be aware of these external challenges in order to design policies that fulfill the company's and the individual's needs. Because medical coverage will be required, cost concerns and the exploitation of medical benefits as a recruitment technique will be significant external hurdles.

Any manager who operates without considering external factors is likely to alienate staff, leaving them unmotivated and unhappy.

Recognizing external variables can sometimes include violating the law, which has its own set of negative consequences.

Reasons for Voluntary Turnover

Before we get into the specifics of retention planning, let's take a look at why people choose to leave an organization in the first place. One common blunder HR professionals and managers make is assuming that people quit their jobs solely because they are unhappy with their pay.

Demotivation of employees might, in fact, be caused by a variety of circumstances, such as too much work and/or uninteresting work, among others. We can build retention tactics to reduce turnover if we understand what causes voluntary turnover.

The following are some of the most typical reasons employees quit organizations:

A Mismatch Between the Task and the Employee's Abilities

This problem is closely linked to the hiring process. When there is such a mismatch, it can cause frustration for both the employee and the management.

Assuring that the recruitment process is viable and sound is the first step toward ensuring that the correct job and the correct employee match always occurs during the hiring process.

A Lack of Development

Some employees feel trapped in their jobs and do not see a path to advancement inside the company. To prevent good employees from leaving, design a training strategy and provide a clearly defined path to employment progression.

Internal Pay Equity

While some employees may not be unhappy with their own compensation at first, they may become unhappy when comparing it to that of others. Therefore, employees at the same job level should be paid equally.

Management

Management is also cited as a reason for many employees' departures. Overmanaging (micromanaging) supervisors, managers who are not fair or favor certain employees, managers who do not communicate well, and supervisors who have unrealistic expectations are all factors that contribute to this.

Workload

Some employees believe their workloads are too high, causing them to be stretched thin and leaving them feeling dissatisfied with their positions. They might think they have a lack of work/life balance.

Job Design, Job Enlargement, and Empowerment

One of the main reasons for job unhappiness is the job itself. When initially hiring a person, it is critical to make sure the individual's skills are matched to the job. A review of the recruitment strategy and review process should be taken into account whenever hiring is conducted.

Job enrichment refers to the addition of relevant duties to a job to make employees' work more satisfying. Allowing a shop salesperson to practice producing eye-catching displays and assigning duties centered on this ability is an excellent example of job enrichment.

Job enrichment can meet a greater level of human requirements while also increasing job happiness. According to research conducted by Richard Hackman and Greg Oldham in this field, employees require the following to feel satisfied at work:

- A wide range of skills or activities as part of the job
- Task identity or the ability to accomplish a single task from start to finish
- Task importance or the extent to which the task affects others, both internally and externally
- Autonomy, referring to the ability to make decisions on the work
- Relevant instructions about performance or feedback

Employment enlargement, which is defined as adding extra challenges or duties to an existing job, can also increase job satisfaction. This can include assigning staff to a specific project or task. However, be aware that certain employees may be unhappy with increased labor and job expansion could potentially demotivate them.

The ideal strategy to achieve retention through job enlargement is to know a person and their goals, then increase work that can help the individual attain those goals.

Employee empowerment includes managers by allowing them to make choices and act on those choices with the organization's backing.

Employees who are not micromanaged and have the freedom to schedule their own workdays, for example, are happier than those who are not. The following are examples of empowerment:

- Encourage fresh ideas and ways of doing things.
- Ensure that employees have access to the information they require to perform their duties; for example, ensure they are not reliant on managers for information when making decisions.
- Use management approaches that encourage employee involvement, feedback, and ideas.

Employee cognitive states are used to achieve employee motivation in process-based theories. Employees are demoralized when they perceive incentive distribution to be uneven, according to equity theory. By applying equity theory, a study discovered two more types of increasing fairness procedures (procedural and interactional) that impact employee reactions and motivation.

Employees are driven by expectancy theory when they feel their efforts will result in a great performance (expectancy), when they think their performance will result in positive outcomes (instrumentality), and when they find the results to be attractive (valence). According to reinforcement theory, behavior is a result of the outcomes of actions.

Leaders can enhance the frequency of desired actions by properly linking rewards to positive behaviors, reducing rewards after poor behaviors, and penalizing negative behaviors. These three theories are especially beneficial when creating reward systems for businesses.

Chapter 9: HR Strategic Planning

Strategic HR management is a forward-thinking approach to planning and implementing HR initiatives targeting and solving business challenges while also contributing directly to important long-term business goals.

HR management used to be primarily an administrative job concerned with day-to-day tasks, such as personnel recruitment and benefits administration. HR business strategies that include hiring and keeping the proper people and providing ethical and cultural leadership are now necessitated by changing trade and innovative business thinking.

Project Management Approaches

1. **Agile**

Agile is one of the most well-known project management approaches used by businesses and is ideally suited for iterative and incremental projects. It is a procedure in which self-organizing and cross-functional teams and their customers work together to develop requests and solutions. Agile was designed in response to the shortcomings of the Waterfall technique, whose processes failed to satisfy the needs of the software industry's competitiveness and continual mobility.

2. **Lean**

Lean emphasizes enhancing customer value while reducing waste. Its goal is to provide more value to customers while using fewer resources. Lean's values are derived from the Japanese manufacturing industry and assume that "as waste is eliminated, manufacturing time and cost decrease."

This approach distinguishes between three categories of waste, known as the 3Ms: muda, mura, and muri.

- **Muda**

Muda refers to an action or procedure that does not have any value and is used to eliminate waste. It can be defined as a waste of time or resources.

- **Mura**

Mura aims to eliminate inconsistencies in workflow processes at the scheduling and operation levels, ensuring that everything runs smoothly.

- **Muri**

Muri implies overburden or excessiveness. It refers to business managers putting undue stress on their personnel and processes due to factors like inadequate organization, ambiguous working methods, and ineffective equipment.

Lean methodology is excellent for any business or organization that is interested in reforming how it conducts business. Lean is often mistakenly believed to apply to only manufacturing industries.

3. Six Sigma

Six Sigma is a project management methodology developed by Motorola engineers in 1986. It seeks to increase the quality of a process by lowering the number of previous errors. It does this by identifying and removing factors that are not working properly and/or are not contributing anything to the process as a whole. This methodology employs a variety of quality management techniques, the majority of which are empirical and statistical, and the experience of people who are experts in these techniques.

Six Sigma Master Black Belts supervise the implementation of two primary Six Sigma approaches called DMAIC and DMADV. DMAIC is used to improve corporate processes, while DMADV is used to create new processes, products, or services.

DMAIC stands for:

- **D**efine the issue and the project's objectives.
- **M**easure the many features of the current process in great detail.
- **A**nalyze data to uncover root flaws in a process, among other things.
- **I**mprove the procedure.
- **C**ontrol how the process is carried out in the future.

DMADV stands for:

- **D**efine the project's objectives.
- **M**easure the process's important components, as well as the product's capabilities.
- **A**nalyze the data and create multiple process designs before selecting the best one.
- **D**esign and test the details of the process.
- **V**alidate simulations and a new program to authenticate the design before turning over the process to the client.

Project Management Processes

The Project Management Institute (PMI) is a nonprofit membership organization that also offers project management certification and standards. The Project Management Body of Knowledge (PMBOK), which is not technically a methodology but a guide defining a set of criteria that describes project management, is produced by the PMI.

PMBOK is a set of standard vocabulary and project management rules. According to the report, five process categories appear in almost every project. They are:

- **Initiating:** Defining the beginning of a project or a new stage of an ongoing project
- **Planning:** Determining the project's scope and objectives and how they will be met

- **Executing:** Carrying out the tasks outlined in the project management plan
- **Monitoring and Controlling:** Keeping track of, reviewing, and regulating progress and performance
- **Closing:** Formally finishing a project or phase; all activities across all process groups must be completed

Work Breakdown Structure

Work breakdown structure (WBS) is a strategy for finishing a complex, multistep project in project management. It is a strategy for breaking down large projects into smaller chunks and completing them more quickly and efficiently.

The purpose of a WBS is to make a complex project more achievable. Breaking it down into smaller parts allows multiple team members to work on the project at the same time, resulting in higher team productivity and simpler project management.

The Best Way to Make a Work Breakdown Structure

It is critical to first evaluate a project's scope by speaking with all stakeholders and essential teams involved before creating a work breakdown structure.

As the project manager, you want to make sure that all key feedback and deliverables are gathered and evaluated openly. To display the hierarchical framework of priority and connectedness between the tasks needed to accomplish the project, you can use Gantt charts, flowcharts, databases, or lists.

Examples of WBS

Each project's WBS may be different.

You need to determine which WBS works best for you and your team. The purpose is to clearly display to everyone involved, whether team members or external stakeholders, the structure of your projects and their progress.

Here are some examples of work breakdown structures. Any of these can be used to create a WBS outline.

- **WBS spreadsheet:** You can use a spreadsheet to organize your WBS, marking the different stages, tasks, or outputs in the columns and rows.
- **WBS flowchart:** A graphical representation workflow can be used to organize your WBS. Flowcharts make up the majority of WBS examples and templates.
- **WBS list**: A straightforward list of tasks, deliverables, and subtasks can be used to structure your WBS. This is the most basic method for creating a WBS.
- **Gantt chart for WBS**: Your WBS can be organized as a Gantt chart, a combination of a spreadsheet and a timeline. You can link project deliverables and show performance objectives with a Gantt-chart-structured WBS.

Process of Strategic Planning Components

The five steps of the strategic planning process are:

1. Initial evaluation
2. Analysis of the situation
3. Develop a strategy
4. Implement the strategy
5. Monitor the strategy

1. Initial Evaluation

The procedure begins with a preliminary evaluation of the company. Managers must identify a company's vision and mission statements at this stage.

A company's vision answers the question: "What do you want to be when you grow up?" A firm's ultimate purpose and direction for its personnel are defined by its vision.

2. Situational Analysis

The appraisal of the company's resources, core capabilities, and operations is part of the internal assessment. An organization has both tangible and intangible assets, such as capital, land, equipment, culture, brand recognition, knowledge, patents, licenses, and trademarks. All of these are located and listed for use during a company appraisal.

Exceptional customer relationship capabilities or efficient supply chain management may be among a company's core capabilities at this stage. Managers examine the value chain and the entire production process while reviewing the company's actions.

As a result of all these actions, a situation analysis characterizes the organization's strengths, weak points, prospects, and threats, revealing a clear understanding of the company's market position.

3. Developing a Strategy

Long-term objectives are developed following a successful situational analysis. Long-term goals can strengthen the company's competitive position in the long run. These goals are stated in specific strategies. For example:

A. Strategy at the Corporate Level – When strategic business units (SBUs), divisions, or small and medium firms select approaches for only one product supplied in only one market, they utilize this sort of strategy.

B. Strategy at the Corporate Level – At this level, top parent company executives decide which items to sell, which markets to penetrate, and whether to purchase or combine with a competitor. Integrative and intense diversification and defensive measures are the options they consider.

4. International/Global Strategy

At this stage, the most important concerns to address are: Which new markets should be developed? How should they be entered? How far should you go with your diversification?

Managers have a variety of strategic options to choose from when trying to create a global company strategy. The options can depend on a company's goals, the findings of a situation analysis, and the level at which the strategy is chosen.

5. Implementation of the Strategy

Even the best strategic plans must be put into action to see how well they work, and only well-executed strategies provide businesses with a competitive edge. Thus, there is always a risk when new strategies are implemented.

Managerial abilities are more crucial than analysis at this point. Communication is critical in strategy implementation because new strategies require pitch-ins from all levels of the business to be successful.

A strong strategic plan gives a company the tools it needs to figure out if it has achieved its aims. Any strategy should contain measurable objectives so that the link between success and the strategy is clear.

As internal and external environments evolve, changes in the strategic plan and goal formulation are required. For example, an HR manager should always keep in mind modifications in forecasts so that the strategy can be adapted as soon as the forecast changes.

Legislative changes may also have an impact on strategic plans and budgets. HR managers must stay on top of these changes and communicate them to their employees as efficiently as possible.

Chapter 10: Structure of the HR Function

Having a detailed strategy, an in-demand product or service, and effective management are essential factors to running a successful business. But be that as it may, the entire business structure relies upon the ability of the individuals inside the organization to execute such strategies with confidence and methodical planning.

All aspects of a business gradually come down to the individuals working in it. By overseeing individuals efficiently, organizations can be more productive and successful, create brand loyalty, and accomplish higher goals. The HR department takes care of all this.

HR refers to a wide range of strategies used in the work environment to smooth workflow. It is the administration of any decisions within an organization relating to the organization's employees.

In the last few decades, the HR function has seen significant growth and has become a fundamental part of every organization. Nowadays, a well-integrated HR system has become more crucial than ever before because it helps the individuals within an organization quickly and efficiently achieve the overall goals and targets set for them.

HR Strategies

The HR team has several kinds of strategies to make the business process efficient and smooth. These strategies can include managerial, operative, and advisory strategies. Each strategy complements the others.

Managerial Strategy

The managerial strategy mainly corresponds to planning, organizing, and directing.

Planning

This is where the HR team determines the organization's goals and chooses the methods or procedures that will be used to reach them. Using efficient measures creates a balance between the number of jobs available and the number of employees available. With a thorough strategy, the HR team can avoid either a surplus or a shortage of employees in the organization.

Organizing

At this stage, the HR team develops a methodology or mechanism that ensures the organization's goals and objectives. It involves assigning responsibilities and jobs to the individuals and creating a chain of command that is necessary for all to adhere to.

Directing

Now, the plans developed in the previous stage are put into effect. The HR manager encourages employees to start working more efficiently to accomplish the organization's goals. This can be done through gentle reminders, motivation, offering salary increases, and much more.

Operative Strategy

Operative strategies are concerned with recruitment, strategy implementation, compensation, training, maintaining order in the organization, maintaining employee records, and developing methods to improve employee working conditions, among other factors.

Recruiting

To start with, the operative function includes the effective running of the recruitment drive where the HR management must shortlist the right people for the job, then analyze each individual before making the final decision. Most organizations believe that attracting individuals with exceptional skill sets and abilities and keeping them for long periods is the hardest challenge.

Analyzing

Job analyzing is another part of this strategy, whereby the HR management describes and identifies the skills and abilities required for a specific job and indicates whether any prior work experience is required, as well as any prerequisites that might be needed to execute a certain task. Some HR departments run a Learning and Development Program to prepare employees for taking up more responsibilities in time.

Compensation and Welfare

Compensation and welfare refer to the HR function that calculates and scales salary levels with corresponding job titles and the type of work a particular job entails. It also includes other benefits, incentives, and compensation to be included in the job description. This function also takes care of other welfare services, such as health-care facilities provided to employees. These are usually provided in insurance plans and are extended to the employees' immediate family members.

Advising Strategy

The advising strategy revolves around HR providing high-level management and individuals with an extremely critical and detailed set of advice when formulating new policies and procedures. This strategy also includes giving employees advice to maintain cordial employee relations and improve the work environment by boosting worker confidence and morale. HR management also extends this strategy to advising the heads of various departments. The advice offered is mainly related to policies that include job descriptions, recruitment, and compensation.

Importance and Key Structural Components of the HR Department

A well-run HR department is highly beneficial, contributes massively to the productivity of an organization, and promotes a healthy work environment. An efficient HR system permits organizations to handle HR issues intelligently. The HR function allows the organization to attract talented individuals, helps the organization's chiefs and workers adjust to hierarchical changes, and enables technology adoption. It also oversees all the employees in the organization, helping them work efficiently and allowing them to assist the organization in achieving the upper hand in the industry.

The tasks that an HR manager or the department itself carry out may vary from organization to organization depending on its size; however, there are a few key elements and components that have to be addressed by every HR department and are pivotal to an organization's productivity levels. Some of the key components have already been discussed in the HR strategies mentioned above, which we will now discuss further.

Selecting the Right Individual

Identifying and hiring the right set of individuals in a limited period is key to achieving the right results and reaching organizational goals and objectives. Hence, a successful HR department requires a structure that can efficiently advertise jobs, locate the right individuals, screen them, conduct the preliminary interviews, and organize recruiting endeavors with managers responsible for making the final decision.

Employee Relations

Employee relations relates to fortifying the employer-employee relationship by measuring levels of job satisfaction and worker commitment, and settling workplace disputes. In a unionized workplace, employee and work-related HR elements might be unified and taken care of by one trained professional, or they could be independent functions overseen by two HR experts.

Training and Development

When hiring new employees, it might be better to provide them with some level of assistance in the form of orientation and preliminary training that will help them make a smooth transition into an organization. For this purpose, most HR departments provide their employees with leadership training. Training might be scheduled for recently recruited individuals and administrators in areas such as performance management and dealing with individual relations matters at the office level.

Payroll

Payroll is an important component of any organization, regardless of how big or small it is. An HR department has to collect relevant employee data for financial purposes (i.e., tax purposes, insurance, payments, paychecks, and deposits).

Personnel

Numerous obligations related to personnel—including recruiting, terminating contracts, and performance assessment activities—are the responsibility of the HR department. HR supervisors and representatives are strongly associated with the progression of a worker's tenure at an organization. They handle and track records, welcome fresh recruits, compile execution assessments, determine worker disciplinary methods, and terminate workers. Most of the time, the HR department is answerable for keeping staff records that make note of all employment actions.

Legal Compliance

Organizations need to keep in compliance with laws that might affect the business or the workplace itself. For that matter, employers and organizations rely heavily on HR departments to ensure that they remain compliant. HR departments are responsible for informing employees of all the employment rights they are entitled to. Some of these federal and state rights include the Family Medical Leave Act (FMLA), the Occupational Safety and Health Act (OSHA) regulations, and many others. Additionally, HR offices are entrusted with documentation relating to employment legislation, including handling employee cases.

Outsourcing HR Functions

Outsourcing refers to when a company hires an external provider who is responsible for certain HR functions. Most organizations outsource HR functions so that the organization's current HR department can focus more on the organization's important issues, such as work-environment relations and growth promotion. Other small duties, such as transactional responsibilities, are taken off the hands of the organization's HR department to decrease its workload and increase efficiency. Outsourcing HR functions may reduce HR costs for some organizations.

Added Benefits of HR Functions

Managing conflicts effectively is another important job of the HR department that helps reduce any visible levels of friction among employees or between employees and their employer. Conflicts are part of every healthy organization, but they need to be taken care of swiftly, and the HR department does that.

HR functions also contribute to strategic management by bringing about positive outputs that lead to organizational success. Individuals who are highly skilled in HR partake in corporate decision-making that underlies HR decisions.

Other benefits of the HR functions include:

- Creating awareness for employees

- Improving organizational culture
- Maintaining a positive work environment
- Managing talent

Summary

HR management is an important tool that must be used in an organization to develop policies to achieve set goals and appease workers. In the long run, HR strategy can drastically impact an organization's overall performance. A good HR strategy can make a company successful; conversely, a weak HR strategy can bankrupt it. Structuring an HR division optimally is necessary for the smooth running of the different HR functions and employee growth.

Chapter 11: Employee and Labor Relations

Employee and labor relations are key to maintaining a healthy work environment in an organization. These two relations help an organization manage itself efficiently, improve relations between employees, and build upon them by bridging communication gaps, conducting performance management, and assisting in settling disputes between employees.

Employee and labor relations both deal with problems that come out of the workplace. They assist in resolving conflicts and preventing any similar grievances from occurring in the future.

Both employers and employees expect something from each other. Therefore, to avoid any conflict, employers should try to create a healthy work environment. Likewise, employees should maintain a work ethic that meets their employer's expectations. This is usually done by meeting deadlines and increasing creativity and productivity levels.

If and when a conflict arises within the workplace or any discrepancies occur, employee and labor relations help in the form of labor unions or third parties outsourced by the organization, which address the concerns of the employees, help bring balance to the employer-employee relationship, and resolve disputes.

Employee Relations

Employee relations (ER) describe the relationship between an employee and employer. It mainly focuses on relationships within a workplace, which can be either paired or, in some cases, collective. ER aims to improve and maintain a healthy relationship between managers and their respective team members. In doing this, ER takes care of the employer-employee relationships' practical, legal, emotional, and physical aspects.

This can be done by:

- Resolving problems between the managers/employers and the staff/employees
- Creating a safe environment where all organization members feel comfortable working, both mentally and physically
- Building a trustworthy and respectful relationship between employees and employers

With employee relations, we can also acknowledge the hard work and efforts of the HR department that is responsible for maintaining and keeping track of relationships between all members of an organization. The effort that the HR department puts in is formalized in the employee relation policies.

Employee Relations (Principles and Practices)

Having successful employee relations is crucial to an organization's development. For that reason, we must consider certain principles and practices that will help with that development.

An organization must consider two key principles while improving employee relations: honesty and keeping promises. It is highly important that while communicating within the workplace, employees and employers maintain a strict code of not making promises they cannot keep and being straightforward with each other. If promises are not kept either by managers or employees themselves, or if a certain piece of information shared within the organization turns out to be false, that will lead to disappointment and negativity all around.

With all this in mind, the HR department or the ER experts must encourage other important practices that will help the relationship between members of an organization.

As discussed before, honest communication is extremely important for all employees. When team members are well informed, it is easier for everyone to communicate and understand each other's ideas. It is also important to discuss an organization's vision and goals. Honesty improves coordination among the employees, as well as the general atmosphere of the workplace as a whole.

It is also important to understand that once a task has been assigned to an employee, the employer or the division manager must not let trust issues get in the employee's way. Rather than checking on the employee every day, a weekly or monthly meeting between the employer and employee is preferable, as it allows both individuals to do their jobs without any interruptions and improves their relationship.

Also, when an employee is aware that their manager/employer trusts them to competently do the work they are assigned, it helps boost the employee's confidence and allows them to excel at their job.

Recognizing and appreciating an employee's hard work and effort is just as important to bettering employee relations. If employees feel that their efforts are not being appreciated, they might not feel as important to the team and may start looking for other employment opportunities. Hence, it is important that employers and other team members often take time out to appreciate their coworkers and maybe even have occasional celebrations to recognize each other's hard work. Showing your appreciation to your employees and making sure that they matter can create stronger employee relations.

What Must Employee Relations Managers Do?

In most cases, the employee relations task remains with the HR department; however, some organizations do hire experts specifically for building employee relations.

Some of the key responsibilities of an ER manager include:

- Urging managers and workers to meet weekly or monthly on a one-on-one basis to build rapport
- Eliminating any issues present between top management and workers
- Conducting regular interviews and taking feedback from employees
- Creating and sending feedback to workers in regard to proposed policy changes
- Considering approaches to show representatives that the organization values and recognizes their efforts
- Listening to employee complaints and making appropriate adjustments
- Organizing company benefits and plans for employees

Labor Relations

Labor relations are engagements between the employees, management, and labor unions that allow them to make beneficial decisions within an organization. The decisions are usually about wages, salaries, working conditions, and working hours. Other key issues, such as welfare, security, and grievances on the part of employees, are also identified under the term "labor relations" and are taken care of by the appropriate labor relations experts.

Unionization

Unionization is the process whereby employees of a firm or organization may become part of a labor union and agree that the union will act as a bargaining tool against the employers in case of any injustice. The union represents all workers who are part of the organization. A labor union allows employees to voice their opinions and makes it easier for employers to address issues.

Organizing a Union

The initial phase in this process is understanding the major problems that employees often suffer. At this stage, employees are assessing and gathering support for taking action. This step distinguishes central problems and makes other employees aware of their union rights.

The second phase of organizing a union is writing a list of demands that employees will make. These demands can include decreased working hours, higher wages, increased health benefits, or any other incentives that will help workers.

Next come the union elections. For a union election to take place, at least 30% of the worker population should sign some sort of authorization form. The higher the percentage of the worker population that signs the form, the stronger the union is. When the 30% worker population requirement has been met, a request to the National Labor Relations Board (NLRB) for conducting elections is made.

The NLRB then takes all things into account before agreeing to and organizing the elections. The NLRB representative conducts a thorough investigation to eliminate any issues that could hinder the elections from taking place. Once all this is done, the NLRB devises an agreement between the election parties, consisting of the balloting date, time, and place.

If the union can gain the favor of the majority of the voters, the NLRB will be officially recognized as a bargaining representative for the workers.

Unfair Labor Practices

Most of the time, organizations abide by all laws applicable to them, which, in turn, creates healthy relationships between organizations and their employees. However, there are instances when either the employer or the union itself violates employment legislation. This is known as unfair labor practices.

Unfair Labor Practices Committed by Employers

The most common sort of violation occurs when the employer or organization does not agree to negotiate with the union representing the employees on a particular matter.

In other cases, employers might discriminate against an employee or a group of employees who actively participate in labor unions. Common examples of discrimination against these employees include preventing promotions, restricting salary package upgrades, making wage cuts, and increasing working hours.

Taking part in a hot cargo agreement is another way employers involve themselves in unfair labor practices. A hot cargo agreement occurs between an employer and the union when the employer agrees to stop doing business with another employer in dispute with the union. The union, in turn, may go easy on the protest and might even agree to some of the unfair laws imposed by the employers. This is unfair to the employees.

Unfair Labor Practices Committed by Unions

Just like employers and organizations, some labor unions also take part in unfair labor practices. These practices may include:

- Coercing or forcing employers to reverse a decision or pass an unfair judgment
- Refusing an opportunity offered by an organization or its employees to negotiate and look for a middle ground
- Using featherbedding, a technique in which unions threaten to require employers to pay for work that the workers have not performed
- Forcing employees to take part in union programs and agreements by threatening them

Taking a Stand

If an organization, employee, or union is under the impression that an unfair labor practice is being committed, they may report it to the NLRB. If the incident or practice has been reported within six months of its occurrence, legal action can be taken against those liable for it.

National Labor Relations Board (NLRB)

The NLRB is a government organization vested with the ability to protect workers' privileges and help them coordinate and decide whether they want to have a union as a negotiating party. The organization also acts to eliminate any unfair labor practices carried out by unions and employers.

What Does the NLRB Do?

The NLRB:

- Investigates any incidents reported or charges made
- Facilitates settlements
- Enforces orders
- Introduces new rules and regulations regarding labor laws and unfair practices
- Decides cases

Unfair labor practices occur on both ends of the spectrum, whether it is the organization and its executives or the labor union and its workers that are conducting these practices. Such practices must be discouraged and stopped with extreme prejudice. Unfair labor practices lead to disruptions within an organization and decrease productivity levels as well as employee morale. The environment within the workplace also starts to deteriorate along with relations between employers and employees.

International Labor Relations (IIR)

IIR are fairly complex. Newly introduced globalization standards and rules have brought IIR under immense pressure, which has led to the better treatment of employees of multinational companies.

Summary

We must understand the importance of both employee and labor relations. Employee and labor relations are one of the key factors that influence an organization's work environment and affect both employee and employer satisfaction. Most companies and organizations nowadays invest in employee relations to maintain camaraderie between their employees and keep conflicts to a minimum. Employees look to actively participate in labor unions that will help them improve labor relations at the organization they work at. All of this leads to an increase in an organization's productivity levels while also maintaining a healthy workplace atmosphere.

Chapter 12: Organizational Effectiveness and Development (OE&D)

Organizational effectiveness and development (OE&D) is a technique that organizations implement to help them increase performance levels and move toward higher levels of growth.

OE&D efforts mainly focus on systematic interventions and changes in policies that restructure an organization and bring workers to a common standpoint that helps achieve the organization's goals and objectives. Team performance, employee growth, efficiency, and productivity are some of the key areas that OE&D emphasizes.

OE&D has become more crucial than ever in today's business. It helps strengthen an organization's ability to achieve better results and improve processes and strategies through useful policies.

Another key feature of OE&D is its use of critical analyses and scientific data. The process does not base its strategies on assumptions; instead, it uses scientific findings as evidence to build a structured and controlled process before moving onto practical testing and implementation.

Both internal and external stakeholders take part in the organization's development process. The internal contributors consist of management and employees, while the external contributors include all business investors, suppliers, customers, communities, and governments.

Organizational Development Goals and Interventions

Every organization has a set of goals or one major goal that it structures its business activities around. These goals may vary from company to company. For instance, a merchandising business or any corporate firm will try to maximize its profits—that will be the organization's main goal. For a hospital or a health service center, coordination and better functionality are a top priority.

There is one common goal that all organizations look to achieve, and that is increasing the firm's competitiveness. Any company wants to excel in its market and take control of it. This is possible only when the organization's resources are used to the fullest extent to achieve maximum efficiency.

This is where organizational goals come in. To increase competitiveness, OE&D allows organizations to better use resources and improve team performance and efficiency. OE&D helps an organization better understand the resources at its disposal and make intelligent use of them. Through analyzing and processing data, OE&D allows organizations to improve performance, results, and productivity, and increase the organization's competitiveness.

However, all of this is achievable only through interventions devised to assist in problem-solving, improving function, and allowing department heads to manage their team and the office atmosphere.

Behavioral Interventions

1. Interpersonal Relations

Interpersonal relations interventions help improve communication between team members and align their goals and objectives so that they are met in a relatively short period. The most common example is training new employees along with other team members, as well as teaching them how to interact with customers and clients.

2. Role-playing

This is a technique used in many development programs where two or more workers are presented with a real-life situation that they role-play. The workers are assigned different roles or personalities. For instance, one worker might be tasked with playing the role of a manager while the other acts as a subordinate. This training method helps new hires learn how to cope with a similar situation when dealing with an actual customer. This technique is mostly used for sales training.

3. Management by Objectives

Managing by objectives is a type of intervention that integrates the organization's goals into its framework to increase profits and achieve sustainable growth. This type of intervention allows managers to take control and contribute to a task and its development as effectively as possible.

Managing by objectives helps increase the accuracy and timeliness of the planning process at the management level. It bridges any gaps present between employee performance and organizational goals. This strategy also increases synergy levels and encourages performance appraisals.

4. Developing the Grid

In almost every organization, managers or departmental heads have a certain preference for productivity and efficiency rather than employee satisfaction. On the other hand, some managers might show more care and appreciation for employees while putting little emphasis on production levels.

The grid development strategy helps managers reevaluate and balance the level of concerns expressed by employees or other business officials regarding productivity. It emphasizes the fact that improving leadership styles will help achieve better results in the future.

Relevant OE&D practices may use surveys and questionnaires to better understand and interpret the existing leadership styles assumed by managers, then help them reanalyze their styles and make suitable adjustments to their styles to make them more effective.

Nonbehavioral Interventions

1. Organizational Structure Redesign

An organization may adjust the chain of command to make it more productive. Similarly, this can also be done by making changes in functional responsibility, such as a move from a product to matrix organizational design.

2. Job Enrichment

Job enrichment is a persuasive strategy that stresses the need for work challenges. It recommends that jobs be restructured so that employees derive some level of fulfillment and satisfaction from them.

Job enrichment allows for altering a job by adding various responsibilities to it from other organizational levels. This makes the job both challenging and interesting for workers while allowing employees to feel a degree of pride at the same time.

Miscellaneous Interventions

1. Team Building

Team building improves a workgroup's effectiveness. It helps improve relationships between members, especially between team leaders and their subordinates. Improving work procedures and interpersonal relationships is the main focus of team building.

The key assumption that this intervention considers is that by increasing workgroups' effectiveness, managers will observe a widespread increase in an organization's effectiveness.

2. Survey Feedback

Surveys and questionnaires are other useful methods used in OE&D methods to increase effectiveness. OE&D methods involve acquiring data related to the organization through surveys, then using that data to make important decisions about the organization.

Feedback collected through surveys is useful for OE&D, as it tends to change employees' and participants' attitudes for the better. Both team building and survey feedback, when used together, make a positive impact on organizations.

The Development Process and Steps

OE&D interventions and techniques go through several processes before they are considered applicable in an organization. The development process uses scientific research and real-life organizational issues so that relevant interventions can be devised.

To start with, any manager or departmental head must first try to *identify* gaps in the current strategies or find room for improvement. This is usually done by monitoring events such as customer complaints, a decrease in profits, poor customer feedback, or frequent employee resignations. Once the issue has been identified, the manager notifies the organizational development officials, who then set up a meeting with the manager. The meeting may include other senior officials of the organization as well.

The second step is the *diagnosis* of the problem. The OE&D officials look at the problem and try to identify what is causing it. To come up with valid assumptions regarding the problem, the experts try to acquire useful data through surveys and questionnaires. They may conduct interviews with the employees to have a better understanding of the problem.

After a detailed inspection and determination of the root cause of the problem, the OE&D experts develop a way to design effective intervention techniques to eliminate or at least try to minimize the occurrence of the problem. The interventions must be designed so that they meet the criteria set by the organization and can successfully tackle the problem and show positive results.

At the *implementation* level of the interventions, a maximum number of participants must be engaged. Also, the participants must be aware of their role in the implementation and have a clear understanding of what needs to be done at each step. In addition, the participants and the organization as a whole must be ready to accept and understand the changes effectively.

Once the interventions have been approved and implemented, the organization gradually starts to see results, which it can analyze to determine the effectiveness of the interventions. If the results show a positive change in team performance, the organization may choose to stick with the interventions. These interventions will gradually improve the state of affairs in an organization and allow managers to make further improvements where they see fit.

Organizational Design Structure

Organizational design refers to designing and structuring an organization. This strategy aims to identify any key issues present in the organizational structure that are affecting an organization's performance of in order to make relevant changes.

There are two types of organizational design structure:

1. Centralized structure
2. Decentralized structure

Centralized Structure

In a centralized organizational structure, all roles, positions, and processes are well established and command is held only by top-level officials. A top-down chain of command is in place. The managers and employees working under the top management are responsible for implementing the decisions made by the top officials and must strictly abide by those decisions.

Communication is easier in a centralized organizational structure, as there is a clear chain of command to which all members of an organization must adhere. Administrative costs are considerably lower, and it does not take much time for managers and employees to implement any changes or decisions top officials make. Moreover, in a centralized organizational structure, employees' overall work quality remains high.

However, some problems may occasionally be observed in a centralized organizational structure. Since the chain of command has to be adhered to, managers may feel they do not have as much control of their divisions as they would like. Employees sometimes also feel disconnected from the organization due to a lack of communication between them and senior officials. Employees are simply following orders and implementing decisions that were made without the workforce having any real say in them.

Decentralized Structure

In a decentralized organizational structure, decisions that top-management officials otherwise would make in a centralized structure are handed over to the division managers and supervisors at the lower and middle levels. This improves efficiency. Also, managers feel valued because they have the authority to make day-to-day decisions themselves. Employees feel happier, as some managers and supervisors ask for opinions on their decisions.

A decentralized organizational structure overall leads to effective communication and customer service. Employees feel motivated and want to perform better. Moreover, when the authority to make quick decisions lies with the manager, it reduces costs because the manager does not have to wait for the top management's approval on every decision; instead, managers make the decision themselves, without wasting time or resources.

Summary

Technology is evolving rapidly, so organizations must learn to adapt consistently to newer business methods. Today, organizational development and effectiveness are extremely important aspects for all organizations. Regardless of the size of an organization, interventions have to be made when things are not working as they should.

When organizational development strategies are being implemented and changes are being made, both the employees and management of an organization must help each other stay ahead of any problems. It is not easy for any member to adapt to change quickly, but the transition can be made smoother with positive attitudes from both management and employees.

Chapter 13: Technology Management

In today's world, the use of technology has become crucial to running a successful business. Organizations tend to put extra effort into incorporating technological resources into their offices to improve efficiency.

Technology management involves adapting to changes in the technological world and trying to incorporate newer inventions into businesses to enhance creativity and productivity. This management revamps a business or an organization by bringing technology into the fold. Product innovation, technology innovation, and research and development (R&D) are some of the core components of technology management.

Nowadays, employees and workers must learn how to consistently adapt to innovation and work with it to achieve a company's objectives. Division managers and supervisors are also under immense pressure to show results in a limited period. Maximizing daily profits, reducing costs, and not exhausting business resources are just some of the tasks that put a lot of pressure on a manager. However, if managers and firms introduce a strategic technology management system, achieving such tasks becomes easier and less time consuming.

Effective technology management techniques help organizations optimize their resources and gain competitive advantages. Organizations can carefully manage their resources by acquiring and interpreting data through the use of innovative technology. However, technology can be useful to a business only if it is managed properly and its management and execution are aligned with an organization's goals and objectives.

Technology Management Strategy

In the last 30 years, with the aid of computers, companies and their employees have managed to produce and acquire more data than in the previous 5,000 years. More and more money is being invested into managing technology that helps retrieve data for companies. That data is then analyzed for the purpose of increasing performance.

A company that lacks an efficient technology management system or a decentralized IT structure may regularly find itself plagued by duplicate data. This usually happens when more than one technological system is performing the same task and the manager or employees are unaware of it.

The major responsibility of managing technological systems lies with the IT department. The goal of this department is to set up a technological system that takes business judgment, technology investment, and expertise into account.

The IT department may start by setting up a meeting with senior company officials and board members to discuss the results the company is in search of. Subsequently, the IT department will devise a detailed plan after speaking to the division managers, each of whom will have a separate set of requirements and demands that must be met.

As a result, the IT department must involve every division manager, as well as the senior officials' strategic objectives, in their plans, then implement the appropriate technological system to attain these objectives.

Technology Planning

Above, we discussed how organizations can use strategies to manage technology systems efficiently. Now we are going to look at how IT departments may use manager and employee feedback to equip them with the appropriate tools to excel at their jobs.

The IT department first acquires data by conducting interviews and assessing the type of work an organization does. The department then takes a look at the organization's objectives.

During the planning process, the experts conduct a detailed analysis of the company's priorities. Implementing a technological system usually consumes a big chunk of an organization's financial resources; so the system that is implemented must be able to help with performance for a long period in order to pay for itself.

Once the technological system has been established, the next step is to evaluate and analyze how effective the system is. This is accomplished through practical implementation and checking whether the system is fulfilling the organization's needs or not. This is crucial because if the objectives are not being met and the tools provided to the employees and workers are not as efficient as they were expected to be, running this system will just be a waste of time and resources.

To avoid this, it is imperative that the experts also evaluate the organization's existing infrastructure and build a technological system around it. A well-planned technological system can still work as efficiently and effectively as the existing infrastructure allows.

Technology management techniques can help improve the organizational decision-making experience and achieve better results. Technology management helps enhance performance as well as productivity. Thus, by bringing together the organization's technological and business sides, we see better utilization of resources from all personnel in the organization.

Once the system has been implemented, system experts, managers, and employees must work to maintain it and look for opportunities to make better use of it.

For the smooth running of the system, it is recommended that workers and experts use the system for comprehensive and flexible processes. The goal is to decrease redundancy.

Strategic Technology Management System (STMS) Technique

The Strategic Technology Management System (STMS) allows for adopting a new technological system, implementing it for use over a long-term period, and managing it until the point of its decline.

The STMS follows a life-cycle approach for managing technology. It consists of the following steps:

1. Technology Creation

This is the first phase of STMS. It involves generating designs for new inventions, then creating them. This phase also involves senior management committing to the task of adopting a new system of technology and offering support for technology creation.

2. Technology Monitoring

During technology monitoring, experts analyze and interpret any technology trends that are present before a new system's implementation. The monitoring process includes implementing information systems and further developing them to look for trends. Experts also conduct a complete competitive analysis to help them understand market competitiveness from an existing set of technologies.

3. Assessment

At this point, IT experts sit down with employees and try to comprehend the market trends with the aid of the technological system. In this phase, the integration of technology and business is taken to the next level, and assessments are made to determine the effectiveness of implementing the technological system for the business.

4. **Technology Transfer**

Once assessments have been made and the decision to implement a technological system has been approved, the next step involves R&D and production. Organizations may look for mergers or enter into alliances with potential suppliers of the technological system.

5. **Accepting Technological Change**

If and when the new technology is implemented, staff and senior management must support this change. The analysis of the impacts and effects of this technological change also falls under this phase. If the impacts are positive for the most part, they may include removing barriers that were otherwise affecting business, reduce the workload on the staff, and other effects.

6. **Utilization**

Now, businesses and employees start to make use of the technological changes. This process involves the effective use of the technology for project execution and management. The main goal of workers in this step is to find ways to maximize utilization of the technology while providing constructive feedback for further improvement.

Improving the System

Something even more crucial than implementing a technological system is trying to manage and improve it. A technological system can be *built* exceptionally well, but it will be of no use to an organization if employees and managers do not use it efficiently.

The best way to manage and modernize such a system is by putting customer value at the top. The system should be set up and managed in such a way that it works in the best interests of the organization's customers. Satisfied customers are crucial to an organization because they have a profound effect on the organization's performance. Hence, the system must provide the best experience to customers. This is usually done by providing customers with better service quality or by changing operating efficiencies that then reduce costs.

Another way to improve the management of the system and help it run better is simplifying its design and structure. Over the past few years, modern technology has come a long way. Instead of deciding between simplicity and offered features, organizations must look for systems that have both. This will not only save resources for the firm, but also improve customer service and time management.

Challenges

There are various factors and risks involved in technology management. These risks can be either internal or external.

The hardest challenge for the technology management team is that they have to come up with the system's design and structure. This process is full of uncertainties about whether the new system will work or not while keeping in mind the amount of time spent and the resources used.

If a system or innovation has been deemed operable and functional, the organization must find a sponsor or an individual to fund the implementation of the technology. A management team is also needed to oversee and help coordinate the whole process.

In many cases, senior officials and managers forget the importance of having a marketing perspective and believe that simply adapting to new technology is the answer to all their problems. As a result, little attention is paid to the implementation of technology, and most of the organization's resources are exhausted in either the purchase of the technology or its development.

Consequently, most technological systems fail as a result of poor implementation efforts.

Another key challenge that organizations may have to face is finding the right set of employees who know their way around the newly installed technology and can use it to benefit the organization.

Summary

For businesses and organizations to run successfully, they must incorporate modern technology in their daily business practices. This is possible only if organizations invest in technology management. A team of expert innovators is crucial for a business to compete in the rapidly changing market, with no room for inadequacy. From senior managers down to employees of an organization, everyone must adapt to technological changes if they are to compete in the market.

Chapter 14: Workforce Management

Workforce management is an integral part of running a smooth business. Organizations tend to incorporate workforce management into their daily business practices to enhance employee performance.

Workforce management helps increase an organization's competency and competitiveness through efficient processing. Workforce management systems allow organizations to gather detailed information about business metrics, ranging from the number of workers required to complete a particular task to knowing daily employee attendance and performance.

A workforce management system takes care of maintenance and all those processes that help a business grow and retain competency and productivity. It also helps the workforce conduct daily tasks with greater efficiency.

Workforce Management Tasks

Data Accumulation

The workforce management system takes care of gathering real-time data, which usually consists of statistical employee performance data and performance management data as a whole. Field service management is another task performed by workforce management, which revolves around taking care of the company's resources.

Managing Employees

Performance, HR, and training management all fall under workforce management. It is important that a workforce management system take care of employee satisfaction and make sure that employee performance and results match those required by the organization. All of this requires rigorous employee training, which the workforce management must conduct.

Forecasting and Budgeting

Forecasting and budgeting are one of the more important tasks and processes of workforce management. The workforce management system's efforts in budgeting and forecasting include analyzing and gathering information to understand the type of resources needed to complete a given task. A workforce management system makes calculated forecasts and assesses budget limits that make it easier for the organization to determine how many resources and staff members it can deploy.

Scheduling

Drawing up schedules is a key aspect of workforce management. Staff scheduling permits organizations to optimize their resources and plan as needed while keeping in mind business variables, such as workload, availability of resources, time of year, and other complexities.

Time Management

A workforce management system allows for a better understanding of time and attendance patterns, which helps companies and their managers predict and plan for any unanticipated staff absences.

Employee Performance

Employee engagement describes how committed an employee is to the job. Workforce management analyzes engagement and looks at factors that help improve performance. By working out the motivation behind all employee engagement in a business, workforce management can assess an employee's commitment to the organization, increase work quality and productivity, and retain top employees.

Recruitment Process

Approaching, interviewing, shortlisting, and selecting candidates are all part of the workforce management hiring process.

Compliance

Every organization has to deal with compliance issues. These may include showing and tracking certifications for roles and positions and meeting the requirements of working conditions and union agreements.

For a workforce management system, compliance is an important yet complicated department. Noncompliance with the government or relevant authorities may leave organizations liable for hefty fines and lawsuits. Making sure agreements remain intact and an organization does not break laws is a crucial responsibility that falls under workforce management.

Workforce Management Benefits

Workforce management is vital for an organization's development. For an organization to excel in the industry and have a say in the market, it must check all boxes for success, such as efficiency, productivity, profit maximization, and team-building. All of this is possible when a firm's resources or an organization are optimized to the maximum, which is possible only through a proper workforce management system. Workforce management is extremely advantageous to an organization because it allows an organization to excel in the market through better employee performance, reduced costs, and better client service.

Some of the key benefits and advantages of workforce management include:

- Analyzing the problem and utilizing the appropriate resources and staff for it. This leads to an increase in productivity and better use of time and resources.
- Complying with the government and relevant authorities at both local and national levels. This allows the organization to run its business without worrying over legal problems, as the workforce management system takes care of all of this.

- Training and tutoring employees and staff on better methods of service provision and teaching them to handle leads to increase customer satisfaction.
- Coming up with techniques to maximize resources and minimize costs without having to sacrifice the quality of service.
- Improving employee motivation and engagement through better communication and increased transparency.
- Optimizing labor costs.
- Making employers and senior officials aware of worker engagement and individual employee performance, which helps management better plan training methods for new and potential employees.

Role of a Workforce Manager

The job of a workforce manager is to determine how to make the most out of the resources available and bring the best out of each employee. A workforce manager will take care of all assessment reports of the company's productivity, then design an appropriate plan to increase productivity.

A workforce manager will analyze daily production levels and labor time, then make valuable interpretations. Based on these interpretations, the workforce manager will make appropriate adjustments. Exceptional communication and problem-solving skills are required on the workforce manager's part so that there is no room for ambiguity.

A workforce manager's job is highly complex and requires immense effort. They must know how to balance an organization by trying to keep customers satisfied while reducing operational costs. No trade-off must be made between costs and customer satisfaction.

Forecasting is a key function of workforce management. Hence, an ideal workforce manager must have the right capabilities to provide the staff with the right motivation, encouragement, and care that will help build morale and improve performance. Overseeing employees and monitoring staff on a day-to-day basis is necessary in order to see results.

Organizational Restructuring

Restructuring usually takes place when an organization is looking to improve its business and maximize profits.

Changes in an organization's structure could be legal, operational, or ownership related. Other organizations looking to restructure usually do so after observing poor results over a certain period.

Organizations may decide to restructure if things are not going smoothly or changes implemented by the workforce management system are not showing results.

Factors Leading to Organizational Restructuring

Affected Business Environment

Businesses are always looking to expand and improve by adapting to newer methods. Incorporating newer methods in a business sometimes requires a specific organizational framework and infrastructure. For this purpose, organizations may think about restructuring so they can bring in newer technology and methods that may be beneficial to the business processes.

Some organizations or industries may suffer due to external factors, such as changes in governmental rules and regulations. A recent example of another external factor is the massive impact of COVID-19 on the tourism industry. In such circumstances, it is hard for an organization to remain afloat, and it may decide to restructure or even rebrand itself.

Financial Takeover

This is a scenario where a buyer or new owner may want to see a change in business proceedings after taking over a company. The new owner may have plans to restructure and rebrand the business and start over. If the owner chooses to go in a different direction, the business may call for a complete restructuring in infrastructure, resources, and employees.

Innovation

Evolving methods in information systems, telecommunication, and other technological advancements all make a huge difference in business productivity.

Organizational Restructuring Types

Financial Restructuring

Financial restructuring refers to changes in an organization's capital structure.

Cost-Saving

When cost-saving is required, restructuring is done to reduce the organization's overall operational costs. This is usually done through downsizing and laying off employees.

Mergers and Acquisitions

When two organizations look to combine or one organization takes over another, it is not surprising that some sort of restructuring may take place, as the vision of the new shareholders or owner may be different from that of the previous owner or shareholders.

Legal Restructuring

Legal restructuring occurs when changes are made to an organization's legal policies. This usually happens when changes are made in governmental rules and regulations, or when a takeover has taken place and the new management wants to make changes to the previous legal framework.

Workforce Management During Organizational Restructuring

In most cases, staff and employees have to face the consequences of restructuring. These consequences come in the form of sudden layoffs, which affect both the employees who have been let go and the ones who remain behind. Unexpected layoffs instill a fear of job insecurity in the employees' minds, so the workforce manager must deal with restructuring carefully.

After the layoffs, the new organizational structure—which must be laid out before the layoff process begins—represents the rebranding of the company and defines the new roles and responsibilities of all personnel. For instance, if the organization is downsizing and looking to keep only technical workers, it must make a list of employees who the workforce management wishes to keep and those it has to let go.

Once the new structure has been laid out and all the new roles and jobs have been defined, the workforce management and the workforce manager must plan how to get the best out of the new structure.

Workforce management must make sure that effective communication is taking place between all employees. To facilitate a higher level of communication, management may hold a few meetings and seminars to brief employees about their new roles.

Chapter 15: Corporate Social Responsibility

What Is Corporate Social Responsibility (CSR)?

The definition of CSR has been widely disputed since its inception in the 1960s. Different parties have different perspectives on what is going on. NGOs (non-government organizations) tend to see CSR as a "greenwash" scheme that misleads consumers into thinking they are more environmentally friendly than they actually are. The government classifies CSR as a disciplinary regulation imposed on companies to ensure a fair share of their profits is shifted to where it is needed. A business graduate would define CSR as simply a business strategy needed for the check and balance of a growing company.

The two most prominent names in defining CSR are Benedict Sheehy and Archie B. Carroll. After researching different viewpoints (e.g., managerial, institutional, and economic), Sheehy settled on "international private business self-regulation," while Carroll decided that CSR was launched because of the rising social concern for corporate relations with ethics. According to the ISO 2600 standards, Carroll's definition is closer to the official definition than Sheehy's.

Four Types of Corporate Social Responsibility

1. Environmental Responsibility

Environmental responsibility means taking measures to cut back on a company's carbon footprint. These measures vary depending on the company's size. Multinational companies tend to have a much bigger impact on the environment because of the resources used during the manufacturing stage of a product. Therefore, their measures include steps like:

- **Reducing greenhouse gases** – This step helps preserve the ozone layer. Over the past few decades, numerous companies have made reductions in emissions by a recognizable percentage. An example would be Ford making more fuel-efficient cars.

- **Preserving natural resources, such as forests** – Through this initiative, companies help preserve species that inhabit nature reserves. Additionally, preserving vegetation helps keep oxygen levels constant and carbon dioxide levels low in the atmosphere. Starbucks has taken a "Go Green" lead by making some of its products and stores through sustainable means.
- **Recycling/going green** – This strategy reduces landfill sites and, in turn, decreases greenhouse gas emissions by encouraging the reuse of waste material. This has become a very common practice among food companies that practice recycling by creating recyclable cutlery, napkins, etc.
- **Switching to renewable energy** – Renewable energy resources include solar panels and wind turbines. By switching to these power supplies, a company can eventually reduce greenhouse gas emissions. Companies like Nike and Google have switched some of their manufacturing plants to renewable energy.

2. **Ethical Responsibility**

In keeping with CSR, a company is bound to follow certain rules and regulations that ensure all of its employees (leadership, investors, employees, suppliers) are treated equally and fairly. This allows no room for discrimination against race, sex, class, etc. This strategy can also be termed "company diversity."

This CSR factor mainly tends to be a point of contention for companies operating on a large scale. In the early 2000s, Nike ignored ethical responsibility by employing underage workers for less than minimum wage. When this practice became known, people were outraged. The massive backlash nearly bankrupted Nike.

Ways in which a company can uphold ethical responsibility include:

- **Ensuring equal pay between male and female employees** – Although a rising concern, there seems to be little improvement on this initiative. However, if seen through, it will make for a much more agreeable workplace and more satisfied employees, which is advantageous to all businesses, according to Maslow's Hierarchy of Needs.
- **Addressing harassment claims in the workplace** – This is another common topic of discussion nowadays. A build-up of unaddressed harassment cases can greatly jeopardize a company's image. A simple solution is to address the problem at lower levels by providing employees with legal aid and, more importantly, enforcing rules that allow all employees to feel safe in their work environment.

3. Economic Responsibility

This is a practice in which an organization chooses to spend its profits in a manner that benefits the business as well as the environment. Consequently, this practice both increases sales revenue and provides gains for the community. A good example of this would be a business determining that using recyclable products during sales and manufacturing is better than the alternative. This decision lowers material costs for the company and consumes fewer nonrenewable resources.

4. Philanthropic Responsibility

This aspect of CSR supports the community beyond just providing jobs. It encourages practices in which a firm dips into its own profits to provide for any number of struggling populations. This is advantageous to a company because it makes the organization look humanitarian.

Monetary donations can be utilized in many ways, such as:

- **National disaster relief** – Just like different governments provide aid during national disasters, businesses can lend a helping hand, too, by funding NGOs that specialize in disaster relief teams.
- **Educational programs** – This is by far the most widely used scheme for philanthropy, and there is no better example than billionaire Bill Gates, whose foundation has consistently worked with international teams to bring technology education to remote parts of the world. Microsoft makes monetary donations and supplies its software free of cost to receivers of Gates Foundation grants.
- **Investing in the community** – This can be done through various modes, but usually there is a difference in how small and big businesses approach this topic. Large-scale businesses can take on large projects (i.e., installing water or power plants in villages), while smaller businesses can hold fundraisers for a local cause. In the end, both firms will benefit because of increased customer and employee loyalty.

The Benefits of CSR

Saving money on operating costs

A smart business needs to learn how to incorporate CSR into its current plan. If this is done effectively, the business will greatly benefit. When a firm reiterates mottos like "go green" or "save the Earth" enough times, it educates employees, which causes them to use resources provided by the company more efficiently and, in turn, brings down operating costs. A common example of this would be asking all employees to save energy by switching off lights and air conditioning when they leave work, or requesting that employees use printer ink and paper responsibly.

Enhancing influence in the industry

When a business follows CSR standards by behaving ethically, it benefits the entire hierarchy of employees (not just the top third of the pyramid) and preserves the natural environment. Additionally, if the CSR strategy is conducted fairly (by integrating it seamlessly with the current business plan), it attracts stakeholders and enhances the company's traction in the industry.

This increased traction is mainly seen between supplier firms and customer corporations. For example, a supplier firm might want to associate only with CSR-friendly firms in order to boost its own economic growth. Starbucks is a company that employs overseas coffee bean suppliers who strictly follow fair-trade policies (which is now a popular CSR tactic).

Funding opportunities

This factor is largely associated with small-scale businesses or start-ups. It is evident from recent statistics that small businesses tend to have a hard time surviving in the first three years of their operation; therefore, it is understandable that owners of such businesses focus solely on profit margins. However, it has been demonstrated that owners who keep CSR a prominent part of their business attract a larger number of opportunities because of the good name CSR gives them.

Therefore, it is recommended that small businesses incorporate CSR in all business practices to maximize their growth. For instance, institutions that offer grant money to start-ups actively look for CSR traits in business plans.

Organizations like the UN and the World Bank have taken it upon themselves to provide financial assistance to start-ups that promise to move forward with a philanthropic strategy.

Risk management

This is a straightforward concept relating to the check-and-balance operations a government runs on businesses. For example, businesses run through safety checks in their manufacturing plants. A significant amount of CSR in the business plan will persuade officials that the business is responsible enough to conduct its own checks and balances.

The elimination of such interference from the government is a principal task for a business. Furthermore, bad press can lead to a sudden decline in revenue. Consequently, rebuilding a business after evidence of fraudulent behavior can be nearly impossible.

Being an "Employer of Choice"

This is a commonly overlooked benefit of CSR but is becoming more and more relevant every year. Graduates looking for jobs are increasingly interested in the scope of CSR-utilizing companies. Therefore, CSR will bring a wider variety of potential employees to any firm.

This applies to the new-hire sector of the company and to current employees. As a population, we are starting to realize the negative impact we have on this Earth, and most of us are actively trying to find ways to negate it. Working for a company that incorporates CSR is a great place to start. The employees of these companies are usually attracted by eco-friendly marketing, but the journey to philanthropy does not end there. Activities like fundraisers and community volunteering are set up to make employees feel like they are actively giving back.

Preserving the environment

Below are some ways CSR impacts the environment positively:

- Encouraging recycling in offices and manufacturing plants reduces a company's waste products. This eventually results in a reduction in the company's carbon footprint.
- Regulations on the expenditure of electricity cause a decrease in energy wastage. Even better, switching to renewable sources of energy improves oxygen quality.
- Reducing the usage of automotive vehicles by increasing the usage of online meetings and memos; asking employees to carpool; and

providing free, shared transportation has a major impact on smog production in certain areas.

Chapter 16: Diversity and Inclusion

Diversity in the Workplace

If an organization is looking to maximize its gains, it needs to start improving the workplace. Diversity plays a crucial role in how efficiently a body of employees functions. Although individuals specifically in charge of selection and recruitment (the HR department) encounter this topic the most, it is no longer a matter just for them. Staff higher up in the hierarchy have also started to address this issue because of its impact on a company as a whole.

Diversity refers to the variation between individuals in a closed environment. It is composed of two basic parts:

- How one identifies oneself
- How one is regarded by one's peers

Examples of diversity include gender, personality, marital status, sexual orientation, ethnicity, race, and even mental and physical conditions.

<u>Inclusion in the Workplace</u>

The awareness of the need for inclusion in a workplace has been around since the sixties, but only recently have reforms been made to actualize this concept. The word *inclusion* is often grouped with *diversity* or *equality* but, in fact, inclusion encompasses both of these things. Through inclusion, we have access to additional opportunities to achieve equality and diversity in the workplace. SHRM's definition for inclusion is:

> The achievement of a work environment in which all individuals are treated fairly and respectfully, have equal access to opportunities and resources, and can contribute fully to the organization's success.

On an individual level, this definition translates to employees feeling confident and secure in expressing their individualism in their work environment.

Diversity vs. Inclusion

We will discuss the differences between these two aspects in this section, but it is important to remember that the implementation of these traits works synergistically. The difference in work efficiency is seen only when both aspects are incorporated smoothly.

The effects of diversity extend only to respecting and recognizing differences among individuals, while inclusivity is a practice in which the same individual is given equal opportunities in all official roles.

The practice of diversity was executed a lot earlier than inclusion because it is relatively easier to enforce. For example, American firms started to hire African American individuals in the sixties; however, these individuals' presence in the firm did not mean they had equal opportunities. They rarely received managerial positions and had very little say in the working of things compared to their counterparts.

Inclusion refers more to an employee's psyche and how it benefits from equal work distribution and equal creative power.

Benefits of Diversity

1. Wider Variety of Applicants During Recruitment Phase

When a company chooses not to discriminate between potential hires at a personal level, it automatically increases the pool of selection for the recruitment agencies. Rejecting differences like race opens up the selection to individuals who might show great potential. Not only this, but having a wider selection of candidates decreases the amount of time taken to fill key roles, saving the company precious time and money.

2. Enhancements to the Employer Brand

When consumers find out that a certain company is diversifying its workforce, this news positively impacts the company's image. This positive image translates into increased sales revenue. Customers are more likely to have a personal connection to a brand/product when they find out the people behind it are like them.

3. Improved Outreach to International Markets

Different language skills and cultural experiences can make it easier to market to different demographics. Individuals with work experience in different parts of the world are beneficial not only to the firm, but also to new target demographics.

4. Enhanced Creativity

It is statistically proven that the more diverse a group of people is, the higher their level of creativity. The explanation for this trend lies in the fact that people of different cultures and backgrounds introduce their own traditional ideas to the workplace. This, in turn, causes an integration of the different cultures, giving rise to a hybrid approach. This approach will target different demographics simultaneously.

Benefits of Inclusion

1. Increased Job Satisfaction

A company that makes inclusion its mantra will allow employees to cultivate a greater sense of self. This inclusion increases people's confidence and contributions to the firm. Additionally, an individual who is satisfied in the workplace will be a more loyal employee and dedicate more time and effort to the job, which will increase the person's work efficiency.

2. Lower Turnover

This is arguably the most lucrative benefit of practicing inclusion. A firm that preaches treating all its employees fairly and appreciates them for their efforts causes a decrease in turnover rate, meaning employees will refrain from leaving. This reduces the costs directed toward the recruiting agency and whittles the pool of employees so that only the most talented and dedicated individuals remain.

3. Higher Productivity

Inclusion has a direct relationship to productivity because when employees receive affirmation in the form of bonuses and other offers, it motivates them to dedicate more of their effort and time. This change happens not only on a personal level, but also company-wide—it increases the company's net efficiency.

4. Increased Organizational Flexibility

Organizational flexibility refers to a firm's ability to survive fluctuations in its vicinity without being affected itself. When management consistently practices inclusion, this creates a more apt workforce; employees will put more effort into collaborative measures when faced with hurdles.

Managing Diversity and Inclusion in the Workplace

Measures like diversity and inclusion might seem easy to establish, but in reality, it takes several years before a firm can see the fruits of its labors. Below are some ways this can be carried out:

1. Educating Employees in Managerial Positions

Managers play the most integral role in practicing diversity and inclusion. It makes sense that the person in charge needs to be aware of how to implement these practices to put them into effect. Managers not only have a stake in the employees' tenure, but are also seen as mentors. Therefore, employees in a position of power can either pressure their subordinates into following diversity and inclusion because they have power, or they can choose to set an example by abiding by the regulations of diversity and inclusion and using their influence as an educational tool.

However, the company has to realize that employees in management positions are also just part of the workforce. Many people in these positions fail to understand exactly how diversity and inclusion work, and their own personal biases cloud their better judgment. As a result, they are unable to appreciate the benefits this strategy brings about.

A straightforward way to tackle this problem is to organize workshops and training programs aimed at teaching these individuals how to integrate diversity and inclusion into their current work ethic. Additionally, firms should consider strict vetting processes for positions that involve leadership roles. Lastly, the only way of maintaining anything is through checks and balances; regular evaluations assessing improvement and relaying constructive criticism regarding diversity and inclusion should take place throughout the year.

2. Acknowledging Cultural/Ethical Differences

Through this method, a business learns to accommodate employees of all religious/cultural groups equally. This will lead to a greater sense of belonging and acceptance among peers and seniors. There are many ways to implement this task. For example, the concept of floating holidays is an allotted number of days that employees can take at any time of year to celebrate various religious holidays (Christmas, Eid, Hannukah, etc.).

3. Addressing Gender Inequality

Gender inequality has started to surface as a major problem in large-scale corporations. There are many aspects in which a workplace can be home to gender inequality, but the major problem lies in pay inequality.

Solving this issue is a multistep program that should be initiated by the simple acknowledgment of the pay gap. Once this is established (by making salaries an easy topic to talk about), a discussion needs to be held between subordinates and seniors, encouraging the presentation of contentions related to pay. Consequently, there should be meetings to review policies and shift profits to benefit everyone equally.

4. Redacting Biases in Promotions and Evaluations

The majority of individuals let their own personal biases, whether conscious or unconscious, infiltrate their work ethic. A system needs to be put in place to minimize this occurrence. This system will eliminate biases during opportunities like promotions and in-house assessments like evaluations. It will secure judgment based solely on a person's work-related skills and experience.

Strategies to minimize bias include:

- Being selective over the words used in internal memos. For example, using gender-neutral terms and descriptions to enforce inclusion.
- Establishing teams to eliminate information about demographic traits before documents like résumés or applications are reviewed.

5. Highlighting Disapproval of Discrimination

The majority of large-scale firms have had antidiscriminatory policies in place for several decades, to no avail. Documentation of such rules and regulations is not enough; it is crucial to actualize them. Employees in leadership positions play a vital role in implementing diversity and inclusion; therefore, it falls upon them to strengthen the practices.

6. Accommodating Various Generations

Nowadays, the workforce is dominated by millennials, but there needs to be an effort to make other generations feel comfortable too. For example, older employees should have training programs to keep up with their younger, computer-savvy counterparts or be provided with extensive health-care plans. On the other hand, younger employees should be offered packages to pay off student debt or be introduced to banking schemes that support installments on major spending.

7. Making Inclusion and Diversity a Daily Practice

Diversity and inclusion should be integrated into even the most minute details of the workplace. The basic message here is to respect everyone's wishes, not just on the official level but on a personal level too.

8. Keeping a Check on Diversity- and Inclusion-Related Laws

The government has assigned certain organizations the task of monitoring diversity and inclusion in workplaces. It should be commonplace for a firm to protect itself by staying abreast of any updates in these laws. This is especially important for larger firms that tend to face a major setback when faced with lawsuits. However, smaller businesses should not take laws lightly. Moreover, firms that have an international presence need to keep tabs on laws according to the laws of the country each branch is operating in.

Chapter 17: Conflict Resolution

In an organization setup or a workplace, conflicts between individuals or parties are fairly common. In broad terms, the term *conflict resolution* refers to settling a dispute among parties by reaching a peaceful and practical resolution.

Often, when an argument is born, the HR department looks to negotiate terms with the involved parties or come up with a resolution that both parties are satisfied with.

Conflict resolution applies to *all* disputes. We come across problems and get into conflicts frequently in our daily lives, and all of these occurrences can be seen as an opportunity to make use of conflict resolution and find a peaceful solution. These conflicts could be either household arguments between families or fights between friends or coworkers. These issues can be resolved through better communication or by putting effective conflict resolution strategies to use.

However, when problems are much bigger and more complex, exceptional critical thinking and negotiation skills may be required to reach a resolution. This is where conflict resolution helps. When a serious conflict arises, using conflict resolution strategies to negotiate allows both parties to come to terms with each other through a joint solution that will help both parties in the future.

Conflict resolution helps the aggrieved parties better understand one another, and improves decision-making and the ability to look for solutions as fast as possible. Conflict resolution skills can be very useful and are usually required by most organizations across various job sectors.

When working in an organization, arguments might take place between two coworkers, between an employer and employee, or even between management and its employees as a whole. For this purpose, organizations and companies look for exceptional conflict resolution skills among candidates during the hiring process.

Disputes within the workplace reduce productivity and affect employee morale. Individuals who can help resolve disputes are usually reasonable and easy to work with. They also are great negotiators and understand all types of personalities because they are compassionate.

Types of Conflict

Conflicts and disputes are a normal part of every organization. Disagreements between coworkers, missed deadlines, and differences of opinion are causes of conflict in the workplace.

All these disagreements can be categorized into types of conflicts. We discussed this earlier; now we will go into further detail, as this is a key topic in any business.

1. Relationship Conflict

Relationship, or interpersonal, conflict occurs between individuals who do not see eye to eye or who are not on the same page when working on a task. This mostly happens due to the individuals' personalities. They have different styles, goals, and ways of doing things.

Such conflicts are common in organizations. Often, these conflicts happen when individuals who would rather never meet each other outside work are assigned a collective task. And since this sort of conflict pertains to disputes between individuals on a personal level, it is easy for the situation to worsen rapidly.

2. Task Conflict

Arguments may emerge between a group of employees over the course of action that must be taken to perform a certain task. The larger the number of employees in a group, the larger the number of opinions.

When employees do not agree with each other, conflict often occurs. Disagreements are usually related to the task itself, policies, procedures, and work resources.

3. Intergroup Conflict

These types of conflicts usually include two different departments of an organization. There is, however, also the chance of conflict within a group that is not part of the organization. Both horizontal conflict, where workers argue between one another, and vertical conflict, where workers might argue with a subordinate, may occur in such types of conflict.

4. Value Conflict

Value conflicts may arise due to different preferences over values and identities. These preferences may include political parties, religion, or any other important beliefs. Senior management officials might also come into conflict with one another over the implementation of certain policies or programs that might affect the organization's image.

For instance, some senior officials might oppose a merger with an organization that has ties to a corruption scandal or express opposition to taking on a client who is being prosecuted.

Why Resolve Conflict?

The idea behind resolving conflict and reaching a middle ground is to ensure that both parties agree to a mutual decision that will help them in the future. Negotiating as quickly as possible also saves time, which is important to an organization's efficiency.

An important part of negotiations is acknowledging and understanding different opinions, beliefs, styles, and ideas that are not aligned with your own. This tactic allows those involved to look at things from a different perspective.

A healthy relationship between members of an organization or even another organization is always beneficial to a company's long-term stability. Through reconciling with your opponents, you build more allies and improve networking.

What the Conflict Resolution Process Should Include

The conflict resolution process involves several key actions or events that help identify the conflict and try to resolve it.

The most important part of the process is that both aggrieved parties acknowledge and recognize that there is indeed an argument.

Both the groups and individuals involved must agree to address the problem and look to compromise with each other. Moreover, they must put in the effort to resolve the issue, show empathy, and understand one another's point of view.

The role of the HR department and experts in the conflict resolution process is to observe key changes in the behavior and attitudes of both sides. They must try to identify the root of the problem and take the necessary steps to resolve it swiftly.

It is important to note that once the HR representatives or designated mediators have proposed key interventions, the involved parties must make compromises and agree to the resolution while setting aside personal differences and grudges.

Once the resolution has been reached and compromises have been made, both senior management and HR officials should monitor the effects of the agreements.

Senior management may terminate employees who fail to adhere to the new resolution and/or resist efforts to eliminate the problem.

Conflict Resolution Strategies and Methods

Different types of conflicts require different types of resolution strategies and skills. Some disputes are easy to solve and can be taken care of by fixing small communication gaps. More complex issues may require the assistance of HR representatives and mediators.

1. Assertiveness

The expert mediator or HR manager must set up a meeting to find a middle ground between the groups or individuals who have been arguing. Another example of this method is when one of the individuals or groups tries to resolve the issue peacefully by seeking out the other individual or group.

2. Communication

Effective communication is key to resolving conflicts. Both parties must listen to each other's opinions and emotions regarding the situation.

Some key tips for effective communication:

- Let members of the organization contribute. They might have an opinion that will help solve the problem.
- Both groups must speak freely about their emotions. This way, they will be able to be empathetic and understand one another's perspectives clearly.

- Active listening is important. If one party is not able to comprehend the other's opinion, they must make their lack of understanding clear to the other party.
- During negotiations, it is important to be firm but easygoing at the same time.

HR representatives have an important role to play in this strategy. Their job is to conduct interviews and listen actively to both parties, working out the nature of the problem and its root cause.

3. Avoidance

Avoidance usually occurs when people feel that resolving or communicating will be of no use and that it would be better to remain silent. Some may even feel that the atmosphere created by getting into a dispute and arguing is not worth the potential reward of resolving it.

4. Collaborating

Collaboration makes it easier for both parties and the HR department to resolve a conflict. Both groups are assertive and cooperative in this method. Additionally, collaboration saves valuable time.

5. Compromising

Compromising is where the aggrieved parties agree that they cannot have everything. Instead, the parties agree to make do on some things. They take what they can get and leave the rest. This happens in almost all conflict resolutions and is considered the fairest way of dealing with issues. Even if the participants are not completely satisfied, they understand that the decision was fair.

6. Critical Thinking and Brainstorming

Once mediators know what a dispute is and what the interests and demands of those involved are, they critically analyze those interests and demands and look for a conflict resolution.

The HR department may set up a meeting to discuss possible solutions with the two parties. The facilitators must consider certain things, such as:

- Trying to come up with as many solutions as possible and shortlisting the best ones
- Prioritizing the interests of groups involved and looking for solutions that are in their best interests
- Maximizing options

7. Looking for Alternatives

Mediators usually plan alternatives before they start working on appropriate solutions. The pros and cons of each alternative are taken into account before use. The alternatives may be ranked in order ranging from best to worst.

Conflict Resolution Examples

- A mediator/supervisor setting up a meeting between two individuals/groups in a dispute
- Two coworkers agreeing to cooperate with each other to find a peaceful solution to their problems
- HR experts conducting interviews and actively listening to each party's concerns
- An expert mediator successfully helping two individuals or groups understand one another's perspective and reach a mutual agreement
- Redefining the job roles of the aggrieved employees to prevent any further rifts

In conflict resolution, the facilitators' main goal is to generate a solution that works best for both sides. This may not always be possible, but it is still important that the experts try any means necessary to resolve the conflict as smoothly as possible.

Chapter 18: HR in the Global Context

HR management in the global context simply means overseeing a workforce of those organizations and firms that have business spread over several countries or continents. HR management (HRM) is different in every country and operates according to each country's culture and laws.

Global HRM revolves around taking care of employees and workers who work across the globe by managing and supporting them, as well as by implementing identical policies across each organizational branch to ensure fair treatment.

The global HRM team simultaneously takes into consideration the different laws, traditions, and cultures of each country where it manages an organization. Cultural differences often account for problems in workplace facilities, frameworks, and communication.

The workforces in different countries and continents will have different requirements in terms of working hours, wage rates, and salaries. Also, different legislation in different countries means different tax rates, benefits, contractual policies, and appraisal techniques. This is something the global HRM has to take care of.

All of this can be very complex for the global HRM system to deal with, even though the recent invention of global HR software has made it easier for organizations and firms to manage different policies.

To adapt to the changing economy and global requirements, HR professionals must develop new skills and competencies. This can be done by learning more about cultures and the various labor laws, employment legislation, and economic trends that apply to them.

Global HR Management Sectors

Employee Relations

Employee relations cause several challenges for employees working and living abroad. These challenges can relate to employee performance, motivation, or absenteeism. Many global HRM experts deal with these challenges by organizing an employee assistance program (EAP). The program offers solutions to deal with diverse cultural issues that stem from working in different parts of the world. The program also features methods to improve and maintain employee performance.

Labor Relations

Organizations taking their business to other countries or continents must consider the challenges of the labor market. The flexibility of the market and labor unions are extremely crucial to operating in foreign territories. It is important to know how strong the labor unions are and whether they pose any restrictions that may affect the performance of the business.

Business Leadership

Global leadership is key for a successful international business. Today, almost every organization that works locally and internationally is constantly searching for a global leader. With the increasing demand for global leaders, HR experts should look toward creating a global leadership development program. The main goal of this leadership program is to build candidates who manage businesses in other countries and help them adapt to the local culture.

A global leader who can effectively adapt and adjust to different cultures and norms can successfully handle international business challenges. They must also have an open mindset that considers all other cultures and views. It is important that the leader be sensitive toward diversity, including all ethnic, religious, and class groups that may coexist in the workplace. Respecting a region, its people, and its values is what makes a global business leader successful.

Lastly, a global business leader must be able to integrate into the organization workers of different class groups and cultures. After all, a workplace must have a proper corporate culture for the smooth running of operations across all platforms, regardless of any differences in culture, language, or legislation.

Ethics and Social Responsibility

As discussed earlier, CSR has become a crucial part of the modern HR department's activities. CSR is an organization's dedication to providing a quality lifestyle to its workers and the community.

Ethics and social responsibility in a business are crucial to the organization's image in the country where it is running its business. Business ethics and responsibility allow an organization to effectively advertise its employment brand to its employees, as well as to governments of other countries.

Diversity

Cultural backgrounds, ethnicities, and languages are all key variables that factor into a workplace atmosphere. Therefore, an organization and its HR department must conduct full-length research on the different issues and challenges that they may face when they go global.

Many global HRM teams run diversity programs once they finish setting up their business in a different country, so it is easy for members of the company to get to know each other better and build important relationships.

Staffing Management

As organizations look to globalize, they also face some key challenges in global staffing management. This is because actions or decisions that work very well in one country might not be as effective in another country due to differences in cultural norms or government policies and legislations. What is legal in one country might be illegal in another.

Some of the major challenges that global HRM professionals face related to staffing management are global relocation, recruitment, international assignment management, and global outsourcing.

Recruitment

It must be noted that when hiring internationally, job requirements for a specific job may differ from country to country due to differences in cultural norms. Hence, it would be favorable for the HR department to have a deep understanding of the cultural differences in each country to fully comprehend candidates' backgrounds and prior experience.

Employee Development

Employee learning and development are an integral part of an organization. Organizations that have their businesses set up across the globe can use that to their advantage by training employees from other parts of the world. Global business leaders and HR managers also have a duty to ensure that workers coming from a different country have access to all the resources they need to settle into and feel welcome in a new culture and environment.

Training

Training new staff and employees is important because they can get an idea of what their job positions require and what a firm's policies are. However, when training and briefing are done globally, this process can become a little more complex than usual.

To ensure that all employees and staff can understand their briefings, the global HRM experts must use a similar onboarding process at every branch. If need be, HR professionals should hire a translator.

The higher the transparency between the employees and the HR professionals when policies and procedures are being discussed, the better the communication and growth of a company's business will be.

Legal Compliance

HR professionals should clearly understand all government policies that impact their organization and strictly adhere to each country's legal requirements. Rules and regulations vary from country to country, and it is important that HR officials make sure that all rules and regulations are being strictly adhered to in every country the organization is operating in.

Employee Compensation and Benefits

Salaries, benefits, and compensation vary from country to country, so HR experts must ensure that all work and compensation laws are being abided by.

Importance of Global HR Management

HR is a major discipline of an organization that takes care of the most crucial part of the organization—its employees. Global HRM makes the transition for foreign workers with different cultural values, ethnicities and languages easier.

There has been an increasing demand for workforce empowerment in the last few years. In simple terms, workforce empowerment means giving employees the appropriate amount of power or authority that aligns with their responsibilities and job role. For this to happen, alterations will have to take place in the mindset and the skills of the workforce. Global HRM plays a vital role in bringing these changes to life.

Strategic Benefits

Global HR management has brought consistency to today's organizations. This level of consistency allows a company's brand to grow while simultaneously strengthening and making its operations smoother. Additionally, organizations can lay strong foundations for their organizational structure if they do this. Having similar structures at each location makes a company's goals and objectives more prominent and puts them at the forefront.

Having complete control over a company's operations allows the global HR manager to head the company and its operations in their entirety; as a result, the company is better able to run its foreign branches and the company brand itself.

Summary

With the increase in internationalization, global HRM has become more crucial than ever in helping organizations attain their goals and objectives. Organizations and firms that make extensive use of global HRM will have the upper hand in the global market over firms that do not use it. Global HRM helps improve the organization's operations and makes the transition to another country easier.

Additionally, the role of an HR manager is extremely vital in the global organizational movement. Managers must have the ability to show sensitivity and flexibility toward different cultures, backgrounds, and class groups. They must also have a clear understanding of the government laws of the host country and make sure that those laws are not broken.

Global HRM is a difficult process that makes the running of business operations across the world easier. Organizations and firms must take a positive approach toward global HRM in order to achieve stability and growth in the foreign market.

Chapter 19: Risk Management

When an organization sets up its business, it has to be prepared for all kinds of risks and failures, whether it is losing capital, resources getting damaged, or even fights breaking out in the workplace. Any occurrence that could create dissatisfaction in the workplace must be carefully avoided as much as possible.

In HR, risk management involves identifying risks that can harm the organization's business activities in the future and prevent them from happening. Employee conduct, improper management, and hiring are all important factors that may or may not contribute to an organization's failure.

Starting from the bottom, the focus includes even part-time employees and goes up to the senior management. The HR department must take into consideration the behavior of the whole staff to anticipate potential risks and deal with them.

Why Manage Risk?

Risk management on behalf of the HR department is a key aspect of almost every organization. There is a risk management plan in place in every business. Organizations with an established risk management plan fare well in controlling a challenging situation. Organizations with no backup plan to minimize risk may have to deal with reduced income, customer dissatisfaction, and wasted resources.

With the help of an HR risk management plan, an organization can deal with employees who might be a nuisance to the work environment while also improving decision-making during the hiring process. Managing the workforce across the whole organization also becomes a lot easier.

Who Is Involved?

The number of people who are involved in the risk management process and are responsible for devising plans to minimize risk may vary from organization to organization. An organization that works on a large scale may have the resources and finances to host a large risk management department. In a smaller company, by comparison, the responsibility lies mostly on the shoulders of the executive director.

However, once the risk management plan has been put into practice, each member of the organization becomes responsible for the smooth execution and running of the plan.

The Risk Management Process

Every organization needs to have a risk management process in place it can use to easily identify and understand the risks and challenges that it is exposed to and how to deal with them.

1. Identification

The first step of the process is identifying the risk. This involves looking at basic risks that are involved in every business, then further looking into risks specific to the organization itself.

2. Assessment

The next step is determining the probability of the risk and its severity. The risk management team may design a chart organizing the risks involved in order from top to bottom, to highlight both the frequency and severity of those risks.

3. Planning

This process involves the HR management team and the risk management experts (if any) coming together to research strategies corresponding to each risk. Some common strategies include:

Acceptance: This involves the organization coming to terms with the fact that there will be risks involved in certain activities crucial to the business's growth. For that reason, the organization will choose to come up with plans to minimize the damage.

Avoiding: Avoiding is the strategy in which risk management officials suggest that senior management stop certain processes and activities that may pose a serious threat to the business. This is done after determining how damaging the risk would be to the business and whether the business could take such a hit.

Modifying: Sometimes it is beneficial to change a few rules and policies surrounding a business activity to reduce the probability of a risk occurring.

Transferring and Sharing: Another intelligent strategy that organizations often use is transferring risk to another organization by signing a legal agreement whereby the other organization will take full or partial responsibility for any risks involved and bear the consequences.

4. Implementation

Once the strategies have been planned out and selected based on feasibility and practicality, the next step is to communicate these strategies to staff and employees, and highlight their key aspects.

The strategies must be carefully explained to everyone who may need to take part in their execution to achieve maximum benefit. If required, the HR staff and risk management experts may even provide relevant training so those involved can fully grasp the concept of these strategies and what they ought to bring to the table.

5. Observing

The last step of the risk management process is monitoring and observing the strategies once they have been implemented. The experts check whether there has been a decline in the frequency of the risks involved and whether the organization has expanded and improved its services since the risk management strategies were implemented.

The risk management experts also look to introduce upgrades to the strategies, if possible, to further decrease the chances of risk and allow the organization to run its business with more freedom and independence.

Examples of Organizational Risks and How to Deal With Them

An organization has to face several risks and potential challenges and come up with solutions. It is important to know that these risks and challenges vary from organization to organization. However, there are a few risks and challenges associated with every organization that the HR manager must take care of through risk management strategies.

Legal Compliance

Rules and regulations surrounding the business industry are usually very complex. If HR professionals are not fully aware of the laws and legislation an organization should comply with, the organization may face dangerous lawsuits and fines. To deal with this, HR professionals must regularly run comprehensive audits to ensure that an organization is not violating any legislation. Laws can change without prior notice, so the staff in charge of risk management must remain vigilant.

Talent Acquisition

The HR department is usually in charge of hiring. Interviewing, shortlisting, ordering background checks, etc., are all part of an HR professional's job requirements.

However, hiring comes with its own risks and challenges. If the hiring process is not planned and executed properly, it may cause a lot of problems, such as miscalculations in estimates of staff requirements that may lead to understaffing or overstaffing.

To deal with the challenges and risks involved during the talent acquisition process, it is best to establish an efficient recruiting program to make the hiring process easier. Also, it is beneficial if the hiring committee takes referrals from employees and asks them to recommend candidates who would be best suited for a particular job position.

The HR department may even consider a complete restructuring of the onboarding process if it feels job candidates are not able to match the needs the organization demands.

Cutting Losses

Although it might be hard for HR representatives to fire a struggling, underperforming employee, it is in the organization's best interests to let the employee go rather than waste time and resources hoping for an improvement in performance levels.

Employee Development

Risks might be involved in the employee learning and development process. It is a manager's job to make sure employees are growing and learning on the job. If employees are not satisfied with their development and growth in an organization, they might leave if they get a chance to. To minimize the risk of employees leaving, the HR department should set up development programs.

Summary

In the end, it is important to understand that the HR department has an important role to play in making sure that management is aware of the risks and challenges that an organization might be vulnerable to.

A clear understanding of the risks involved and how much damage they could cause to an organization's business are important factors in determining an organization's success rate. It is, therefore, vital that organizations today make the most out of their HR departments and provide them with the influx of resources and capital they need to improve the risk management process.

Chapter 20: Total Rewards

Total rewards refers to all the benefits given to an employee based on performance levels during a given period. These rewards recognize an employee's hard work, dedication, and desire to achieve the best possible results for the organization.

The total rewards system is a strategic business strategy an organization implements to recognize its employees' efforts by compensating them through monetary and developmental rewards.

Senior management and executives know that to retain desirable employees, they must provide competitive salaries and rewards. These rewards usually consist of benefits and compensations such as wage increments, bonuses, and better career opportunities. The total rewards system also has implications for social change, as it can positively impact employee empowerment.

Organizations often use the total rewards strategy to reward their employees. Apart from the usual benefits and compensation offered in total rewards, some organizations use the total rewards distribution as an opportunity and platform to introduce learning and development programs. On top of other benefits, such activities keep employees engaged and reduce the probability of employees leaving.

Total Rewards Strategies

To successfully implement a total rewards strategy, it is important to have senior management and executives on board to develop an approach that drives organizational change. The team, which usually consists of the HR representative and other company employees, should be composed of excellent decision-makers and analysts so that the total rewards plan fits the needs of everyone in the organization.

Developing a smooth total rewards system may involve some of the following strategies.

1. <u>Analyzing</u>

The group members responsible for creating an efficient total rewards system start by assessing and analyzing the current total rewards system. They assess the current list of benefits and rewards and how effective they have been in helping the organization achieve its goals.

The team also takes employee opinions into account by running surveys and conducting interviews. The employees weigh in on how beneficial the current total rewards system is. Also, the total rewards planning team considers employees' opinions on growth and development, the current salary system, benefits, and other compensation methods.

The team also takes a look at the policies and the daily practices that the organization has set. Any recommendations senior management or employees have made regarding policies and practices are part of the assessment report.

The group responsible for generating a new total rewards system must come up with a solution to important questions such as:

- Which types of rewards will suit employees' needs?
- Who is eligible to receive the rewards?
- What level of performance or contribution is required to receive rewards?
- Does the organization have the capital and resources to fund specific rewards and benefits?

2. Designing

This is where a senior executive works with the group tasked to develop the rewards and compensation for the total rewards plan that will be best suited to the workplace.

Different types of rewards will be established for different levels of achievement. These rewards might be monetary and may also include other rewards, such as extended time off from work, flexible working hours, and other development opportunities.

As mentioned earlier, HR professionals often determine nonmonetary rewards to help boost employee morale and assist in employee learning and growth. These rewards are usually given out when employees meet goals or objectives.

3. Executing

The execution process includes the HR representative bringing the new total rewards system into action by communicating and describing the new system's rules and strategies. Employees are made aware of the new performance levels they must reach to be eligible for rewards.

The HR staff and those responsible for coming up with the plan train managers and senior officials to effectively understand and measure achievement levels.

4. Evaluating

Once the total rewards plan has been implemented, it must be evaluated and measured regularly. A report should be compiled and sent to the senior executives. Based on the group's evaluations, further modifications may be suggested for future strategies.

Therefore, a good total rewards strategy includes all the elements that will lead to faster attainment of the organization's goals and objectives. It is important to understand that HR should lead the entire total rewards procedure and all components of the total rewards strategy must address employee benefits, compensation, and development initiatives.

During the development process, employers should work with HR professionals to set up the rewards and benefits to align with the organization's strategic structure. HR plays a key role during the entire process and helps both employers and employees understand the structure of the total rewards plan.

Oftentimes, employees do not consider the number of resources that their employers have invested into a total rewards plan; HR professionals have to help them see this.

Distinguishing Total Rewards

Financial and Nonfinancial Rewards

Financial rewards help ease the financial burden on an employee. They contribute to the employee's financial well-being and usually include bonuses and a raise.

Nonfinancial rewards offer no monetary incentive; instead, they recognize employees' efforts by giving them benefits, including free parking spaces, gym memberships, time off, and childcare.

When choosing between the two, organizations usually prefer to give out nonfinancial rewards. Nonfinancial rewards can be used on a long-term basis compared to monetary benefits, which give only one-time satisfaction. Employees also feel more comfortable discussing rewards and benefits that do not have a monetary value attached to them.

Additionally, organizations can easily meet the cost of nonfinancial rewards. Financial rewards given to employees with similar performance levels generally require a higher investment, which, many times, organizations cannot provide.

Intrinsic and Extrinsic Rewards

Intrinsic rewards are intangible and provide a higher level of job satisfaction to employees. These psychological rewards are a recognition of employees' performance and achievement of significant results.

Intrinsic rewards make employees feel appreciated and valued by the organization. Some important examples include promotions, personal achievements, and praise by senior management. These rewards are intrinsic because an individual achieves them through hard work and persistence. Additionally, these rewards cause sustained behavioral change.

Extrinsic rewards are tangible rewards given out to employees for their performance. They include monetary benefits, such as pay raises, bonuses, and other financial incentives. Extrinsic rewards usually are the result of a collective effort instead of one individual working alone.

Advantages of a Total Rewards System

The key aspects of the total rewards system cater to all the things that an organization can do to retain its employees; attract potential employees; and provide bonuses, incentives, and learning and growth opportunities. An organization benefits greatly from a total rewards system.

Employee Performance

Most total rewards programs offer direct incentives to employees in the form of career growth and development opportunities. These help employees develop new skills, increase their knowledge, and improve their abilities.

Additionally, the total rewards system allows for better employee performance monitoring through employee input. This creates a dialogue between employees and employers, which leads to better understanding between the two; as a result, mutual respect is born.

Employee Retention

During the hiring process, small businesses and firms may show potential candidates the metric by which performance levels are measured. These levels show the levels at which benefits such as bonuses, pay raises, and other intrinsic or extrinsic rewards are given out.

These levels provide an incentive for employee retention. They give candidates and employees a road map to their long-term goals and objectives. Another important benefit is transparency, which puts both senior management and its employees on the same page and helps build relationships and a peaceful work environment.

Value Proposition

The total rewards system allows the organization to better communicate the level of investment it has put in to come up with the total rewards. Most employees are unaware of the substantial amount of costs organizations bear to introduce bonuses, pension plans, and other monetary and nonmonetary incentives.

For this purpose, employers sometimes hand out a total rewards statement to their employees. This statement emphasizes the cost and value of all other benefits and incentives that the organization offers employees apart from salary.

Program Administration

The total rewards system also helps HR organize and administer all employee concerns related to benefits and other incentives. In organizations and businesses that lack a proper total rewards system, the system of compensation and rewards can be poorly structured. For example, health-care administration occurs on a separate schedule from salary, and bonuses and company benefits take place on a different schedule than learning and development. In a well-established total rewards system, all these elements can be administered at one place and time without any discrepancies.

Summary

Every employee or staff member works best if the organization provides an incentive, whether it is financial or nonfinancial. The total rewards strategy and plan is crucial; in fact, it can be the factor that allows the organization to attain a competitive advantage in the market.

Additionally, it must be understood that a basic salary is not an employee's sole motivator. An organization must acknowledge that tangible and intangible rewards and benefits motivate an employee to work harder.

The total rewards strategy contributes to an employee's financial well-being and development. It strengthens employee and employer relationships and improves communication in the organization as a whole. It brings satisfaction to the employees and improves overall morale.

SHRM-CP Test 1

(1) For HR professionals, understanding core aspects of a business is crucial because:

(A) It allows them to design long-term strategies that are in alignment with the goals and objectives of the business.

(B) It allows them to hire the right people.

(C) Both A and B.

(D) None of the above.

(2) Which of the following is not required in deciding business acumen?

(A) Knowledge of the most profitable aspects of the business

(B) Knowledge of the current market situation

(C) A thorough understanding of the respective niche

(D) A focus on quantitative research versus qualitative research

(3) Face-to-face communication is encouraged because:

(A) Most companies find it difficult and time consuming to personalize emails.

(B) It allows for better integration of different companies or departments.

(C) Customers may also get a chance to voice their opinions.

(D) It allows for effective decision-making that may save time.

(4) Which of the following suggestions may not help in the development of business acumen?

(A) Familiarity with the current business strategy

(B) An understanding of the company's finances

(C) Know-how of the technical aspects of the business

(D) An understanding of the business environment

(5) An HR professional must:

(A) Possess technical know-how

(B) Understand business finances

(C) Make practical decisions

(D) Both B and C

(6) An HR consultant is not required to have which of the following characteristics?

(A) Business management skills

(B) Marketing abilities

(C) Dependence on the parent company or organization

(D) Ability to manage an office, customers, the business, and its finances

(7) Why must HR consultants be aware of the legal aspects of a business?

(A) They may choose to work alone.

(B) They may have to deal with the administrative aspects of the business.

(C) Both A and B.

(D) None of the above.

(8) An HR consultant's critical evaluation helps:

(A) Improve the documentation process

(B) Understand the bigger picture

(C) Evaluate the decision quality

(D) Both B and C

(9) HR consultants look for smaller companies to work with because:

A) Such companies help them formalize long-term relationships.

B) Such companies lessen the burden of publicity.

C) Such companies lessen the competition in a respective niche.

D) Such companies offer more chances to succeed and grow independently.

(10) Why should an HR consultant stay current with the latest trends?

A) Older trends become redundant over time.

B) It helps them attract customers.

C) It helps them stay ahead of the competition.

D) It allows them to work for larger companies and corporations.

(11) Which of the following sets of three words best describes *ethical practices*?

A) Moral principles, employee behavior, everyday business practices

B) Health, safety, moral principles

C) Employee behavior, everyday business practices, health

D) Business growth, moral principles, employee behavior

(12) Which of the following statements is untrue regarding integrating cultural effectiveness and ethical practices into a business?

(A) They both create a strong and reliable brand image, which attracts investors.

(B) They both give employees a sense of belonging.

(C) They both guarantee the protection of the ecosystem/environment.

(D) They both make the sales department humbler, which can win brand loyalty.

(13) Which of the following actions could be untrue in regard to ethical practices?

(A) Keeping employees accountable

(B) Maintaining the secrecy of certain private documents

(C) Hiring people of all ethnicities, irrespective of their past

(D) Keeping a very close eye on new-world developments and directives

(14) There is a constant learning process that happens in a workplace. This process enhances a person's interpersonal skills and ability to enhance other skills, like being aware of surroundings and staying humble.

What does this statement best explain?

(A) Personal growth encouragement

(B) Business growth encouragement

(C) Enhancing self-belief

(D) Enhancing ethical beliefs

(15) Why is it so important for a business workforce to be aware of the cultural differences in a firm?

(A) Cultural differences help in decision-making.

(B) An intercultural office allows a company to target a bigger audience.

(C) Cultural differences help with the creation of a legal structure.

(D) None of the above.

(16) Organizations are able to successfully meet their goals if leadership incorporates maintenance requirements and task needs into the workforce schedule.

Which of the following is not a maintenance role of leadership?

(A) Praising, acknowledging or recognizing worker performance

(B) Resolving any contradictions or differences between group members

(C) Stating the approach and attitude expected from the group members

(D) Passively following the audience or group's approach and welcoming its ideas

(17) Which of the following motivational theories highlights the cognitive process that enables individuals to interpret factors that bring about their final decision or course of action?

(A) Expectancy theory

(B) Theory of self-determination

(C) Goal-set theory

(D) Attribution theory

(18) Which group of higher-order needs ensures that tasks set are deemed intrinsically motivating when at least one of those needs is met?

(A) Independence, expertise, and affiliation

(B) Security, rest, and prestige

(C) Expertise, safety, and shelter

(D) Affiliation, expertise, and security

(19) Which of the following is an assumption of expectancy theory?

(A) All individuals are rational.

(B) Individual behavior is determined by the desirability of the outcome.

(C) Both A and B.

(D) None of the above.

(20) How does hedonism link to the expectancy theory of motivation?

(A) All individuals are rational decision-makers.

(B) Individuals act in ways that decrease their pain and increase their pleasure.

(C) Goals are more likely to be met when individuals are involved in the goal-making process.

(D) None of the above.

(21) The Situational Leadership Theory® constitutes which four leadership styles?

(A) Participating, delegating, and coaching

(B) Supporting, directing, and participating

(C) Coaching, supporting, delegating, and directing

(D) None of the above

(22) Which of the following is an essential component during the recruitment process?

(A) Understanding labor markets and the factors that influence them

(B) The needs of the public

(C) The company's financial standing

(D) The candidate's qualities

(23) Which of the following is a step in a job-based analysis?

(A) Seeing whether or not a candidate fits the requirements of the job vacancy

(B) Cold-calling customers three times a day

(C) Calling customers back

(D) Analyzing market trends and the market situation

(24) What type of testing is not part of the recruitment process?

(A) Job knowledge tests

(B) Cognitive ability tests

(C) Language tests

(D) Work samples

(25) Which of the following is not an internal factor during the recruitment process?

(A) Financial restrictions

(B) Employee unions

(C) Increase or decrease in sales

(D) Changes in technology

(26) Which of the following is the first step of the recruitment process?

(A) Acknowledging a job vacancy

(B) Making use of a staffing plan

(C) Creating a recruitment strategy

(D) Determining the most effective methods of recruitment

(27) Which of the following is a distinction between conventional HR management and modern HR management?

(A) Modern HR management's fundamental focus is on everyday tasks, whereas conventional HR management involves recruiting people well suited for the job and ensuring ethical leadership via innovative business strategies.

(B) Both modern and conventional HR management are similar, but the latter is more focused on innovative business strategies.

(C) Conventional HR management's fundamental focus was on daily tasks, whereas modern HR management involves recruiting, encouraging leadership, and creating strategies.

(D) None of the above.

(28) Which of the following steps in the process of strategic planning constitutes an overview of an organization's position in the market?

(A) Developing a strategy

(B) Analyzing the situation

(C) Implementing the strategy

(D) None of the above

(29) Of the following, which cannot be used to create an outline for a work breakdown structure (WBS)?

(A) A flowchart

(B) A PowerPoint presentation

(C) A spreadsheet

(D) All of the above

(30) Monitoring and controlling is one of the five process categories. What does this process category entail?

(A) It states a new project's beginning or the new beginning of an ongoing project.

(B) It performs the tasks described in the project management plan.

(C) Both A and B.

(D) It reviews and modulates a project's performance.

(31) Lean is a project management approach that:

(A) Suggests business managers subject personnel and processes to excessive stress due to unclear working methods, poor equipment, and insufficient organization

(B) Is designed to counter the limitations of the Waterfall technique

(C) Highlights the significance of customer value while reducing waste by using fewer resources

(D) Both A and C

(32) The term *corporate social responsibility* is best defined as:

(A) Investing in the community

(B) Ethical conduct

(C) Environmental practices

(D) All of the above

(33) Corporate social responsibility includes:

(A) Recognizing that being ethical requires extensive financing

(B) Requiring a company to be held socially accountable to its investors

(C) Recognizing that a critical analysis of performance is very important

(D) Recognizing that only the natural environment should be taken care of

(34) __________ is a very common practice among food companies in order to reduce the overall environmental impact of their business practices and to be more efficient and responsible toward the environment.

(A) Going green

(B) Using renewable energy

(C) Ensuring equal pay between employees

(D) Promoting Earth Day

(35) Business contributions for charitable purposes are what type of corporate social responsibility?

(A) Corporate charities

(B) Corporate investments

(C) Donations

(D) Philanthropy

(36) Which of the following is a benefit of taking into consideration the aspects of corporate social responsibility?

(A) Profit maximization

(B) Preserving the environment

(C) Clashing of business objectives

(D) Both A and B

(37) What is the result of employees having a relaxed relationship with their coworkers?

(A) Stronger communication

(B) Collaboration

(C) Cooperation

(D) All of the above

(38) What kind of conflict arises when one person's or group's thoughts and feelings are different from the thoughts and feelings of others?

(A) Behavioral conflict

(B) Cognitive conflict

(C) Affective conflict

(D) Goal conflict

(39) Where does interpersonal conflict occur?

(A) When a person is at odds with himself or herself

(B) When two firms in the same sector are in disagreement

(C) When two groups disagree over goals or resource-sharing

(D) None of the above

(40) Which of the following techniques is not included in the Thomas-Kilmann Model of dispute resolution options?

(A) Accommodating

(B) Defending oneself

(C) Making concessions

(D) Working together

(41) According to Riverbark, 2010, almost 90% of managers believe that employees leave an organization because of:

(A) Money

(B) Problems with the boss

(C) Tight schedules

(D) Unhealthy working conditions

(42) If managers do not take into account external factors, this will likely lead to:

(A) Greater independence of employees

(B) Alienation of employees

(C) Greater productivity

(D) Less teamwork but swifter action

(43) Employees within an organization are driven by which theory?

(A) Equity theory

(B) Reinforcement theory

(C) Expectations theory

(D) Rewards system theory

(44) HR professionals and managers are often mistaken in their beliefs as to why employees leave. The reason they cite for resignations is:

(A) Uninteresting work

(B) Too much work

(C) A mismatch between the tasks and the employee's abilities

(D) Low pay packages

(45) Which of the following is not an external factor that influences HR?

(A) Flexible working hours

(B) Telecommuting

(C) Health-care costs

(D) Technological advancements

(46) Organizational effectiveness and development (OE&D) focuses on which aspect of a business to improve its growth, performance, and success?

(A) Business ethics and public relations

(B) Product and research development

(C) Internal business policy and structure

(D) Data and forecasting

(47) Employees and good team performance are necessary factors contributing to organizational effectiveness. As such, many interventions help in achieving this goal.

Which of the following is an example of a nonbehavioral intervention?

(A) Management by objectives

(B) Role-playing

(C) Interpersonal relations

(D) Job enrichment

(48) To judge a business's performance and the effectiveness of its policies, obtaining the best decision data is very important. Which form of data collection is a miscellaneous intervention that could aid in the accomplishment of this goal?

(A) Survey feedback and questionnaires

(B) Secondhand data from the internet

(C) Newspapers and local magazines

(D) Government publications

(49) Organizational development is a process done in steps. As the head of a supermarket and retail chain, assume that you are to initiate this process.

Which of the following is the first action you should take to formally start the development process?

(A) Look at employee resignations and labor turnover in poor-performing branches.

(B) Distribute detailed surveys asking for the opinions of various employees, such as cashiers.

(C) Implement new policies and strategies designed to combat identified problems.

(D) Design interventions, such as job enrichment and rotations, to boost worker motivation.

(50) Which of the following are examples of organizational design structure?

(A) Matrix structure

(B) Vertical and horizontal structure

(C) Divisional design structure

(D) Centralized and decentralized structure

(51) What is the concept of technological management?

(A) Making innovative products with the latest technologies installed in them

(B) A business strategy in which maximum resources are poured into research and development

(C) A concept that entails adapting to technological changes and integrating them into the business

(D) A process that enables cost-saving by avoiding the use of the latest, often expensive technology

(52) Which of the following departments is a core player in bringing technological change and management to a business?

(A) The marketing department

(B) The IT department

(C) The manufacturing department

(D) The quality control department

(53) The Strategic Technology Management System (STMS) allows for the adoption of a new technological system or change and its implementation and management until its eventual decline or replacement. It is a process done in steps.

Which of the following is not an STMS step?

(A) Technology creation

(B) Technology utilization

(C) Technology removal

(D) Technology transfer

(54) A competitive advantage between organizations arises from an individual's:

(A) Competency

(B) Efforts

(C) Quality of work

(D) Hard work

(55) Who should have the most say when it comes to technology management?

(A) The customers

(B) The CEO or head of senior management

(C) The IT department and a team of innovators

(D) The average employee

(56) From which of the following areas are new employees recruited during the hiring process?

(A) The employment association

(B) The employment line

(C) Labor schemes

(D) The labor market

(57) An organization's goal to introduce new systems and mechanisms in career planning mainly focuses on employee:

(A) Career progression

(B) Self-development

(C) Economic development

(D) Skill enhancement

(58) What may be the cause of a gap in the communication and cohesiveness of a group?

(A) The frequency of interactions

(B) Agreeing to the group objective

(C) A large group size

(D) All of the above

(59) Arrange the following career growth and development processes, starting from first to last.

(I) Need (II) Vision (III) Results (IV) Action Plan

(A) IV, I, II, III

(B) I, III, IV, I

(C) I, II, IV, III

(D) IV, III, I, II

(60) Which of the following factors is linked to the working conditions of an organization?

(A) Fair wages and salary

(B) Work environment

(C) Development opportunities and career growth

(D) All of the above

(61) Which department in a company is responsible for hiring employees and keeping checks on their performance?

(A) The finance department

(B) The research and development department

(C) The HR department

(D) The creative department

(62) Which of the following is not a part of diversity, referring to the variation between individuals in a closed environment?

(A) How one identifies oneself

(B) How one is regarded by one's peers

(C) Both A and B

(D) None of the above

(63) Which of the following refers to an employee's psyche and how this benefits from equal work distribution and equal creative power?

(A) Inclusion

(B) Diversity

(C) Exclusion

(D) None of the above

(64) Different language skills and cultural experiences can make it easier for a company to become multinational. Marketing helps a company grow in which type of market segmentation?

(A) Psychographic

(B) Demographic

(C) Geographic

(D) Both A and C

(65) What is the efficiency at which a company or economy can transform resources into goods, potentially creating more from less?

(A) Lower turnover

(B) Increased organizational flexibility

(C) Increased job satisfaction

(D) Increased productivity

(66) Conflict resolution may help:

(A) Improve understanding, decision-making, and solution-seeking

(B) Avoid further conflicts

(C) Bring about interdepartmental harmony

(D) Make use of all available resources, thereby improving productivity

(67) Which of the following is not part of the HR department's process during conflict resolution?

(A) Observing key changes in behavior and attitude

(B) Taking hardline steps against those in conflict to prevent further conflicts

(C) Identifying the root of the problem

(D) Taking necessary steps before the situation gets worse

(68) Which of the following is one of the fairest ways of resolving a conflict?

(A) Assertiveness

(B) Communication

(C) Compromise

(D) Collaboration

(69) What type of conflict in an organization takes place on a deeper and more personal level?

(A) Value conflict

(B) Task conflict

(C) Intergroup conflict

(D) Relationship conflict

(70) Which of the following is a result of conflict resolution?

(A) It improves relations by bringing the parties to agreement.

(B) It may worsen the dispute.

(C) Both A and B.

(D) None of the above.

(71) Organizations tend to incorporate ___________ into their daily business practices to enhance employee performance and make better use of the resources at their disposal.

(A) Workforce management

(B) Time management

(C) Data collection

(D) Managing employees

(72) Which of the following is not included in workforce management tasks?

(A) Time management

(B) Data accumulation

(C) Employee performance

(D) Organizational structure

(73) Staff __________ permits organizations to optimize their resources and plan as needed while keeping business variables, such as workload, availability of resources, time of the year, and other complexities, in mind.

(A) Compliance

(B) Time management

(C) Scheduling

(D) Recruitment

(74) Organizations must stay current with the technological world to remain successful. This process is known as:

(A) Financial takeover

(B) Innovation

(C) Business environment

(D) None of the above

(75) What usually happens when regulatory changes or a takeover takes place, and the new management wishes to make changes to the organization's previous legal framework?

(A) Legal restructuring

(B) Cost-saving

(C) Mergers and acquisitions

(D) Financial restructuring

(76) What are some of the challenges HR professionals face pertaining to staffing management?

(A) Global relocation

(B) Recruitment and global outsourcing

(C) International assignment management

(D) All of the above

(77) The HR department is concerned with managing a company's:

(A) Employees

(B) Funds

(C) Brand

(D) All of the above

(78) Which of the following is the benefit of HR management?

(A) It lays a strong foundation for the organizational structure.

(B) It makes the organization's goals and objectives clear.

(C) Through the application of HRM, a brand grows and operations get smoother.

(D) All of the above.

(79) Global HRM takes into account:

(A) The care of employees working across the globe

(B) The different laws, traditions, and cultures that exist across the globe

(C) Both A and B

(D) None of the above

(80) What is the main goal of a business leadership program?

(A) Outsourcing labor to different parts of the world

(B) Building strong candidates who can manage businesses in other countries

(C) Dealing with labor unions

(D) All of the above

(81) Which of the following correctly defines total rewards?

(A) All those benefits that might be given to employees based on their performance levels during a given period

(B) All those benefits that might be given to a company based on performance levels during a given period

(C) All those benefits that might be given to executives based on their performance levels during a given period

(D) All those benefits that might be given to management based on their performance levels during a given period

(82) For the successful implementation of the total rewards strategy, it is important that:

(A) Senior management and executives develop an approach that will drive organizational change.

(B) The team, which consists of the HR representative and other company employees, is composed of excellent decision-makers and analysts so that the total rewards plan fits the needs of all the members of the organization.

(C) The employees determine the rewards.

(D) Both A and B.

(83) Which of the following correctly describes the execution process of the total rewards system?

(A) The HR representative brings the new total rewards system into action and describes the new system's rules, strategies, performance levels, and rewards.

(B) The HR staff trains managers and senior officials to understand and effectively measure the level of employee achievement.

(C) Both A and B.

(D) None of the above.

(84) What is the difference between financial and nonfinancial rewards?

(A) Financial rewards help ease the financial burden on an employee. They contribute to the employee's financial well-being. These monetary rewards usually include a bonus and a raise in salary. Nonfinancial rewards are very similar to financial rewards.

(B) Financial rewards help ease the financial burden on an employee. These monetary rewards usually include a bonus or a raise in salary. Nonfinancial rewards offer no monetary incentive but recognize the employee in some manner.

(C) Financial rewards do not help ease the financial burden on an employee. They do not contribute to the employee's financial well-being. Nonfinancial rewards help employees with their financial burdens.

(D) Financial rewards have the form of assets and nonfinancial awards are based on equity.

(85) What is the impact of a total rewards system on employee performance?

(A) It uses employee input to allow for better employee performance monitoring. This creates a dialogue between employees and employers, leading to better understanding between the two, so mutual respect is born.

(B) It worsens employee performance monitoring. It makes the employees greedy for the next reward. It creates conflicts in the workplace and makes the workplace environment stressful.

(C) It makes a firm's managers angry with its employees. The managers think that all the employees want is money in exchange for their work, which is not true.

(D) Both A and C.

(86) Which option best describes risk management in HR?

(A) It is the process of trying to identify and recognize risks that have the potential to harm the organization's business activities in the future and preventing them from happening.

(B) It is the process of trying to identify and recognize risks that have the potential to harm employees and dealing with those risks.

(C) It is the process of trying to identify and recognize risks that have the potential to harm the company's brand identity and dealing with them.

(D) It is the process of trying to identify and recognize risks that have the potential to harm the company's financial success and dealing with them.

(87) Why is it important to manage risks?

(A) In every business, a risk management plan is assembled in case of a disaster.

(B) An organization can have an efficient business plan, resources of the highest quality, and huge amounts of capital, but if it does not hire the right employees with the skills and capabilities to execute the plan, the organization will not succeed.

(C) Organizations with an established risk management plan fare well in controlling a challenging situation.

(D) All of the above.

(88) Who is involved in the process of risk management?

(A) There is a special team dedicated to this purpose in many companies.

(B) The executives of the company are responsible for this process.

(C) Each member of the organization is responsible for the smooth execution of the plan.

(D) Both B and C.

(89) Which of the following options best explains the planning part of risk management?

(A) HR teams and the risk management experts (if any) research and create strategies corresponding to each risk.

(B) The company accepts the risk, then tries to find a way to avoid the risk.

(C) The HR team and risk management experts modify the rules and some processes happening in the business.

(D) All of the above.

(90) What is legal compliance?

(A) It takes place when HR professionals regularly run comprehensive audits to make sure that the organization is not violating any legislation and is complying with the country's rules and regulations.

(B) It takes place when the company undergoes major restructuring and assesses whether it is meeting all employees' needs and acknowledging their opinions.

(C) It happens when legal actions against an employee take place.

(D) All of the above.

(91) A quantitative technique in the job evaluation process is:

(A) Job classification

(B) Alternative ranking method

(C) Aligned ranking method

(D) Point method

(92) Which of the following is not a centralized communication network system?

(A) The circle network

(B) The chain network

(C) The wheel network

(D) The X-shaped network

(93) An organizational confrontational meeting is an example of:

(A) Human process intervention

(B) Technostructural intervention

(C) Strategic intervention

(D) HR intervention

(94) The type of third-party intervention in which an arbitrator dictates and determines the terms of a settlement is classified as:

(A) Medication

(B) Impasse

(C) Fact-finder

(D) Arbitration

(95) Strategic HR planning is:

(A) The process of formulating HR strategies and establishing programs to implement them

(B) Responding appropriately to HR problems

(C) A dying practice as more companies move to TQM

(D) The responsibility of HR professionals

(96) An organization is looking to introduce strategic management sessions for possible directions to move in the future. What would ideally be the role of the HR manager in the planning sessions for this new direction the company is thinking of moving in?

(A) Acquiring useful data about the industry the organization is looking to move into

(B) Acquiring information that would help support the HR department's motives for the company's future growth

(C) Focusing on the important HR issues and not paying attention to the organization's objectives

(D) Thinking about the direction that the organization chooses to go in and how it would affect the HR department

(97) An organization is looking to introduce strategic management sessions for possible directions to move in the future.

What is the most important phase of the HR manager's contribution to this new direction the company is thinking of moving in?

(A) The strategy formulation

(B) Partaking in a SWOT analysis while developing the strategy

(C) The strategy evaluation process

(D) Initiative for strategy implementation

(98) An organization that promises a delivery service that is faster than the production department's ability to produce lacks an understanding of:

(A) The organization's reputation

(B) Organizational structure and leadership

(C) The relationship between the organization's functional areas and the organizational strategies

(D) Synergy among business units

(99) The CEO and senior management of a large-scale corporation are discussing and strategizing the process of STMS to implement new technology and improve the implemented system for the long-term betterment of the corporation's profits and performance.

Which of the following approaches should be adopted when trying to modernize and improve a large-scale corporation's technological systems?

(A) A cost-saving approach

(B) Replication of competitors' and rivals' technological systems

(C) Replicating industry standards and approaches to STMS

(D) Focusing on customer values and satisfaction

(100) As an HR manager, you are meeting with senior management to discuss the use of HR to gain a competitive advantage over other firms in the market. You are discussing:

(A) The firm's HR strategy

(B) The business environment that the firm must operate in

(C) The legal environment that the firm must operate within

(D) The individual problems relating to the HR plan

(101) Andrew works as a clerk in a company's finance department. He has been given a time card and receives additional pay for working overtime. Andrew is:

(A) An exempt line employee

(B) An exempt staff employee

(C) A nonexempt staff employee

(D) None of the above

(102) Due to increasing workload and burnout within a company, workers are starting to face higher stress levels.

What would be the ideal solution to this problem?

(A) Introduce stress management courses for all employees

(B) Allow employees to work from home

(C) Increase lunch-break hours

(D) Let the employees know about the possible job stress during the hiring process

(103) Jim and Melinda are discussing the company's HR strategies to deal with a sexual harassment lawsuit.

This specific HR environmental challenge stems from:

(A) Workforce diversity

(B) Globalization

(C) Legislation

(D) Organizational culture

(104) A production company is discussing how to introduce a niche for itself by specializing in a particular product. The company is discussing the costs of the specialization and the increase it would see in cash flow after the specialization.

The production company is discussing:

(A) Decentralization strategies

(B) HR strategies

(C) Organizational restructuring

(D) Total quality management (TQM)

(105) Senior management wants to transfer the decision-making responsibility from the central office staff to those nearest a problem that demands attention.

This would be considered:

(A) Decentralization

(B) Corporate restructuring

(C) Downsizing

(D) Outsourcing

(106) Anderson and Toby make jam. They have decided to work with Seaside Farm to produce Seaside Farm Preserves.

This sort of partnership is known as:

(A) Cooperative marketing

(B) A joint venture

(C) Downsizing

(D) A business cooperative

(107) Most companies are now able to able to monitor their employees' utilization of email and the internet.

Keeping this in mind, which of the following would be a legislative concern?

(A) A decline in productivity

(B) Privacy issues concerning individuals

(C) Using the employees' personal information to plan parties and surprises

(D) Potential for information to be used to compile mailing lists for different corporations

(108) Parish Construction builds one house each month. Mr. Parish and John execute all the structural work by themselves and hire another company for the plumbing and electrical work.

This is an example of:

(A) The growth of small businesses

(B) Organizational restructuring

(C) Time efficiency

(D) Outsourcing

(109) Tim is organizing a report that includes the challenges his firm is currently facing.

What would Tim not include in his report as a challenge?

(A) Determining individual performance

(B) Disciplining employees for wasting time

(C) Whether to increase the fit between employees and their jobs

(D) Outsourcing a job

(110) A company is trying to deal with an ethical issue. It would be reasonable to say that:

(A) It is always tough to differentiate between what is ethical and unethical.

(B) Problems always resolve themselves into right and wrong choices.

(C) Employees always expect the least.

(D) Implementing ethical codes significantly helps organizations with ethical struggles.

(111) Carl is looking to improve his company's productivity by emphasizing employee competence. He is focusing on the ____________ factor of productivity.

(A) Ethical

(B) Ability

(C) Empowerment

(D) Motivation

(112) You are discussing a certain employee named Kim with the manager of an organization. The manager speaks highly of Kim and explains how she strongly desires to get the best results and puts in maximum effort.

The manager is describing Kim's:

(A) Capabilities

(B) Ability

(C) Motivation

(D) Productivity

(113) A management information system employee has just left to work for a competitor. The employee also took a proposal for a better MIS system that would speed up the data handling process and reduce costs.

This is an example of:

(A) Empowerment

(B) Brain drain

(C) Competitive advantage

(D) Organizational restructuring

(114) Many profitable organizations look to eliminate jobs every year. This trend can be attributed to which of the following factors?

(A) The need for fewer service and production workers in a more technological society

(B) The increasing dissatisfaction of firms with long-term employees

(C) Increasing competition in the industry

(D) The companies' need for more diverse work communities

(115) Toby heads a large company that has just experienced a major brain drain. He increases compensation for new employees and gives each employee with over five years of experience an extra three days of paid vacation per year.

This is an example of:

(A) A reactive HR strategy

(B) Downsizing

(C) Organizational restructuring

(D) Strategic HR planning

(116) Jim is focusing on recruiting qualified employees for his firm, reviewing benefit plans to offer handsome compensation packages, and is generally very involved with a number of urgent HR needs.

Jim is:

(A) Concentrating Excessively on day-to-day problems

(B) Coping with the external environment

(C) Reinforcing overall business strategies

(D) None of the above

(117) Knotts Publishing wants to introduce and implement a new HR strategy. To succeed, Knotts Publishing's HR department should ensure:

(A) Its managers' commitment to the strategy

(B) Increased diversity in the workplace environment

(C) That a backup strategy has been created in case the initial strategy fails

(D) That maximal efforts to control everyday issues are ongoing

(118) The manager in your company tries to solve everyday problems that arise in the workplace based on his personal views and experiences.

What risk is the manager running?

(A) Alienating employees who want to contribute to the decision-making process

(B) Making assumptions about the business and economic environment that are untrue, thereby threatening the company's profitability

(C) Threatening the company's profitability by encouraging centralized decision-making processes

(D) Undermining the company's goals by being too independent

(119) As an HR manager, what will be your biggest challenge in strategic HR planning?

(A) Developing strategies that allow the firm to sustain a competitive advantage

(B) Getting employees to accept empowerment strategies

(C) Lowering labor costs

(D) None of the above

(120) While working on his HR strategic plan, Tim is thinking about whether to recommend specific job descriptions or broad job classes, and detailed or loose work planning.

Tim is considering:

(A) Workflow

(B) Performance appraisals

(C) Staffing

(D) None of the above

(121) A company is looking to improve its strategic HR choices in the staffing department.

What should the main focus be?

(A) Imposing a hiring freeze to avoid laying off workers

(B) Detailed work planning

(C) Enabling supervisors to make hiring decisions

(D) None of the above

(122) As a company manager, what should you consider most when looking at HR strategies concerning employee separations?

(A) Whether to use layoffs or voluntary changes to downsize a firm

(B) Whether to empower supervisors to make hiring decisions

(C) Whether to compensate long-term employees more than recent hires

(D) None of the above

(123) While working on performance appraisals, a firm must make strategic HR decisions regarding:

(A) The appraisal system that would be most suitable for the firm

(B) How data will be used in job descriptions

(C) How to maintain the privacy of managers and employees while collecting data regarding their job performance

(D) None of the above

(124) An HR department is considering whether it should use discipline as a proactive measure to encourage professional behavior.

In which HR function is the department considering its strategic choices?

(A) Workflow

(B) Employee rights

(C) Employee separations

(D) Performance appraisal

(125) A firm is evaluating the _______ it currently gives employees, including stock options, benefits packages, and raises based on performance.

(A) Employee rights

(B) Salary

(C) Compensation

(D) Worker awards

(126) An evolutionary corporation would exhibit which of the following key features?

(A) It would be a mixture of several different industrial companies.

(B) It would be decentralized and flexible.

(C) It would have moral commitments.

(D) It would have a long-term career development program for employees.

(127) Which of the following strategies would be most suitable for a cost leadership business strategy?

(A) Innovation and flexibility

(B) External recruitment

(C) Performance appraisals

(D) None of the above

(128) Your firm is currently working in a very volatile and uncertain environment.

As an HR professional, what HR strategy would you suggest the firm will benefit from?

(A) Variable pay and flexibility

(B) Control emphasis and fixed pay

(C) Centralized pay decisions

(D) Uniform appraisal procedures

(129) Your firm is currently working in a very stable and comparatively less volatile environment than it did before.

As an HR professional, what HR strategy would you suggest the firm will benefit from?

(A) Variable pay and flexibility

(B) Control emphasis and fixed pay

(C) Loose work planning

(D) Low dependency on superiors

(130) A firm that is considering the volatility of its product market, the degree of change that its product is experiencing over time, and the number of competitors with which it is competing is probably examining its HR strategy's:

(A) Fit with organizational characteristics

(B) Fit with the environment

(C) Defender capabilities

(D) Fit with organizational capabilities

(131) Thurmont's steel mill is looking to implement a new HR strategy.

Which of the following would be the most crucial element of the new HR strategy?

(A) Implementing generic job training

(B) Implementing job-specific training

(C) Instituting more flexible HR strategies

(D) None of the above

(132) Steve is looking to purchase a new computer system. He notices that Shell processors offer a reasonable price with an excellent warranty.

Steve is focusing on the company's:

(A) Fit with the market

(B) Consumer appreciation

(C) Distinctive competencies

(D) Consumer enjoyment

(133) You are a manager of a firm and have recently hired new HR staff.

What steps would you take to foster a healthy relationship between yourself and the HR staff?

(A) Require some management experience as part of HR professionals' training

(B) Develop a tough-minded mentality among HR professionals

(C) Hire independent HR consultants to assist the new HR staff

(D) None of the above

(134) Which of the following competencies would an HR department and its professionals require to become full strategic partners?

(A) Content skills

(B) Knowledge of the business

(C) The ability to think tactically

(D) Qualitative skills

SHRM-CP Test 1: Answers and Explanations

(1) (C) Both A and B.

For an HR professional, it is imperative to formulate business strategies that align with the organization's goals and objectives. Moreover, the professional also needs to keep the financial situation at the forefront, hire the right people, and carry out various other tasks to streamline the organization's goals.

(2) (D) A focus on quantitative research versus qualitative research

Incorporating and focusing on <u>both</u> qualitative and quantitative research in an organization's business acumen is crucial for success.

(3) (A) Most companies find it difficult and time consuming to personalize emails.

Face-to-face communication is an important aspect of a company's internal and external communications. Often, many businesses find it extremely hard to produce emails with the right amount of personalization. Such hurdles are overcome by face-to-face communication. If that is not possible, then the next best alternative might be video meetings.

(4) (C) Know-how of the technical aspects of the business

For an organization to operate efficiently and effectively, its employees—such as HR professionals—must be familiar with the organization's goals and objectives. Moreover, it is important for HR professionals to be aware of the organization's finances and current market situation. However, they do not have to fully understand the technical aspects, as that is not their field and will not help develop business acumen.

(5) (D) Both B and C

It is not necessary for an HR professional to be aware of the technical aspects of the business, but knowledge and understanding of the financial aspect and the market situation of the business is crucial. Moreover, HR professionals must make practical decisions for the company's sake.

(6) (C) Dependence on the parent company or organization

A dependence on the parent company or organization is not a characteristic an HR consultant requires. HR consultants must possess certain skill sets that allow them to carry out business decisions that may streamline the company's functioning, such as hiring the right people, making practical decisions, and functioning in accordance with the business's goals and objectives. The consultants must also be well aware of the financial side of the business in order to make fair judgments of the company's financial standing.

(7) (C) Both A and B

HR consultants must always be aware of the legal aspects of the organization they work for. If HR representatives choose to work independently, it is their responsibility to carry out the different administrative tasks, such as the legal and financial tasks and responsibilities for the business.

(8) (D) Both B and C.

Critical evaluation is crucial for HR consultants, as it allows them to carry out a number of tasks effectively and appropriately. It also allows them to look at the bigger picture, make better-informed decisions, and approach a problem with the right mindset, among other various important functions.

(9) (A) Such companies help them formalize long-term relationships.

HR consultants usually prefer to work alone or with smaller companies. This allows them the chance to formalize new and longer-lasting relationships with their customers, which may also stand to benefit the HR consultants in the long run even if they choose to work for corporations in the future.

(10) (A) Older trends become redundant over time.

As time moves on, the old ways of approaching a certain job become redundant. This is because people's needs keep evolving with time, which gives birth to newer innovations. Hence, an HR consultant must be fully aware of the latest trends in order to comprehend the needs of customers.

(11) (A) Moral principles, employee behavior, everyday business practices

Ethical practices describes the systematic rules/moral principles upon which a business operates daily. It is how common moral principles are unified into everyday business practices. Employee behavior plays a huge part in the establishment of ethical practices.

(12) (C) They both guarantee the protection of the ecosystem/environment.

This is untrue because nothing is guaranteed in the business environment. Although protecting the environment does fall under ethical practices, it is still not 100% assured.

(13) (C) Hiring people of all ethnicities, irrespective of their past

As much as it is advisable to hire people of diverse backgrounds and ethnicities, this statement is incorrect, as it includes the phrase "irrespective of their past." The hiring process must always take into account any past wrongdoings that the candidate committed. This is for the safety of the company and its employees.

(14) (A) Personal growth encouragement

Personal growth encouragement is mainly about personal development.

(15) (B) An intercultural office allows a company to target a bigger audience.

People are more attracted to workplaces where a diverse ethnic group is operating. Furthermore, being aware of cultural differences helps HR establish policies that foster a healthy work environment.

(16) (C) Stating the approach and attitude expected from the group members

Maintenance entails feeling involved with the group that an individual is a part of through sharing group values and acknowledging different viewpoints. Option C does not incorporate participation from the group; rather, it merely states what is expected from the group members, which is not a quality of a leader.

(17) (D) Attribution theory.

Based on Fritz Heider's work, attribution theory discusses how people attribute their actions to various external and internal forces that occur within a stable environment.

(18) (A) Independence, expertise, and affiliation

Higher-order needs include self-fulfillment or self-actualization needs, psychological or self-esteem needs, and basic safety and physiological needs. Option A is correct because it states all three higher-order needs.

(19) (C) Both A and B.

Expectancy theory assumes all individuals are rational decision-makers who always weigh the benefits and costs of the options presented to them. Additionally, it also assumes that individuals will choose the option to behave and will act in ways that will help them achieve their desired goals.

(20) (B) Individuals act in ways that decrease their pain and increase their pleasure.

Expectancy theory links to our natural hedonism, as we tend to maximize desired outcomes, such as a pay increase, and consequently seek to minimize undesirable outcomes, such as a job loss.

(21) (C) Coaching, supporting, delegating, and directing

Option C correctly states the four leadership styles that are part of the Situational Leadership Theory®. Directing is the first and most crucial style of leadership, followed by coaching, supporting, and delegating.

(22) (A) Understanding labor markets and factors that influence them

An essential component of the recruitment process is a thorough understanding of the labor markets and the factors that influence them. The needs of the public are external factors that have nothing to do with the recruitment process. The company's financial stability is an important requirement that needs to be known and understood by HR management. The candidate's qualifications are also something that goes without saying, as only fitting candidates are encouraged to apply.

(23) (B) Cold-calling customers three times a day

Cold-calling customers three times a day is an important part of the job analysis process, as it means approaching those customers who have not expressed any prior interest in the company.

(24) (C) Language tests

Language tests are rarely needed, except for international applicants. Job knowledge tests, cognitive ability tests, and work samples are all three very important tests in the process of job recruitment. These tests may include aptitude tests, drug tests, tests that are focused on whether a candidate can match the abilities required for the job, and tests that check a person's understanding of the job.

(25) (D) Changes in technology

Changes in technology are beyond an organization's control. They have nothing to do with the internal factors of the recruitment process and are classified as external factors.

(26) (A) Acknowledging the job vacancy

The first step of the recruitment process is acknowledging that a vacancy for a job exists within a company. This may be filled from within the company or by an outsider. The staffing plans and recruitment strategy may vary in accordance with the job vacancy; hence, they do not come first. These are followed by the determination of the most effective methods of recruitment.

(27) (C) Conventional HR management's fundamental focus was on daily tasks, whereas modern HR management involves recruiting, encouraging leadership, and creating strategies.

Option C is the correct answer because it presents the correct distinction between modern and conventional HR management. Option A is incorrect because it gets the definition of HR management backward, and Option D is wrong because it states that all definitions are wrong. Option B defines conventional HR management wrong.

(28) (B) Analyzing the situation

Strategic planning calls for analyzing the situation. This includes an overview of the company's strengths, weaknesses, potential opportunities, and threats (i.e., market position).

(29) (B) A PowerPoint presentation

PowerPoint presentations have never been used to create an outline for a work breakdown structure. Option B is the correct answer, as the typical examples of work breakdown structures include Gantt charts, lists, flowcharts, and spreadsheets.

(30) (D) It reviews and modulates a project's performance.

Option D is the correct answer because monitoring/reviewing a project and regulating/modulating its progress are crucial in this process category.

(31) (C) Highlights the significance of customer value while reducing waste by using fewer resources

Option C is the correct answer because it defines the Lean approach best. Option A defines the Muri approach, Option B defines the Agile approach, and Option D is false as it suggests Option A as a possible answer.

(32) (D) All of the above

Corporate social responsibility is a type of socially accountable business self-regulation. Organizations are responsible for the impact of their decisions and activities on society and the environment, which further results in ethical behavior, contributing to the environmental practice of being sustainable, and investing in the community.

(33) (C) Recognizing that a critical analysis of performance is very important

Corporate social responsibility is a mode of self-regulating business. It requires a company to be held socially accountable to all its shareholders. The basic purpose of CSR is to give back to the community and provide positive social value. Part of this involves critically analyzing a business's performance and adapting it as necessary.

(34) (A) Going green

Food companies going green pursue practices that lead to more environmentally friendly decisions and lifestyles, which help protect the environment. Food companies practice recycling and going green by creating recyclable cutlery, napkins, etc. They further play a role in being more responsible toward society by using nontoxic materials in packaging. This type of responsibility falls under environmental social responsibility.

(35) (A) Corporate charities

Business contributions for charitable purposes are a type of corporate charitable behavior. Philanthropic corporate social responsibility is described as a charitable act for the good of society. Option B is a way of giving monetary funds. This aspect of CSR looks at supporting the community beyond just providing jobs. Philanthropic responsibilities include things such as funding educational programs, supporting health initiatives, donating to causes, and supporting community development. The two other options are just synonyms of one word and fall under philanthropy as a whole.

(36) (B) Preserving the environment

Option B is correct. One of the many benefits of practicing CSR is preserving the environment. The biggest advantage provided by CSR is enhancing the longevity of the planet. Waste production is reduced, regulations on the expenditure of electricity cause a decrease in energy wastage, and a reduction in the use of automotive vehicles results in less air pollution. Options A and C are both disadvantages of considering corporate social responsibility. Hence both are incorrect. So is Option D, which erroneously states that both Options A and B are correct.

(37) (D) All of the above

Employees need to have a work atmosphere that allows them to be inspired and innovative to perform to the best of their abilities. Both employee performance and productivity increase when employees have a relaxed and comfortable relationship with their coworkers. When this relaxed relationship progresses, employees will exhibit qualities such as communicating, collaborating, and cooperating.

(38) (C) Affective conflict

When an individual's or a group's thoughts, opinions, or feelings are in disagreement with those of others, affective conflict arises. Affective conflict occurs when there is an inability to communicate or to include two or more people. It is a difficulty that emerges in interpersonal relationships among coworkers.

(39) (D) None of the above

Interpersonal conflict is a type of conflict in which two individuals disagree with each other in terms of opinions, thoughts, or something else.

(40) (B) Defending oneself

Defending oneself is one of the five types of conflicts rather than a dispute resolution option. The five main types of conflict resolution in the Thomas-Kilmann Model are staying away, accommodating, making concessions, competing, and working together.

(41) (A) Money

According to Riverbark, 2010, 90% of managers believe that employees leave their places of work due to problems pertaining to pay packages. However, evidence from research disputes this opinion and points toward other issues, such as problems with the boss, tight schedules, an unhealthy work/life balance, and unhealthy working conditions.

(42) (B) Alienation of employees

Managers need to take into account external factors, as a refusal to do so may lead to the alienation of employees. The manager must do this so that the team may gel and become more integrated, allowing it to work toward a unified goal that leads to the fulfillment of the company's aims and objectives.

(43) (C) Expectations theory

The expectations theory states that if results are expected of employees, they will work toward their goal with greater vigor, thereby producing better results. They will also expect better results from themselves, and, upon successfully achieving their aims, they will perform even better. Equity theory is related to the demoralization of the employees; if the same level of workers are not paid equally, the workers who are being paid less may feel that they are being slighted, which can engender resentment toward management.

(44) (D) Low pay packages

Managers and HR professionals often mistake pay packages as the reason why employees leave an organization. However, the real reasons are contrary to popular belief and have more to do with the level of work; a mismatch between skill level and task; a work/life imbalance; and monotonous, uninteresting work.

(45) (D) Technological advancements

Health-care costs, flexible working hours, and telecommuting are all external factors that stand to influence HR. However, technological advancements are one external factor that may have very little or nothing to do with HR in an organization.

(46) (C) Internal business policy and structure

Options A and B are irrelevant; though these concepts contribute to business success, they are not a direct representation of the organizational effectiveness concept. Option C best reflects the focus of O&E on "systematic interventions and changes in policies that would restructure that organization and bring workers to a common standpoint that would help achieve the organization's goals and objectives."

(47) (D) Job enrichment

While the first three interventions focus on the employee side, the last option focuses on nonbehavioral interventions. The emphasis is on the job and its nature so that rather than preset standards and tactics, employee motivation (gained due to job enrichment) contributes to success in organizational effectiveness.

(48) (A) Survey feedback and questionnaires

The correct answer is Option A, which is a miscellaneous intervention that collects required data. Options B, C, and D pertain to outside information that will not be useful in judging the organization's performance and policies.

(49) (A) Look at employee resignations and labor turnover in poor-performing branches.

The correct option is Option A, which is the first step of identifying the problem or gaps for improvement. The other options are not correct, as they do not mention the first step. Options C and D talk about designing and implementing fixes after the problem is identified. Option B is the second step of diagnosing the problem.

(50) (D) Centralized and decentralized structure

Option D is the clear answer, as these are the two forms of organizational design structure asked for in the question. Options A, B, and C involve other concepts that are either not truthful or not related to the organizational design structure concept.

(51) (C) A concept that entails adapting to technological changes and integrating them into the business

Option C represents the core concept of technological management. Options A and B are scenarios or strategies that are components of technological management, not the concept in itself. Option D, meanwhile, is the opposite of the concept.

(52) (B) The IT department

The major responsibility of managing a business's technological systems lies with the IT department. The other departments can benefit from technological change, as can any aspect of the business; however, the role is largest for the IT department.

(53) (C) Technology removal

Replacing old technology might occur, but technology removal is not the focus of STMS. The first step of STMS is technology creation, followed by the other steps concerned with implementing and assessing new technology, not removing it from use.

(54) (C) Quality of work

The quality of an employee's work must be very good. Competency, hard work, and effort are all key to producing quality work, which helps a firm gain a competitive advantage over other firms.

(55) (C) The IT department and a team of innovators

Though the concerns and needs of various stakeholders like employees must be taken into account, the best people for the job are the innovation team and the IT department, which must handle technological management. They should have the most say when it comes to technology management and its implementation. Customers are external and often do not understand the inner workings and technicality of a business. Similarly, senior management may also not have the exact technical know-how required for technological management and implementation, nor would the average employee have this knowledge.

(56) (D) The labor market

Potential employees are always recruited from the labor market. The labor market is where the supply for jobs meets the demand, and firms hire accordingly.

(57) (A) Career progression

New systems and development programs introduced by organizations always focus on employees' career progression by enhancing their skill sets and knowledge.

(58) (C) A large group size

As the number of workers inside a group increases, it becomes difficult to communicate with everyone, leading to communication gaps and a lack of synergy between coworkers. Hence, to improve cohesiveness and communication within a group, keeping the group as small as possible is preferable.

(59) (C) I, II, IV, III

While developing a career growth plan, the first step is always to identify the needs of the program. This is followed by the organization's vision. In the third step, the action plan is set up and implemented. Lastly, once the plan is set, the effectiveness of its results is evaluated.

(60) (D) All of the above

All of the mentioned factors are heavily linked to an organization's working conditions. Appropriate wages, work environment, and career growth opportunities for employees all contribute to healthy working conditions.

(61) (C) The HR department

An HR department is tasked with maximizing employee productivity and protecting the company from any issues that may arise within the workforce. HR responsibilities include compensation and benefits, recruitment, firing, and keeping current with any laws that may affect the company and its employees.

(62) (D) None of the above

Diversity in a closed environment is composed of two basic parts: personal identification and public identification. None of the options suggest this answer; therefore, they all are wrong.

(63) (A) Inclusion

Inclusion can be defined as a work environment in which all individuals are treated fairly and respectfully, have equal access to opportunities and resources, and contribute fully to an organization's success.

(64) (B) Demographic

Demographic segmentation refers to the categorization of the target market based on specific variables like age, education, and gender. It is a type of market segmentation that helps businesses understand their consumers better and meet their needs more effectively.

(65) (D) Increased productivity

Increased productivity means more output is produced from the same amount of inputs. To generate meaningful information about the productivity of a given system, production functions are used to measure it.

(66) (A) Improve understanding, decision-making, and solution-seeking

Conflicts that arise in organizations need to be resolved through negotiations and critical thinking. This is done to bring the participants of the conflict onto the same page and improve understanding between them. This will help in seeking better solutions and lead to swifter decision-making in the future.

(67) (B) Taking hardline steps against those in conflict to prevent further conflicts

All the options mentioned in the question are a crucial part of conflict resolution except for Option B. This is because conflicts are bound to arise in the future and cannot be ruled out of the equation; hence, Option B is impractical and not feasible. It is also not a step that is taken during the process of conflict resolution.

(68) (C) Compromise

Compromise is one of the fairest ways to resolve a conflict because each group puts forward demands and every party walks away with as much as they can and leaves the rest. This also is the fairest way for the negotiators to come to a resolution.

(69) (D) Relationship conflict

Relationship conflicts occur on a deeper level between the employees of an organization. These people will not see eye-to-eye on most issues, and problems are rooted on personal levels. Intergroup conflicts exist between groups or departments. Task conflicts arise between employees who may not agree on the course of action that needs to be taken in order to complete a task. Value conflicts arise between people of different ideologies, such as religion or politics.

(70) (C) Both A and B.

Conflict resolution is a necessary action that needs to be taken at the right time to avoid disruptions and drops in employee productivity and morale. Hence, if done right, conflict resolution may also improve relations between the two parties, who now have a better understanding of each other. However, it may also lead to a worsening of the dispute and argument.

(71) (A) Workforce management

Workforce management (WFM) is an integrated set of processes that a company uses to optimize employee productivity. WFM involves effectively forecasting labor requirements, and creating and managing staff schedules to accomplish a particular task on a day-to-day and hour-to-hour basis.

(72) (D) Organizational structure

An organizational structure is a system that outlines how certain activities are directed to achieve an organization's goals. These activities can include rules, roles, and responsibilities. The organizational structure also determines how information flows between levels within the company. It is not included in workforce management tasks.

(73) (C) Scheduling

Scheduling is the process of arranging, controlling, and optimizing work and workloads in a production or manufacturing process. Scheduling is used to allocate plant and machinery resources, plan HR, plan production processes, and purchase materials.

(74) (B) Innovation.

Innovation involves ideas that have been transformed into practical reality. For a business, these are products, processes or business concepts, or combinations that have been activated in the marketplace and produce new profits and growth for the organization.

(75) (A) Legal restructuring

Legal restructuring happens when a company makes significant changes to its financial or operational structure, typically while under financial duress. Companies may also restructure when preparing for a sale, buyout, merger, change in overall goals, or transfer of ownership.

(76) (D) All of the above

Staffing management is one of the facets pertaining to HR management; hence, HR professionals also have to face some of the challenges associated with it, such as global relocation, recruitment, outsourcing, and international assignment management of staff. Hence, in this case, the correct answer is Option D, which accounts for all of the above.

(77) (A) Employees

A company's HR department is concerned with the company's employees and everything associated with them. This includes taking care of employees, recruiting them, and relocating them to different parts of the globe.

(78) (D) All of the above.

The HR department has many benefits for a company. Not only does it allow a company to lay strong foundations for its organizational structure, but it also makes the organization's goals and objectives clear to its employees due to increased transparency between the higher-ups within a company and its staff and employees. This transparency leads to smoother operations and allows the brand image to grow. Companies that pay attention to HR outperform companies that do not. Hence, the correct answer is Option is D.

(79) (C) Both A and B

Global HRM considers both the care of its employees who are working across the globe and the legal issues that exist around the world. Something that would be permissible and lawful in one part of the world may be unlawful elsewhere. This would also account for traditions and cultures that exist throughout the world. Hence, the correct answer is Option C.

(80) (B) Building strong candidates who can manage businesses in other countries

The business leadership program is another facet of HR. The main goal of this program is to create new candidates who are fit to run the company's operations in different parts of the globe. Options A and C are related to the duties of the global HR department, but the question strictly pertains to the main goal of the business leadership program, which is Option B.

(81) (A) All those benefits that might be given to employees based on performance levels during a given period

Total rewards refer to all those benefits given to an employee based on their performance levels during a given period. These rewards are a recognition of an employee's hard work, dedication, and desire to achieve the best possible results for the organization.

(82) (D) Both A and B.

To successfully implement a total rewards strategy, it is important to get senior management and executives on board and develop an approach that will drive organizational change. This strategy is created by a team that mostly consists of the HR representative and other company employees. The team should be composed of excellent decision-makers and analysts so that the total rewards plan fits the needs of all the members of the organization.

(83) (C) Both A and B.

The execution process includes the HR representative bringing the new total rewards system into action by describing the new rules and strategies of the system. Employees are made aware of the new performance levels that they must reach to be eligible for these rewards.

The HR staff trains managers, senior officials, and those responsible for coming up with the plan so that they can understand and measure the level of achievements effectively.

(84) (B) Financial rewards help ease the financial burden on an employee. These monetary rewards usually include a bonus or a raise in salary. Nonfinancial rewards offer no monetary incentive but recognize the employee in some manner.

Financial rewards help ease the financial burden on an employee. They contribute to the employee's financial well-being. These monetary rewards usually include bonuses and a raise in salary.

Nonfinancial rewards are different from financial rewards. They offer no monetary incentive; instead, they recognize and appreciate employees' efforts by giving them benefits, such as free parking spaces, gym memberships, time off, or childcare.

(85) (A) It uses employee input to allow for better employee performance monitoring. This creates a dialogue between employees and employers, leading to better understanding between the two, so mutual respect is born.

Most total rewards programs offer direct incentives to employees in the form of career growth and development. Apart from the program's financial incentives, other important and more long-term benefits include professional and performance development and training. All of these help employees develop new skills, increase their knowledge, and improve their abilities.

(86) (A) It is the process of trying to identify and recognize risks that have the potential to harm the organization's business activities in the future and preventing them from happening.

In HR, risk management involves trying to identify and recognize risks that can harm the organization's business activities in the future and prevent them from happening.

(87) (D) All of the above.

Risk management is a key aspect of almost every organization in case of any future disaster. Every business venture has to be risk-checked, and the probability of it failing is determined through the gathering of quantitative data.

(88) (D) Both B and C.

The number of people involved in the risk management process who are responsible for devising plans to minimize risk may vary from organization to organization, depending on the organization's size. An organization that works on a large scale may have the resources and finances to host large risk management teams to handle the processes. In comparison, in a smaller company, the responsibility lies mostly on the shoulder of the executive director to come up with plans on how to reduce risk.

Once the strategies have been designed and the risk management plan has been put into practice, each member of the organization becomes responsible for the smooth execution and running of the plan to achieve the desired outcome. Therefore, both Options B and C are correct.

(89) (D) All of the above.

All of the options combine to define the planning phase of the risk management process.

(90) (A) It takes place when HR professionals regularly run comprehensive audits to make sure that the organization is not violating any legislation and is complying with the country's rules and regulations.

Rules and regulations that surround the business industry are usually very complex and require a thorough understanding. If HR professionals are not fully aware of the laws the organization should comply with, they may face dangerous lawsuits and fines.

To deal with this, HR professionals must run comprehensive audits. Managers and employees in the HR department responsible for managing risk must also stay current with legal news so that they can adjust as quickly as possible to any changes in the law. Laws can often change without prior notice, so the staff in charge of risk management must remain vigilant.

(91) (D) Point method

This is the most broadly utilized method of job evaluation. It includes a quantitative and scientific way to deal with the estimation of occupation satisfaction.

(92) (A) The circle network

The circle is a decentralized communication network because there is a free flow of information among its members.

(93) (A) Human process intervention

Human process intervention is a cycle that helps representatives understand their own conduct and other people's conduct in order to work on the advantages through critical thinking.

(94) (D) Arbitration

The type of third-party intervention in which an arbitrator dictates and determines the terms of a settlement is classified as arbitration.

(95) (A) The process of formulating HR strategies and establishing programs to implement them

Designing a plan to meet an organization's needs and requirements is the main focus of strategic HR planning. After the plan is set up, its implementation is the next important aspect of strategic HR planning.

(96) (A) Acquiring useful data about the industry the organization is looking to move into

Option A best describes the role of HR managers as it looks toward working in the best interests of the organization and does not put the HR department's interests first. The HR department's most important purpose is to help an organization grow.

(97) (B) Partaking in a SWOT analysis while developing the strategy

The most important phase is represented by Option B. An HR manager has to influence decisions before the final strategy has been made in order to completely address any HR concerns.

(98) (C) The relationship between the organization's functional areas and the organizational strategies

An organization that promises a delivery service that is faster than the production department's ability to produce lacks an understanding of the relationship between the organization's functional areas and the organizational strategies. It is important to have transparency between an organization's functional areas and the organization's strategies so that management is better able to understand how much the organization can produce and deliver in a specific period.

(99) (D) Focusing on customer values and satisfaction.

Customer satisfaction is an important factor that leads to clear benefits for a business. A pure cost-saving approach or replication of a competitor's ideas may not necessarily be the best approach and could backfire. Similarly, Option C, which means simply doing what everyone else does, does not give the business an edge or differentiation with its technological system; hence, this option is also incorrect. Therefore, the correct answer is Option D.

(100) (B) The business environment that the firm must operate in

It is important for a start-up or a firm that is moving into another industry to understand the industry's business environment and how it operates.

(101) (C) A nonexempt staff employee

Nonexempt employees are eligible to earn minimum wage and are also entitled to receive overtime pay when they work beyond their allotted hours.

(102) (A) Introduce stress management courses for all employees

The ideal option would be to introduce stress management courses so that employees learn how to deal with stressful situations. All other options would give employees some level of comfort but would not eliminate the problem itself.

(103) (C) Legislation

Employment legislation takes care of all employees' rights and regulates the relationship between employees and their employer. Hence, this specific HR challenge stems from employment legislation.

(104) (D) Total quality management (TQM)

Total quality management often improves cash flow. It discusses all those aspects that are related to eliminating any errors in the product or during manufacturing, and improving the supply chain management system as a whole.

(105) (A) Decentralization

Decentralization is the process whereby an organization may choose to transfer a role or activity to several other offices rather than to just one.

(106) (B) A joint venture

When two organizations with different businesses partner for their mutual benefit, they enter into a joint venture in which they are equal partners in the business.

(107) (B) Privacy issues concerning individuals

It is important to protect employee privacy. Legally speaking, an employee's actions or correspondence can be monitored only to a certain extent.

(108) (D) Outsourcing

Outsourcing is when a firm hires third parties to perform a task. This is exactly what Parish Construction is doing when it hires another company for the tasks it is unable to carry out. Outsourcing also reduces costs and improves efficiency.

(109) (B) Disciplining employees for wasting time

Tim should not include disciplining employees in his report as a challenge, as this is something that can easily be resolved by implementing proper rules. Other challenges are more serious and could affect the organization's performance.

(110) (D) Implementing ethical codes significantly helps organizations with ethical struggles.

All organizations have to deal with ethical problems. The best solution is to implement and maintain a set of ethical rules that will help the organization quickly come to a conclusion about the problem and take appropriate corrective measures.

(111) (B) Ability

The ability to understand how to perform a certain task and use the appropriate skills and available knowledge are important for increasing a company's productivity levels.

(112) (C) Motivation.

The key characteristics that the manager uses to describe Kim all relate to her motivation levels.

(113) (B) Brain drain

Brain drain occurs when an employee or worker leaves an organization or firm in search of a better work environment that might include improved wages and benefits and access to superior technology.

(114) (C) Increasing competition in the industry

To remain competitive, many organizations have to keep their profits and revenue up. With better technological systems being introduced almost every year, many organizations choose to lay off workers whose work can be performed by technological systems. This cuts costs and allows organizations to remain competitive.

(115) (A) A reactive HR strategy

A reactive HR strategy is when a company may not hire new employees until it is necessary. Instead, the company looks to find solutions to problems rather than advertise employment opportunities.

(116) (A) Concentrating excessively on day-to-day problems

All the challenges mentioned above are examples of what an HR professional deals with almost every day. Jim has to deal with reviewing, recruiting, and all the other HR needs on a day-to-day basis.

(117) (A) Its managers' commitment to the strategy

It is important to have managers who are dedicated to the task and working just as hard as the HR team to implement new plans and strategies.

(118) (B) Making assumptions about the business and economic environment that are untrue, thereby threatening the company's profitability

It is important for a company manager to listen to the opinions and views of employees and gain valuable feedback. Always relying on oneself and one's own experiences and not listening to others can harm a company's performance and profitability.

(119) (A) Developing strategies that allow the firm to sustain a competitive advantage.

HR managers have to devise plans and strategies that help companies remain at the top of the market. This way, they are able to compete actively with other companies.

(120) (A) Workflow

Workflow is a series of tasks divided into steps to make the job easier for workers. This breakdown increases workplace efficiency and helps ease the burden on employees.

(121) (C) Enabling supervisors to make hiring decisions

Enabling supervisors to make hiring decisions will help smooth the decision-making process.

(122) (A) Whether to use layoffs or voluntary changes to downsize a firm

When looking at HR strategies concerning employee separations, Option A could relieve the firm of its extra expenses and help it run more efficiently.

(123) (A) The appraisal system that would be most suitable for the firm

To check employee workplace efficiency, an appraisal system is important for the firm because it acts as a criterion upon which every employee can be examined fairly.

(124) (B) Employee rights

HR is considering employee rights, thinking about whether the HR department should reinforce discipline in order to bring the employees in line. HR managers know how to handle the matter of employee efficiency in a way that jeopardizes neither the company nor the employees' interests.

(125) (C) Compensation

Compensation is the extra bonus a firm allocates to its employees when they have acted in the company's interest and allowed the firm to secure a profit.

(126) (D) It would have a long-term career development program for employees.

Long-term career development is vital for the training of employees. This is a hallmark of an evolutionary corporation.

(127) (C) Performance appraisals

Without creating extra expenses for the firm, performance appraisals allow the firm to analyze its weaknesses and strengths while keeping a check on the quality of its workforce.

(128) (A) Variable pay and flexibility

Variable pay and flexibility will allow the firm to have enough room for improvisation and uncertain developments.

(129) (B) Control emphasis and fixed pay

Control emphasis and fixed pay will lower the burden on the firm's capital reserves and allow the company to focus on the tasks at hand more effectively.

(130) (B) Fit with the environment

Adapting to ongoing market trends is vital for the growth of a firm and its products. If the firm does not adapt accordingly, its rivals will take advantage of this weakness.

(131) (B) Implementing job-specific training

Implementing job-specific training will help the firm hire specialized workers for the tasks. They should be skilled enough to benefit their own department and focus on their own tasks more effectively.

(132) (C) Distinctive competencies

Steve is focusing on the company's distinctive competencies. A distinctive competency is a specific product or service that differentiates a business from its competitors. If a firm is offering 70% off on a pressure washer, then that is the firm's specialty or competency—the thing it does well.

(133) (A) Require some management experience as part of HR professionals' training

As part of HR professionals' training, every candidate should have some management experience in order to understand the management's views and suggestions on HR matters. This helps foster a healthy relationship between HR and management.

(134) (B) Knowledge of the business

HR reps' knowledge of the business is very important, as this is the backbone of all business dealings done on behalf of the firm. Without knowledge of the environment, a business cannot excel in its market.

SHRM-CP Test 2

(1) Which of the following is an important aspect of HR consultation?

(A) Business management

(B) Administrative functions

(C) Licensing requirements

(D) All of the above

(2) How can you narrow down the competition for your business in the HR consultancy market and make marketing easier?

(A) By selecting a specific niche

(B) By investing a large amount of money

(C) By offering generalized HR consultancy services

(D) None of the above

(3) To start a consultancy business and work as an independent HR consultant, which of the following environments is most suitable?

(A) A well-functioning and well-established office

(B) An apartment or house

(C) Anywhere you can strike a balance between your personal and professional life

(D) Not working as an independent HR consultant

(4) What percentage of American workers refuse to work with companies that are negligent in cases of sexual harassment, even if the workers are provided higher salaries?

(A) 79%

(B) 15%

(C) 25%

(D) 67%

(5) Which age group is ideal for employment in a business?

(A) 30 to 40

(B) 50 and above

(C) Any age

(D) 20 and above

(6) What are the two types of leaders present in an organization?

(A) Formal and informal

(B) Senior and junior

(C) Leader and subleader

(D) All of the above

(7) "People will perform much better at work if they have demanding, defined, and agreed-upon performance goals or targets."

Which of the following theories states this?

(A) Expectancy theory

(B) Attribution theory

(C) Goal-set theory

(D) Leadership theory

(8) According to expectancy theory, when presented with two or more options, which should a person choose?

(A) They should choose the option mentioned first.

(B) They should choose the option mentioned last.

(C) They should choose the most appealing option.

(D) It depends on the person.

(9) Upon whose work is attribution theory primarily based?

(A) Fritz Heider

(B) Albert Einstein

(C) Both A and B

(D) None of the above

(10) Which of the following is the most fundamental level of leadership style in the Situational Leadership Theory® model?

(A) Coaching

(B) Supporting

(C) Delegating

(D) Directing

(11) What describes the process by which managers assess job performance and individual performance rankings?

(A) Coaching

(B) Performance calibration

(C) Consultation

(D) Talent calibration

(12) Which of the following leadership traits is considered culturally dependent?

(A) Confidence

(B) Vision

(C) Team-orientedness

(D) Participation

(13) Apart from the fact that talent management calibration is built on the foundation of performance calibration, what is another major difference between the two?

(A) Talent calibration is future-oriented, and performance calibration is about a specific time period's efficiency.

(B) Talent calibration scales people on the basis of their talent, and performance calibration scales people on the basis of their performances.

(C) Both A and B.

(D) None of the above.

(14) Which form of conflict arises when a person or group wishes for a different conclusion than the one another person or group desires?

(A) Affective conflict

(B) Cognitive conflict

(C) Goal conflict

(D) Behavioral conflict

(15) What best describes the word *level* in a conflict?

(A) The position of the person involved

(B) The number of people involved

(C) The number of days since the conflict started

(D) All of the above

(16) When two people disagree with each other, what type of conflict occurs?

(A) Interpersonal conflict

(B) Intrapersonal conflict

(C) Intergroup conflict

(D) Cognitive conflict

(17) According to the Thomas-Kilmann Model, how many options exist for resolving a conflict?

(A) Four

(B) Five

(C) Six

(D) Ten

(18) Which of the following is part of conflict management?

(A) Collaborating

(B) Competing

(C) Compromising

(D) None of the above

(19) An HR manager should be good at recruiting eligible job candidates. What is the first step in the recruitment process?

(A) Select an individual from the internal candidates

(B) Acknowledge the job vacancy

(C) Call random people for an interview

(D) All of the above

(20) Internal and external factors are used to forecast business changes that might occur in the future.

Which of the following is not an internal factor?

(A) Levels of production

(B) Financial restrictions

(C) Unemployment rates

(D) Increase in sales

(21) What is a disadvantage of using websites as a recruiting tool?

(A) They are expensive.

(B) They are time consuming.

(C) Only a limited number of résumés are available.

(D) A large number of résumés are available, so it is difficult to filter out good candidates.

(22) Testing is an amazing tool that HR management can use to identify the right candidate for the available vacancy.

Which of the following is an unreliable test and should be avoided to save time and resources?

(A) Honesty test

(B) Personality test

(C) Job knowledge test

(D) Cognitive ability test

(23) What does PDC stand for in regard to job recruitment strategies?

(A) Microsoft's Professional Developer Conference

(B) Personal Digital Certificate

(C) Protective Device Coordination

(D) Post-Dated Check

(24) Which of the following are reasons why 90% of employees leave a company?

(A) Unhealthy working conditions

(B) A new job

(C) Problems with their boss

(D) Both A and C

(25) __________ are the things over which a company has no direct influence.

(A) External factors

(B) Internal factors

(C) All issues

(D) None of the above

(26) Which of the following is a common misconception among HR managers regarding employees who leave their jobs?

(A) Employees are affected by the workload.

(B) Employees are unhappy with their paychecks.

(C) Employees find their work uninteresting.

(D) Employees left because of management issues.

(27) What is the name of the project management approach that came into existence as a result of the shortcomings of the Waterfall technique?

(A) Lean

(B) Muri

(C) Agile

(D) Six Sigma

(28) What are the three Ms that constitute Lean?

(A) Make, Manage, Mine

(B) Muda, Mura, Muri

(C) Make, Muda, Manage

(D) Manage, Manage, Manage

(29) Which of the Ms of the Lean approach refers to the waste of resources and time?

(A) Mura

(B) Muda

(C) Muri

(D) All of the above

(30) When was the Six Sigma methodology developed by Motorola engineers?

(A) 1986

(B) 1896

(C) 1999

(D) 2020

(31) Which of the following strategies is adopted by HR management to make the business process more efficient?

(A) Managerial

(B) Operative

(C) Advisory

(D) All of the above

(32) Job analysis is an important part of the recruitment process. Which of the following strategies is adopted by HR management during this time?

(A) Operative

(B) Directive

(C) Managerial

(D) Financial

(33) Apart from scaling salary levels, what else does the HR function of compensation and welfare offer employees?

(A) Job analysis

(B) Health care

(C) Recruitment

(D) Learning

(34) Which of the following departments is responsible for finding a solution for issues concerning payments to employees?

(A) HR management

(B) Marketing

(C) Sales

(D) Finance

(35) What does NLRB stand for?

(A) New Labor Regulation Board

(B) National Labor Relations Board

(C) Both A and B

(D) None of the above

(36) Which of the following best describes unionization?

(A) It is the process of forming a labor union.

(B) It is the process of a firm or organization becoming a part of a labor union.

(C) It is the process of terminating a labor union.

(D) It is the process of uniting two firms.

(37) Team building allows for improvement in the effectiveness of a workgroup. Apart from team building, what other method can help HR increase effectiveness?

(A) Surveys

(B) Questionnaires

(C) Both A and B

(D) None of the above

(38) Identification of gaps in the current strategies is the first step in the development process. What is the second step?

(A) Implementation

(B) Intervention

(C) Correction

(D) Diagnosis

(39) There are two types of organizational design structures. The first type is the centralized structure. Which of the following describes the second type?

(A) Top-level structure

(B) Lateral structure

(C) Decentralized structure

(D) Senior structure

(40) What does a decentralized organizational structure lead to in a company setup?

(A) Well-established processes

(B) Effective customer service

(C) Lower costs

(D) Both B and C

(41) What is the first phase of STMS?

(A) Assessment

(B) Utilization

(C) Technology creation

(D) Technology transfer

(42) What is the process called when the legal policies of an organization are changed?

(A) Financial restructuring

(B) Cost-saving restructuring

(C) Legal restructuring

(D) None of the above

(43) Which of the following can be a consequence of restructuring in an organization?

(A) Sudden layoffs

(B) Downsizing

(C) Mergers

(D) Both A and B

(44) What is a greenwash scheme?

(A) It is a scheme that enables people to plant more trees.

(B) It is a scheme that promotes more environmentally friendly means of business.

(C) It is a scheme that misleads people into believing that a technique is environmentally friendly when it is not.

(D) It is a scheme that ignores the idea of showing concern toward the environment.

(45) What is another name for corporate social responsibility?

(A) Corporate citizenship

(B) Corporate rules

(C) Social obligations

(D) Corporate essentials

(46) Which of the following people are known for defining corporate social responsibility?

(A) Archie B. Carroll

(B) Benedict Sheehy

(C) Both A and B

(D) None of the above

(47) Apart from ensuring equal pay between male and female employees, what is another way in which a company can uphold its ethical responsibilities?

(A) Providing aid during national disasters

(B) Addressing harassment claims in the workplace

(C) Spending profits wisely

(D) Enhancing influence in the industry

(48) How can implementing corporate social responsibility positively impact the environment?

(A) It causes a decrease in energy wastage.

(B) It causes a reduction in a company's waste products.

(C) It causes a reduction in smog.

(D) All of the above.

(49) Which organization provides financial aid to start-ups that intend to move forward with a philanthropic strategy?

(A) World Bank

(B) United Nations Security Council

(C) NATO

(D) International Labour Organization

(50) Which of the following best describes the difference between *diversity* and *inclusion*?

(A) Both terms are synonymous with each other.

(B) *Diversity* refers to recognizing differences between individuals, and *inclusion* refers to providing them with equal opportunities.

(C) *Diversity* refers to providing equal opportunities to people, and *inclusion* refers to respecting everybody who is different in society.

(D) *Diversity* and *inclusion* are the exact opposite of each other.

(51) Which of the following is an important benefit of inclusion in a company?

(A) Higher productivity

(B) Enhanced creativity

(C) Improved reach to international markets

(D) Variety of applicants

(52) What type of conflict is associated with arguments between a group of employees regarding the course of action needed to be taken to perform a certain task?

(A) Relationship conflict

(B) Value conflict

(C) Task conflict

(D) Intergroup conflict

(53) What is the role of HR in the conflict resolution process?

(A) HR should not get involved in these matters.

(B) HR should complain to higher authorities.

(C) HR should observe changes in the attitudes on both sides.

(D) All of the above.

(54) What is another name for relationship conflict?

(A) Intrapersonal conflict

(B) Interpersonal conflict

(C) Intergroup conflict

(D) Intragroup conflict

(55) In a company, people have different preferences and perspectives regarding politics, religion, and identities. What are the types of conflicts that arise due to a difference in opinion on these controversial topics?

(A) Relationship conflict

(B) Interpersonal conflict

(C) Value conflict

(D) Intrapersonal conflict

(56) Which of the following best describes the method by which an expert mediator or HR manager tries to set up a meeting between groups that are in conflict?

(A) Communication

(B) Collaboration

(C) Compromise

(D) Assertiveness

(57) Which of the following is an important sector of global HRM?

(A) Business leadership

(B) Diversity

(C) Labor relations

(D) All of the above

(58) Apart from making a company's goals and objectives more prominent, what is another important strategic benefit of global HRM?

(A) It brings consistency to the organization as a whole.

(B) It increases international sales.

(C) It brings in people from all regions of the world.

(D) It reduces conflicts among people.

(59) What is the approximate number of people involved in an organization's risk management process?

(A) Five.

(B) Ten.

(C) It varies in each organization.

(D) None of the above

(60) Who carries the responsibility in an organization for devising risk reduction plans?

(A) Junior manager

(B) Executive director

(C) Finance manager

(D) Sales manager

(61) Identification is the first step of a risk management process. What is the last step?

(A) Planning

(B) Implementation

(C) Monitoring

(D) Assessment

(62) Which of the following is not the job of an HR representative?

(A) Firing employees

(B) Shortlisting employees

(C) Interviewing employees

(D) None of the above

(63) What can the HR department do to ensure that the organization is not violating any laws and is complying fully with all rules and regulations?

(A) Run audits regularly

(B) Follow the rules prescribed specifically for the HR department

(C) Set strict punishments for violators

(D) Use company spies to watch suspicious employees

(64) Which of the following is an example of a financial reward?

(A) A raise in salary

(B) Provision of childcare

(C) Free parking spaces

(D) Certifications

(65) Intrinsic rewards are intangible rewards given to employees to boost their confidence; in comparison, extrinsic rewards are tangible.

Which of the following is an intrinsic reward?

(A) Bonuses

(B) Financial incentives

(C) Pay raise

(D) Promotions

(66) Apart from better employee performance and greater employee retention, what is another major advantage of a well-functioning total rewards system?

(A) Better program administration

(B) Decrease in sales

(C) A lesser chance of conflicts

(D) All of the above

(67) What describes business acumen the best?

(A) The accumulation of businesses in a market

(B) The way an organization decides to deal with a business situation

(C) The merger of a business into a labor union

(D) The number of years since a business has been established

(68) Which of the following is a prerequisite of deciding business acumen?

(A) Current market situation

(B) Understanding of the respective niche

(C) Both A and B

(D) None of the above

(69) According to reputable research, 74% of American employees believe they do not have access to important company information.

Which of the following is the reason behind this?

(A) Lack of communication between the leadership and employees

(B) Low salaries

(C) Misunderstanding

(D) Lack of training

(70) Disputes are very common in a business environment. Which means of communication, provided that it is easily accessible, can effectively reduce disputes?

(A) Email

(B) Face-to-face communication

(C) Phone calls

(D) Letters

(71) Which of the following mediums best preserves agreement and contracts?

(A) Word of mouth

(B) The note app in a cell phone

(C) Proper documents

(D) Agreements and contracts do not need to be preserved.

(72) Which of the following leaders and/or managers are not chosen by the organization?

(A) HR managers

(B) Formal leaders

(C) Sales managers

(D) Informal leaders

(73) __________ operate as formal leaders in a business environment.

(A) Sales managers

(B) Finance managers

(C) HR managers

(D) All of the above

(74) What are the three higher-order needs of an organization?

(A) Management, attitude, talent

(B) Expertise, independence, affiliation

(C) Management, expertise, talent

(D) None of the above

(75) What is the difference between intrinsic and extrinsic motivation?

(A) Intrinsic motivation is another name for tangible awards, and extrinsic motivation is another name for intangible rewards.

(B) Intrinsic motivation refers to doing something for the sake of the activity itself, and extrinsic motivation refers to doing something for the sake of achieving the desired result.

(C) Intrinsic motivation is the motivation to work within the office premises, and extrinsic motivation is the motivation to work in the field.

(D) Intrinsic motivation is the motivation to work within a closed circle, and extrinsic motivation is the motivation to work in a limitless environment.

(76) When tasks fulfill any one of the three higher orders of need, they are:

(A) Intrinsically motivated

(B) Extrinsically motivated

(C) Both A and B

(D) None of the above

(77) Which of the following stages of the Situational Leadership Theory® model is dominated by followers?

(A) Supporting

(B) Delegating

(C) Coaching

(D) Directing

(78) The path-goal theory of leadership is attributed to which of the following researchers?

(A) Robert House

(B) Fritz Heider

(C) Both A and B

(D) None of the above

(79) How many tools do transformational leaders have at their disposal to influence employees and build their dedication to a company's objectives?

(A) Six

(B) Seven

(C) Four

(D) Five

(80) What type of people do personal appeals work best with?

(A) People you know and like

(B) People you do not know but are fond of

(C) People you know but do not like

(D) People you neither know nor like

(81) Which of the following best describes rational persuasion?

(A) The use of facts, evidence, and logical arguments to convince people

(B) The use of exaggeration to convince people

(C) The use of wrong information to persuade people

(D) All of the above

(82) A plan for global expansion is a/an ___________ used to forecast changes that might be needed in the future.

(A) Internal factor

(B) Recruitment strategy

(C) Job description

(D) External factor

(83) Apart from preparing reports, which of the following is a step that might be included in a task-based analysis?

(A) Writing performance evaluation reports for employees

(B) Answering incoming phone calls

(C) Assisting customers with product-related questions

(D) All of the above

(84) Compared to a task-based analysis, a competency-based analysis is:

(A) Less objective

(B) More clear

(C) Inviolable

(D) More objective

(85) Which of the following can be a costly option for recruiting new employees in a company?

(A) A temporary staffing firm

(B) Websites

(C) An executive search firm

(D) Social media

(86) Which of the following can be a great place to find people for entry-level employment positions?

(A) Colleges

(B) Universities

(C) Both A and B

(D) None of the above

(87) According to reinforcement theory, what results from the outcomes of actions?

(A) Problems

(B) Behavior

(C) Tasks

(D) Efforts

(88) According to equity theory, what are the two types of procedures that can increase fairness in an organization?

(A) Procedural and interactional

(B) Rational and motivational

(C) Procedural and behavioral

(D) Approachable and reliable

(89) Apart from increasing job satisfaction for employees who might be tired of their repetitive work, what is another positive effect of employment enlargement?

(A) Encouragement for employees

(B) Adds extra challenges to their existing jobs

(C) Labor exploitation

(D) Reduced burden for senior employees

(90) Agile is a famous project management approach. What kinds of projects is Agile ideally suited for?

(A) Less time-consuming projects

(B) Iterative and incremental projects

(C) Procedural projects

(D) Projects that require a lot of documentation

(91) Lean methodology is an excellent approach for businesses looking to reform themselves. What is a common misunderstanding associated with it?

(A) Lean reduces waste.

(B) Lean increases waste.

(C) Lean specializes only in the manufacturing industry.

(D) Lean does not apply to the manufacturing industry.

(92) How can the Six Sigma methodology increase the quality of a process going on in a company?

(A) By reducing waste

(B) By lowering the number of previous errors

(C) By overburdening employees

(D) By firing non-serious employees

(93) There are two primary approaches associated with the Six Sigma project management methodology. These approaches are DMAIC and DMADV.

What is DMADV used for?

(A) To create new processes, products, or services

(B) To improve the existing corporate processes

(C) To investigate the features of the current processes

(D) To control how the current processes are being carried out

(94) In project management, when is a work breakdown structure used?

(A) When there is a complex, multistep project on the table

(B) When deadlines are nearing

(C) When the number of employees is large

(D) When the number of employees is small

(95) Identify an example of a work breakdown structure from the following:

(A) Initial evaluation

(B) Gantt chart

(C) Flowcharts

(D) Both B and C

(96) The world has witnessed a large movement in support of the LGBTQ+ community in the last few years. What should be the role of a company and specifically its HR department in such changing times?

(A) They should avoid involving the company's name in controversial scenarios.

(B) The HR department should make the workplace inclusive for people belonging to the LGBTQ+ community.

(C) They should choose the popular side even if it is against the movement.

(D) None of the above.

(97) At times, employees do not file important complaints to HR because they fear repercussions from their seniors. This practice can prove seriously damaging for the business. How can the HR department fix this issue and encourage employees to report any wrong they see happening around them?

(A) They should provide a platform for employees to file anonymous complaints.

(B) They should install CCTV cameras on the office premises.

(C) They should leave spies around suspicious employees to keep a check on them.

(D) They should establish punishments for those who do not report problems.

(98) A task has been assigned to two employees in a company. They fail to find common ground, so a conflict arises between them. What should be the stance of the HR department representative in conflict resolution?

(A) The representative should not get involved in the dispute.

(B) The representative should be on the side of the employee they are friends with.

(C) The representative should maintain neutrality and hear the opinions of both the involved parties.

(D) The representative should take the matter to a higher department.

(99) A talented 45-year-old candidate applies for a job among several other candidates. The experience and talent of the 45-year-old are greater than those of the rest of the applicants. What should the HR department do?

(A) They should shortlist the 45-year-old for the interview.

(B) They should filter the 45-year-old out of the list.

(C) Both A and B.

(D) None of the above.

(100) A company's HR department takes on a very important project, and there is no room for mistakes. The project has to be communicated to employees. What mode of communication should HR use to avoid any misunderstandings?

(A) Email

(B) Indirectly through another senior employee

(C) Directly via face-to-face communication

(D) Phone call

(101) Almost a year ago, you started an HR consultancy home business covering a wide range of niches. The persistent issue you are facing is a limited number of clients. This number does not exceed a certain level even though you have created a perfect balance between your personal and professional life. How can this issue be fixed?

(A) Choosing a specific niche

(B) Immediately setting up an office to work in

(C) Expanding the number of niches you are working in

(D) Waiting for a year or two

(102) An employee reaches out to you and is under much stress due to the workload and the repetitive nature of his job. How should the HR department react to this situation?

(A) Ignore the employee

(B) Show sympathy toward the employee

(C) Complain about the employee to higher authorities

(D) Scold the employee for complaining

(103) You, as an HR manager, are assigned to persuade a client, who is someone you have never met, to sign a deal with your company. How can you accomplish this?

(A) Make a personal request to the client

(B) Adopt a rational approach and provide factual evidence related to your company's business

(C) Try to please the client with exaggerations and false information

(D) Send the client to some other manager who is good with persuasive strategies

(104) The government announces changes in employment legislation that will henceforth only allow the hiring of candidates below the age of 38. What precautions from the end of the HR department could have prevented this new law?

(A) The department should only have hired candidates below the age of 38.

(B) The department should have included people from all age groups.

(C) The HR department should have tried to find information about the law before it was passed.

(D) This is an external factor that the HR department could not have controlled or prevented.

(105) A company wants to create and add new processes to its operations. The HR department decides to use Lean as the project management approach to achieve the desired target. Even after several months, though, the department fails to invent new processes. What is the reason behind this?

(A) Six Sigma is the correct project management approach for the creation of new processes.

(B) It will take a few more months to achieve such a target.

(C) The people involved are not competent enough to attain positive results.

(D) Agile is the correct project management approach for the creation of new processes.

(106) A company takes on an extremely complex project that is incredibly lengthy and constitutes several steps. The task needs to be divided into several parts so that it is quickly and efficiently done. The HR department will require tools to break down the task and maintain a record of it. How can this be done?

(A) Word of mouth

(B) Use a spreadsheet to organize the different stages, tasks, or outputs in columns and rows

(C) Both A and B

(D) None of the above

(107) The managerial strategy mainly corresponds to planning, organizing, and directing organizational processes. If a person is assigned the wrong task or responsibility, where has the HR department shown itself lacking?

(A) Planning

(B) Directing

(C) Organizing

(D) None of the above

(108) Due to unavoidable circumstances, a company decides to downsize several of its employees after two months if certain issues still persist. What can the HR department do to prepare the employees who will be retained for the additional responsibilities they might have to carry out in the near future?

(A) Immediately initiate learning and development programs for all employees

(B) Inform the employees that will be retained about the extra responsibilities awaiting them

(C) Wait for the two months to pass before saying anything

(D) None of the above

(109) An employee is caught red-handed sending important confidential information to the company's competitor. This is a serious violation of the law. What should the HR department do to prevent such violations in the future?

(A) Provide access to confidential information only to trustworthy employees

(B) File a case against the employee to instill fear among other employees

(C) Ensure greater security for confidential data

(D) None of the above

(110) What is the responsibility of the HR department if it finds out that a union is threatening to make employers pay for work that the workers have not done?

(A) Do not get involved in such matters

(B) Report it to the National Labor Relations Board and seek legal action against the union

(C) Convince higher authorities to give in to the unfair demands of the union

(D) Ignore the threats

(111) Organizational development extends over a vast spectrum and is essential in achieving better results and improving the currently running processes in a company. To improve communication between team members and align their objectives so that they are quickly met, what behavioral intervention should the HR department take?

(A) Role-play

(B) Interpersonal relations interventions

(C) Develop a grid

(D) Manage by enforcing the objectives

(112) A company wants to make some important decisions and requires relevant data about its organizational structure that is authentic and reliable. What should the HR department do to ensure this?

(A) Carry out surveys and questionnaires

(B) Take risks

(C) Make decisions based on hypotheses

(D) None of the above

(113) A new technological system is introduced in a company, but a large number of employees do not respond positively to its introduction. What should the HR department do?

(A) Remove the system

(B) Issue warnings to the employees responding poorly to the system

(C) Inform employees of the positive qualities of the system

(D) Ignore those negative responses and move ahead with the system

(114) A new technology is an important part of the company, but the majority of the employees do not know how to use it. If the situation persists, the technology will get wasted. What should be done to ensure complete implementation of the new technology?

(A) Fire the employees who do not know to work with the new technology

(B) Initiate training programs to help employees learn how to use the new technology

(C) Remove the technology, as it is just a waste of money

(D) Hire trained employees who are be experts in the operation of new technology

(115) To keep up with competitors in the market, a new technological system is essential. However, a certain company cannot afford to install it due to a limited budget. What should be done to solve this problem?

(A) Look for funds and sponsorships

(B) Drop the idea of getting the new technology

(C) Cut down on the company's spending to save money

(D) None of the above

(116) A company is facing a financial crisis due to poor sales. How can it save costs?

(A) Downsize some employees

(B) Take loans from established firms

(C) Shut down the company

(D) None of the above

(117) How can a small office with a limited budget play its part in the protection of the environment?

(A) Turn off unused lights in the office

(B) Run the office on solar energy

(C) Small offices cannot help the environment

(D) The environment is not companies' problem

(118) A city suffers an earthquake, and many people lose their lives and homes. The situation is terrible, and people are in dire need of help. What can a business do in such a situation?

(A) Fund NGOs that help with disaster management

(B) Not take on a responsibility that is not up to the company

(C) Issue a statement to show solidarity with the grief-stricken people

(D) Send employees to help in the removal of debris

(119) How can an HR department ensure gender equality on company premises?

(A) Ensure equal pay for both male and female employees

(B) Address any harassment claims immediately

(C) Hire females in higher positions

(D) All of the above

(120) How can a food business play its part in protecting the environment from damage?

(A) Use paper bags instead of plastic

(B) Run the office on solar power

(C) Use recyclable cutlery such as paper straws

(D) All of the above

(121) If a Black person with immense talent applies to your company along with several White candidates, what is your responsibility as an HR manager?

(A) Immediately filter out the Black candidate

(B) Hire the Black candidate to create a popular image for your company

(C) Shortlist the Black candidate for an interview based on their talent, not their race

(D) Hire only Black candidates

(122) A company says it supports the BLM movement but does not have any Black people working for it. Which of the following terms can the HR department use to describe the behavior of the firm?

(A) Diverse

(B) Inclusive

(C) Both A and B

(D) None of the above

(123) Two individuals with drastically opposed political beliefs get into a serious argument on company premises. Despite several attempts at communication, the arguments still persist. These two individuals are supposed to work on the same project together. What should the HR department do to resolve the dispute?

(A) Fire both the employees

(B) Ask employees to avoid discussing politics in the office

(C) Have someone else complete the project

(D) Not involve itself in such conflicts

(124) In global HRM, a very common issue is ineffective employee relations. It is difficult to manage employees and their performance when they are spread all across the globe. What can the global HR department do to avoid challenges regarding employee relations?

(A) Organize an employee assistance program (EAP)

(B) This problem cannot be solved

(C) Appoint separate HR managers in each country

(D) None of the above

(125) A new system was introduced in a company, and it collapsed the day after its launch. What could have been done to prevent this from happening?

(A) An unreliable system should not have been launched.

(B) Risk management should have been done beforehand.

(C) This was an unpredictable scenario that could not have been avoided.

(D) The right people should have been asked to install the system.

(126) In risk management, it is important to determine the chances of a risk taking place and its severity. What can the HR department do to rank risks?

(A) Prepare a chart to highlight the frequency of every risk from top to bottom

(B) Write risks down on a piece of paper

(C) Not organize risks

(D) List the risks on a cell phone notepad

(127) What can a new start-up with an extremely low budget do to reward its employees?

(A) Observe the lack of requirement for start-ups to reward their employees

(B) Give nonfinancial rewards such as gym memberships, time off, free parking spaces, etc.

(C) Give financial rewards such as incentives, bonuses, pay raises, etc.

(D) None of the above

(128) An employee performs exceptionally well the entire year. What should the HR department reward this person with?

(A) A promotion

(B) An incentive

(C) Nothing, because the person did what she was paid for

(D) Anything that the company can afford at that moment

(129) The HR manager of a company treats the company's customers with incredible kindness. However, the manager is rude and mean to the employees and does not communicate with them properly. What should be done with the HR manager?

(A) The manager should be removed, and a responsible manager should be hired.

(B) This is not a problem that needs to be addressed.

(C) The employees should show more tolerance toward the stressed manager.

(D) None of the above.

(130) A company is going bankrupt, but the HR department approves a handsome loan for an employee. What understanding from the end of the HR representatives could have avoided this problem?

(A) Understanding of the current business markets

(B) Understanding of the finances of the company

(C) Both A and B

(D) None of the above

(131) You are in a meeting. Your colleague, who works with you in the same HR department and has been extremely collaborative with you for the past year, suddenly starts acting weirdly toward you. The colleague is also quick in disagreeing with any suggestions you give during the meeting. How should you react to this situation?

(A) Ignore your colleague's behavior and move on with your own work

(B) Complain about your colleague's attitude to higher authorities

(C) Call your colleague out in front of the entire meeting room

(D) After the meeting, politely ask your colleague why he is behaving in such a way and try to resolve any issue that comes up

(132) You have recently hired a new employee. A few days after being hired, the person does something that is not appreciated in the culture and practice of your office. What is your responsibility as an HR representative?

(A) Immediately fire the employee for breaking the rules

(B) Call the employee to your office and issue a strict warning

(C) Give the employee some time to get familiar with the company's practices

(D) Punish the employee by cutting some amount of money from the first month's salary

(133) A group in the company rebels and seeks a 50% increase in their salary. This is going against the company policy even though the group's officially appointed leader is completely loyal to the business. Whom should the HR department hold accountable for this rebellion?

(A) The formal leader

(B) The informal leader trying to influence the group

(C) The employees

(D) None of the above

(134) In some cases, due to formal ways of communication, such as emails and face-to-face scheduled meetings, employees are unable to build a relationship of trust with their bosses, so the work environment remains stressful for them. How can the HR department step into such a situation and ease it for the employees?

(A) Introduce a culture of phone calls

(B) Put more pressure on the employees so they perform better

(C) Respect not having a role to play in such situations

(D) Introduce a social hour for employees and management

SHRM-CP Test 2: Answers and Explanations

(1) (D) All of the above

HR consultation works independently and provides relevant people to companies that wish to outsource all of their HR work. HR consultation businesses lead these companies to external service providers.

HR consultation also has a variety of aspects. Apart from business management, administrative functions, and licensing requirements, those aspects include dealing with numbers, choosing areas of expertise, working independently, getting familiar with legal aspects, etc.

(2) (A) By selecting a specific niche

Niche-specific HR consultancy is always a better option than HR consultancy that caters to a broad range. Selecting a specific niche narrows down the competition in the market—as there are several different types of niches in existence—and brings in a relatively greater number of clients to the HR firm.

(3) (C) Anywhere, if you can strike a balance between your personal and professional life

HR consultancy is an independent business, and you own it. You are the one who will decide the place where you want to set up based on your preferences. Even if you can afford to open an office, you may feel more creative in your home. If you are able to strike a balance between your personal and professional life, you can choose this option.

(4) (A) 79%

This percentage is high because of the increasing importance of including ethical practices in a business. People are becoming more kind, compassionate, and considerate toward fellow human beings. They do not tolerate discrimination against anyone anymore. Therefore, companies have a duty to make it a habit to practice ethics and morals and be on the right side of history.

(5) (C) Any age

In a lot of cases, due to age restrictions, a huge number of talented individuals are left behind despite their level of experience and skills. This practice should come to an end, and age should become just a number in all workplaces. Companies should start being inclusive of people from all age groups, as this will result in positive effects.

(6) (A) Formal and informal

There are two types of leaders in an organization: formal and informal. A formal leader is the official leader of a group and is appointed by the organization. An informal leader is not appointed by the company but is a person in a team, group, or department who acts as the boss of all members and guides them through tasks. This person's influence on the group can bring positive or negative outcomes.

(7) (C) Goal-set theory

According to goal-set theory, it is assumed that people are inclined to work better if they have properly set goals. The foremost tenet of this theory is that people try hard to achieve the objectives they set for themselves. This theory recognizes that people with goals are more driven than those who do not keep track of what they want to do in their life or job and are therefore not motivated.

(8) (C) They should choose the most appealing option.

It is human nature to seek the option that attracts us the most. This is exactly what the expectancy theory of motivation reaffirms. It further states that the more appealing an option is, the more likely it is that employees will prefer that option. Therefore, companies need to provide attractive options that appeal to their employees if they really want them to be motivated and productive.

(9) (A) Fritz Heider

Attribution theory describes the process by which people try to understand the reasons or causes behind their actions. This theory is attributed to Fritz Heider, who further claims that conduct is determined by a combination of both internal and external factors.

(10) (D) Directing

In the Situational Leadership Theory® model, directing is the most fundamental level of leadership style. It is a leader-driven stage that primarily focuses on employees who have little or no experience in their new positions. As the name suggests, this leadership style directs such employees through their job requirements, tasks, challenges, and responsibilities.

(11) (B) Performance calibration

Managers, usually from the same department or function, use a consistent set of criteria to document individual employee performance rankings. Talent calibration is used to assess the overall health of a company's talent pool; coaching is for individuals who have enhanced their competence, and consultation involves seeking help from a more informed person regarding a certain issue or task.

(12) (A) Confidence

Vision, team-orientedness, and, to an extent, participation, are leadership traits that are universal—anybody can have them. In comparison, confidence is a trait that not everybody has; it is culturally dependent. The surroundings you grew up in and the way you were brought up can play a great role in shaping your confidence.

(13) (A) Talent calibration is future-oriented, and performance calibration is about a specific time period's efficiency.

It is important to be able to differentiate between these two different types of calibrations. Performance calibration is tied to compensation in some way, while talent calibration measures the health of an organization's talent pool and is built on the foundation of performance calibration.

(14) (C) Goal conflict

Goal conflict arises when two groups or two people argue over whose objectives and conclusions will be considered or pursued. When the ideas of two groups or two people are different, cognitive conflict arises. When the thoughts and feelings of two groups or two people are in direct conflict with each other, affective conflict arises; when a person or group does something that is undesirable to the other, behavioral conflict arises.

(15) (B) The number of people involved

There are numerous levels of conflicts, and they are all categorized on the basis of the number of people involved. When people face an issue with themselves, the conflict is referred to as intrapersonal. When two people are involved, the level is interpersonal. When two groups are at odds, the resulting conflict is considered an intergroup conflict. When two organizations are having a dispute, the conflict is called an interorganizational conflict.

(16) (A) Interpersonal conflict

Interpersonal conflict occurs when two or more people disagree over something.

(17) (B) Five

According to the Thomas-Kilmann Model, there are five options for dispute resolution. They include staying away, accommodating, making concessions, competing, and working together.

(18) (D) None of the above

Conflict management techniques include changing team members, creating a common enemy, using majority rules, problem-solving, and changing organizational structures to avoid built-in conflicts.

(19) (B) Acknowledge the job vacancy

The first step that an HR manager takes in the recruitment process is acknowledging a job vacancy. At this stage, the manager figures out the job specifications and assesses whether the job description is complete. When the HR manager completes their research, they move on to the next step, which is to prioritize any internal employees.

(20) (C) Unemployment rates

Unemployment rates, along with changes in technology; changes in law; shifts in population; shifts in urban, suburban, and rural areas; and competition are external factors used to forecast changes that might be needed in the future. Factors such as financial restrictions, increases or decreases in sales, and production levels are internal factors.

(21) (D) A large number of résumés are available, so it is difficult to filter out good candidates.

Websites are a relatively cheap recruiting tool that start-ups can use. However, the biggest drawback of websites is that they bring in a huge influx of people who want to get the job, and many may be unqualified.

(22) (A) Honesty test

Cognitive ability tests and personality tests are reliable. They provide authentic information about employees. However, honesty tests are unreliable and waste time, money, and resources, as these tests can easily be passed through manipulation, deception, and cleverness.

(23) (A) Microsoft's Professional Developer Conference

Microsoft's Professional Developer Conference (PDC) is an annual conference in July. A huge number of web developers and other professionals attend it to meet new people, make more contacts, and, most importantly, update their skills.

(24) (D) Both A and C

Unhealthy working conditions and problems with the boss are among the most common reasons why 90% of employees leave their workplaces.

(25) (A) External factors

As the name suggests, external factors influence a company from the outside. They can be anything unpredictable, and, as a result, a company usually does not have any control over them.

(26) (B) Employees are unhappy with their paychecks.

A common misconception held by HR managers is that employees leave their work because of unsatisfactory salaries. However, this is actually not the case. Rather, managerial issues, boring work, and unfair workloads are the most common reasons people leave a company.

(27) (C) Agile

The Waterfall technique failed to satisfy the needs of the competitiveness of the software industry and its continual mobility. As a result, Agile was created.

(28) (B) Muda, Mura, Muri

Lean is a project management approach that focuses primarily on enhancing the value of a customer while reducing waste. The three Ms—Muda, Mura, and Muri—are the three categories of waste. Muda refers to the waste of resources and time. Mura aims to eliminate inconsistencies in the workflow processes of scheduling and operations. Muri refers to excessiveness.

(29) (B) Muda

Muda refers to the waste of resources and time.

(30) (A) 1986

Six Sigma is a project management approach that focuses on increasing and improving the quality of a process by lowering the number of previous errors. Motorola engineers invented the approach in 1986.

(31) (D) All of the above

There are several different strategies that HR teams usually adopt to make a company's business run smoothly and efficiently. Three of the most common and most effective strategies are managerial, operative, and advising.

(32) (A) Operative

HR teams are always trying to improve their company's business. They adopt several different strategies, including managerial, operative, and advising on priority strategies. Planning, organizing, and directing form the aspects of the managerial strategy. The advising strategy refers to providing high-level management and advice to employees, while the operative strategy includes recruiting, job analysis, compensation, and welfare.

(33) (B) Health care

Compensation and welfare provides welfare services to employees, including health-care benefits for their well-being. These benefits are usually provided in the form of insurance plans that extend to immediate family members.

(34) (A) HR management

It is the responsibility of the HR department to look into employee payment issues.

(35) (B) National Labor Relations Board

NLRB stands for National Labor Relations Board, which is broadly assigned the task of conducting union elections.

(36) (B) It is the process of a firm or organization becoming a part of a labor union.

Unionization refers to how the employees of a firm decide to become a part of a labor union and agree that the union will act as a bargaining tool against their employers in case of any injustice and also represent them. Employees also are assured that the union will allow them to voice their opinions.

(37) (C) Both A and B

Both surveys and questionnaires provide HR with an efficient way of increasing effectiveness. The people concerned with organizational development acquire relevant data through these surveys and questionnaires to figure out the managers' leadership styles, reanalyze those styles, and make important decisions regarding the business.

(38) (D) Diagnosis

After identifying gaps in the current system, the next step is to diagnose the problem. The organization looks at the problem and tries to figure out its root causes using surveys, questionnaires, and, at times, interviews to find out the most relevant cause associated with the emerging problem.

(39) (C) Decentralized structure

There are two types of organizational design structures: centralized and decentralized. In a centralized structure, all the roles, positions, and commands are held by top-level officials. In a decentralized structure, decisions that the officials in a decentralized structure would have made are handled by lower and mid-level company officials.

(40) (D) Both B and C

The advantage of a decentralized organizational structure is that it leads to effective customer service and lower business costs.

(41) (C) Technology creation

STMS stands for Strategic Technology Management System. It is a technique that follows a life-cycle approach to manage technology in a company. The first phase of STMS is technology creation. It involves creating new designs for new inventions, then consequently inventing them.

(42) (C) Legal restructuring

As the name suggests, legal restructuring occurs when changes are made in a company's legal policies. Financial restructuring is the restructuring of an organization's capital structure. Under the cost-saving strategy, changes are made overall in the organization to reduce costs.

(43) (D) Both A and B

One of the major drawbacks of restructuring an organization is that sudden layoffs and downsizing have to occur. Sudden layoffs and downsizing cause job insecurity among remaining employees.

(44) (C) It is a scheme that misleads people into believing that a technique is environmentally friendly when it is not.

Greenwash is a term used for techniques and processes projected as being environmentally friendly but that in reality are not. NGOs tend to see corporate social responsibility as greenwash.

(45) (A) Corporate citizenship

Corporate social responsibility is also known as corporate citizenship.

(46) (C) Both A and B

The definition of corporate social responsibility has been severely disputed ever since the term surfaced in the 1960s. In recent times, the two prominent names that have defined the term are Benedict Sheehy and Archie B. Carroll. Sheehy refers to CSR as international private business self-regulation, whereas Carroll says that CSR was launched because of rising social concerns. Carroll's definition is closer to the official definition.

(47) (B) Addressing harassment claims in the workplace

There are four types of corporate social responsibility: environmental, ethical, economic, and philanthropic. There are ways to uphold each of these types of

CSR. To uphold ethical responsibility, addressing harassment claims in the workplace is important. If this is not done, employees will suffer and the image of the company can be seriously jeopardized.

(48) (D) All of the above.

One very important responsibility that falls under CSR is environmental responsibility. By implementing environmental responsibility, a company's waste production can be reduced; energy waste can be decreased, and since the use of automotive vehicles is also reduced, smog production can be controlled.

(49) (A) World Bank

The World Bank offers loans to countries all over the world. It offers financial assistance to start-ups on the condition that they move their operations forward with a philanthropic strategy, such as providing natural disaster relief, education programs, etc.

(50) (B) Diversity refers to recognizing differences between individuals, and inclusion refers to providing them with equal opportunities.

Though the words *diversity* and *inclusion* seem synonymous, there is a major difference between the two. Diversity occurs when you respect the differences among individuals and recognize them. Inclusion happens when you provide individuals who are unlike you with opportunities in your company and include them in your circle. As a company, you need to be both diverse and inclusive.

(51) (A) Higher productivity

Higher productivity is a benefit of inclusion, whereas enhanced creativity, variety of applicants, and wider reach to the international market are benefits of diversity.

(52) (C) Task conflict

When groups of employees come into conflict regarding the course of action that must be taken to do a certain task, this is called a task conflict. Relationship conflicts occur when individuals are not on the same page about a task. Intergroup conflicts arise when conflicts arise not only within the groups, but also between groups. Value conflicts arise due to differences in opinions and personalities.

(53) (C) HR should observe changes in the attitudes on both sides.

The HR department is of great importance. It cannot pass any issue to higher departments, stay neutral, or take sides when conflict arises the employees. It has to play the role of a mediator and negotiator. To do this, it should observe changes in attitudes on both sides, hear both sides of the story, and fix the issues as soon as possible.

(54) (B) Interpersonal conflict

Relationship conflict, also referred to as interpersonal conflict, arises between individuals who are not on the same page when working on a particular task. Intrapersonal conflict arises when a person is in conflict with himself or herself. Intergroup conflict occurs between two groups, and intragroup conflict arises within a group.

(55) (C) Value conflict

When people are in disagreement due to their difference in opinions on certain issues, this is considered to be a value conflict.

(56) (D) Assertiveness

There are several conflict resolution strategies. The strategy in which an expert mediator makes efforts to set up a meeting between groups that have been arguing is called assertiveness. Communication happens when parties talk to each other to solve the problem, collaboration happens when the groups in conflict are cooperative, and compromising happens when parties agree to compromise on some things.

(57) (D) All of the above

Global HR management revolves around taking care of employees and workers around the globe. There are several sectors to it. Apart from diversity, some other important factors are labor relations and business leadership, employee relations, staffing management, recruitment, ethics and social responsibility, training, employee compensation and benefits, and legal compliance.

(58) (A) It brings consistency to the organization as a whole.

Consistency is a very important strategic benefit of global HRM. Consistency allows a company's brand to grow and strengthens business operations.

(59) (C) It varies in each organization.

The number of risk management employees will vary in each organization depending upon the size of the organization, the types of risks, and the skills and experiences of the people involved.

(60) (B) Executive director

The executive director is responsible for devising risk reduction plans.

(61) (C) Monitoring

Every organization needs to have a risk management process to easily identify and understand the risks involved with business decisions. Assessment is the second step of the process, planning is the third, and implementation is the second-to-last step. The last step is monitoring the strategies that have been implemented to fix any errors that might pop up.

(62) (D) None of the above

The job of the HR department extends over a very large area of work. The professionals are responsible for recruiting, interviewing, and shortlisting the right candidates for the business. Sometimes HR professionals must also fire employees.

(63) (A) Run audits regularly

Regular audits are the most effective way of finding out a company's level of compliance with the law. A regular and constant check is maintained this way. It is relatively easy to convince people to follow the rules and regulations.

(64) (A) A raise in salary

As the name suggests, financial rewards have to do with raising employees' compensation levels and helping them with any money-related problems they might be facing. A raise in salary is a popular example of such rewards. Free parking, childcare, and certifications are examples of nonfinancial rewards.

(65) (D) Promotions

Intrinsic rewards are given out to make an employee feel appreciated and part of the company. Promotions, personal achievements, and words of appreciation from senior executives are some examples of intrinsic rewards. Extrinsic rewards are, in comparison, monetary rewards, such as bonuses, pay raises, incentives, etc.

(66) (A) Better program administration

A well-functioning total rewards system in a company that honors its employees has multiple advantages besides employee performance and employee retention. When there is a properly working reward system, it becomes easier to administer business programs without discrepancies.

(67) (B) The way an organization decides to deal with a business situation

Business acumen is the way an organization decides to deal with a business-related situation to bring out the best results.

(68) (C) Both A and B

Deciding on business acumen or deciding how an organization will deal with a business-related problem requires the organization to know the profitable aspects of its business, the cash flow, the current market situation, and its respective niche. If a business is well versed in all of these, it will easily come up with effective business acumen.

(69) (A) Lack of communication between the leadership and employees

Communication is key in every aspect of life, especially in a business. Lack of communication between leaders and employees can result in many issues. The employees will not feel appreciated, and they will not work with the same energy they would otherwise. They will also think that they are not being provided with the information they deserve to know. This dissatisfaction can cause disputes and conflicts, which can disrupt healthy work environments.

(70) (B) Face-to-face communication

In today's technologically controlled world, lack of communication has become a huge issue. Emails, letters, and phone calls can bridge barriers, but the most effective means of communication is sitting face-to-face with the person you want to have a conversation with. In business setups, effective communication is essential, and if possible, one should definitely have face-to-face conversations, as they almost eliminate the chances of misunderstandings.

(71) (C) Proper documents

Legal contracts and agreements are the most important business documents. They cannot be treated informally and need to be properly documented in a very formal way. You cannot save them on cell phones, as they could easily get lost or stolen.

(72) (D) Informal leaders

Every manager and formal leader is officially appointed by the organization. The other kinds of leaders, called informal leaders, are usually self-appointed leaders of a group. They are not official leaders and are not chosen or appointed by the company.

(73) (D) All of the above

Formal leaders are appointed by an organization as official agents and representatives, whereas informal leaders are self-appointed guides of a group. Every manager in the company is a formal leader of their department, as the company officially hires them.

(74) (B) Expertise, independence, affiliation

The three higher-order needs of an organization are expertise, independence, and affiliation.

(75) (B) Intrinsic motivation refers to doing something for the sake of the activity itself, and extrinsic motivation refers to doing something for the sake of achieving the desired result.

According to the self-determination theory, there are two types of motivation: intrinsic and extrinsic. Intrinsic motivation refers to doing something for the sake of the activity itself, and extrinsic motivation refers to doing something for the sake of achieving the desired result.

(76) (A) Intrinsically motivated

When tasks meet any of the three higher-order needs, these tasks are said to be intrinsically motivated.

(77) (B) Delegating

Delegating is the final level of leadership style in the Situational Leadership Theory® model. Employees in this case are extremely capable and driven. Therefore. the leader is required to keep only a minimal and superficial check on them.

(78) (A) Robert House

Researcher Robert House is known for laying the foundations of the path-goal theory of leadership. The expectation theory is based on his work.

(79) (C) Four

Transformational leaders motivate their employees and followers to focus on the company's success more than they focus on their personal achievements. They have four tools that help them do this. These are charisma, inspiration, intellectual stimulation, and individualized consideration.

(80) (A) People you know and like

A direct appeal works best when it is addressed to people you both know and like.

(81) (A) The use of facts, evidence, and logical arguments to convince people

Rational means "logical"—something that makes sense to everyone. Therefore, an approach is considered rational when you try to talk to someone and sway them to your viewpoint through factual evidence and logic. This is by far the most widely used technique to influence people. Rationality is also linked to favorable job performances by several types of research and studies.

(82) (A) Internal factor

There are two types of factors that are used to predict the changes that a company might have to make in the future. They are external and internal factors. Plans for global expansion, financial restrictions, employee unions, production levels, and increase or decrease in sales are considered internal factors.

(83) (D) All of the above

There are usually two types of job analyses: task-based analysis and competency-based analysis. The steps usually included in a task-based analysis are writing performance evaluations for employees, preparing reports, answering incoming phone calls, assisting customers with product questions, and cold-calling at least three customers a day.

(84) (D) More objective

In comparison with a task-based analysis, a competency-based analysis is less clear but more objective. It is, therefore, done for specific and high-level job positions in a company.

(85) (C) An executive search firm

There are several recruiting strategies common in companies, including hiring recruiters, associating the company with an executive search firm or a temporary recruitment or staffing firm, contacting corporate recruiters, conducting campus recruiting, using websites and social media SIGs, referrals, and events. Out of all of these, associating your company with an executive search firm is the costliest because these firms usually demand 10–20% of the first-year wages of the employee being appointed, which is quite a lot to ask for.

(86) (C) Both A and B

Colleges and universities are ideal places to find people for entry-level job positions. Campus recruiting at these places helps you find these people easily.

(87) (B) Behavior

According to reinforcement theory, behavior is a result of the outcomes of actions.

(88) (A) Procedural and interactional

According to equity theory, two types of procedures can increase fairness among employees: procedural and interactional. Together, they impact both employees' motivation and their reaction toward any wrong or right happening to them.

(89) (B) Adds extra challenges to their existing jobs

Usually, employees get bored if they are provided with the same work every day. Employees who want to challenge themselves every day will enjoy job enlargement, as it adds new challenges to their existing jobs. For example, an employee can be assigned a new project or task that increases their job interest and increases their motivation.

(90) (B) Iterative and incremental projects

Agile is one of the most famous project management approaches in the world. It is used for iterative and incremental projects in which cross-functional teams and their customers work together to find solutions.

(91) (C) Lean specializes only in the manufacturing industry.

Lean is an excellent project management approach that focuses on increasing the value of customers by simultaneously reducing waste. The values of this methodology are derived from the Japanese manufacturing industry. A common myth associated with this approach states that Lean specializes only in the manufacturing industry, which is completely false.

(92) (B) By lowering the number of previous errors

Six Sigma is a project management methodology that was developed back in 1986 by Motorola engineers. The technique works by increasing the quality of a process by lowering the number of previous errors. It does this by identifying those errors and removing them from the system simultaneously.

(93) (A) To create new processes, products, or services.

DMAIC is used to improve already existing processes, while DMADV creates new processes, products, or services by creating, analyzing, and testing the thought-out designs.

(94) (A) When there is a complex, multistep project on the table

A work breakdown structure requires you to divide any task into smaller parts so that it can easily be finished without compromising on quality. This strategy is used when a complex, detailed, lengthy, and multistep task has to be done because it allows employees to do their work more efficiently.

(95) (D) Both B and C

Work breakdown structure is a technique used to break down a complex and multistep task into smaller chunks so it can be completed quickly and efficiently. There are several ways to create a WBS outline and keep track of the chunks being created. Some examples can include a spreadsheet, flowchart, list, and Gantt chart. All these serve as platforms where you can easily maintain a record of your project and organize the entire project and the parts you have broken it down into.

(96) (B) The HR department should make the workplace inclusive for people belonging to the LGBTQ+ community.

The world is becoming more kind, compassionate, and considerate toward people. You can lose extremely talented employees if you stay silent in the face of important social justice movements. Therefore, making your workplace inclusive for such people will show your support for them and their cause.

(97) (A) They should provide a platform for employees to file anonymous complaints.

Many things do not get recorded on cameras. Moreover, establishing punishments after a mess is made is not productive conflict resolution. Also, spying on your own employees is unethical. Therefore, the best way to give your employees the freedom to voice their complaints is to provide a platform on which they can register anonymous complaints.

(98) (C) The representative should maintain neutrality and hear the opinions of both the involved parties.

One of the most important roles of the HR department is to bridge gaps and maintain healthy communication among employees. They should not stay away from conflict resolution and should also not pick sides based on their personal preferences.

(99) (A) They should shortlist the 45-year-old for the interview.

Age should just be a number in a company. Age should not matter if an individual possesses the right level of talent and skills for the job.

(100) (C) Directly via face-to-face communication

The most effective form of communication is face-to-face communication—when people sit across each other to have a conversation. There is a chance of misunderstandings in phone calls, emails, and indirect modes of communication because you cannot look at or read the body language or expressions of the people you are talking to. They might tell you that they have understood the task when they are still having doubts.

(101) (A) Choosing a specific niche

Waiting for another year will only exert more pressure on your already limited resources, and so will the addition of more niches. Setting up an office is not necessary if you are able to strike a balance between your personal and professional life. However, it will help narrow down the competition and attract more clients to your business if you choose a particular niche and stick to that.

(102) (B) Show sympathy toward the employee

Sending the employee away, scolding the person, or complaining about the individual will only add to the employee's stress and disrupt the work environment. Showing support and sympathy to employees is important for maintaining a healthy work environment.

(103) (B) Adopt a rational approach and provide factual evidence related to your company's business

Making a personal request to the client or sending another person in your stead will not impress anyone. Furthermore, flattery or exaggeration can cause clients to immediately lose interest and/or trust in your firm. Only facts and logic can help you win people over.

(104) (D) This is an external factor that the HR department could not have controlled or prevented.

Governments come and go. They establish their own laws that can be neither predicted nor prevented by anyone. The only thing that can be done is to abide by those laws, as they are uncontrollable external variables.

(105) (A) Six Sigma is the correct project management approach for the creation of new processes.

Six Sigma is a project management approach that increases the efficiency of organizational processes by lowering the number of previous errors. It consists of two primary approaches: DMAIC and DMADV. DMADV is used to create new processes.

(106) (B) Use a spreadsheet to organize the different stages, tasks, or outputs in columns and rows

The work breakdown structure technique needs to be used for complex multistep processes because it cuts down the work into smaller chunks. This makes it easier to complete the work. A proper spreadsheet containing all the divisions of the work should be used to organize this data.

(107) (C) Organizing

There are three components of managerial strategy: planning, organizing, and directing. When you are organizing, you are assigning people in the company tasks and responsibilities they are supposed to carry out. If a person is assigned the wrong task or a responsibility that would be better carried out by someone else, the HR department is lacking in organizational skills.

(108) (A) Immediately initiate learning and development programs for all employees

Waiting for two months to pass is risky and a waste of time. Informing people behind doors is not ethically and morally correct. The best thing to do is to initiate training programs for all employees so that the employees who will be retained are prepared to bear the burden of any extra responsibilities.

(109) (B) File a case against the employee to instill fear among other employees

The best way to avoid being held in serious contempt of the law is to establish strict punishments so that the other employees think twice before committing any similar violations.

(110) (B) Report it to the National Labor Relations Board and seek legal action against the union

Some unions carry out illegal labor practices, such as forcing employees and employers to accept unfair demands. To keep them under control, one can simply report the misconduct to the NLRB, which will take legal action if the practice was conducted over a period of six months.

(111) (B) Interpersonal relations interventions

As the phrase itself suggests, these interventions are made to improve interpersonal relations between two individuals so that the company's objectives are met without any conflict or hurdles.

(112) (A) Carry out surveys and questionnaires

Surveys and questionnaires are fairly trustworthy sources of relevant and reliable information about a company. Taking risks or operating based on hypotheses is foolish when the option of questionnaires and surveys is available.

(113) (C) Inform employees of the positive qualities of the system

Removing the system when it is important will drastically affect your employees. Removing the employees or ignoring their responses will reflect poorly on the communication and relations between management and employees. Carrying out awareness programs to convince those individuals reluctant to use the technology of the new system's benefits is the best solution.

(114) (B) Initiate training programs to help employees learn how to use the new technology

If most of the employees are unable to operate new technology, it is unfair to fire a large majority of people and hire new ones. Doing this will also exhaust your resources. Training employees about the functions of the technology is the most effective solution.

(115) (A) Look for funds and sponsorships

Cutting down on expenditures to save the required amount of money will take time. Similarly, dropping the idea is not advised if the technology is essential.

The best idea is to seek out funds and sponsorships for a company with a limited budget.

(116) (A) Downsize some employees

It is a difficult decision, but taking out loans will only add to the pressure, as the company cannot predict how long the financial crisis will persist. Shutting down the company is equivalent to giving up when there are other solutions still available. Therefore, downsizing is the best alternative for a company that finds itself in this kind of situation.

(117) (B) Run the office on solar energy

Environmental damage can be averted, and everyone can play a part, as small as it may be. Companies have a responsibility to use ethical environmental practices as much as possible. Shutting off unused lights is not a long-term measure. Instead, running the office on solar power will allow you to light the office without harming the environment.

(118) (A) Fund NGOs that help with disaster management

When someone is struck by a disaster, everyone who is safe and can help should play their part, including companies. Issuing mere statements when you can afford to offer more concrete help is highly insensitive. Moreover, sending people who are not capable of removing heavy debris will also not help the situation and may actually worsen it.

(119) (D) All of the above

Gender equality is a hot topic these days, and you can play your part as a company in several different ways, including ensuring equal gender pay, addressing harassment claims immediately, and hiring females for higher positions.

(120) (D) All of the above

Everyone can play their part in preserving the environment. Restaurants can use paper bags, run their machines on solar power, and use recyclable utensils like paper straws to preserve the environment.

(121) (C) Shortlist the Black candidate for an interview based on their talent, not their race

Filtering out the candidate is racist behavior. Hiring a Black person just to make your company look good is equally racist. Hiring only Black candidates is not any better. The only viable behavior here is to shortlist the Black candidate for an interview based on their talent and aptitude for the job, not their race.

(122) (A) Diverse

Diversity means respecting and recognizing the differences among individuals. *Inclusion* is providing those individuals with opportunities in your company. If you are only respecting them and not making them a part of your business, this will make your company only diverse, not inclusive.

(123) (B) Ask employees to avoid discussing politics in the office

Firing the employees is not the right thing to do, as conflicts cannot be completely eliminated. Separating the employees will also not be appropriate because if they are talented individuals, they should not be deprived of the chance of working on a project. Therefore, you can only ask the employees to moderate their behavior by not discussing such things in the workplace.

(124) (A) Organize an employee assistance program (EAP)

To avoid challenging employee relations, HR should organize an EAP. Hiring separate HR managers will not resolve any issues, as the employees will all still have to report to a single HR manager. Instead, training employees to deal with all the managers spread across the globe is an effective way of solving this issue.

(125) (B) Risk management should have been done beforehand.

There is no 100% reliable system. If the right people install the system but risk management is not done on it, any system may collapse. Identifying the errors in a system and reducing them can help prevent such a problem from occurring.

(126) (A) Prepare a chart to highlight the frequency of every risk from top to bottom

It is important to rank the identified risks in order to keep a track record of them. Writing them down informally on a piece of paper or a notepad app on a cell phone might cause you to lose the data. Therefore, all important data should be entered into an organized system.

(127) (B) Give nonfinancial rewards such as gym memberships, time off, free parking spaces, etc.

Businesses with limited budgets and other businesses prefer nonfinancial rewards, as they tend to last longer than any monetary reward. They can also be provided to employees with little to no cost to a company.

(128) (D) Anything that the company can afford at that moment

Employees always crave appreciation. The more they feel valued, the more they are motivated to work hard. The appreciation can be provided in any form.

(129) (A) The manager should be removed, and a responsible manager should be hired.

Effective communication is the primary responsibility of an HR manager. As a result, an HR manager needs to be of good character and act polite, kind, tolerant, etc.

(130) (B) Understanding of the finances of the company

If HR had had adequate information about the company's finances, which includes the profits, losses, spending, etc., the department would not have approved the loan.

(131) (D) After the meeting, politely ask your colleague why he is behaving in such a way and try to resolve any issue that comes up

Ignoring your colleague, calling the person out, or complaining about the individual without even communicating with them will reflect poorly on your attitude. Instead, you should wait for an appropriate time, such as after a meeting, to politely inquire why your colleague is now acting in this manner when previously your relationship was cordial and productive.

(132) (C) Give the employee some time to get familiar with the company's practices

Scolding employees, warning them, punishing them ,or firing them are all extreme behaviors, especially when an employee has just been appointed. If you exhibit these behaviors toward a new employee, you will create the impression that your company's work environment is tense and strict. New employees should be allowed some time to make themselves comfortable in a company's culture.

(133) (B) The informal leader trying to influence the group

Informal leaders are self-appointed people who take command of a group and guide its members through issues.

(134) (A) Introduce a culture of phone calls

It is the prime responsibility of the HR department to build effective workplace communication. Phone calls are a good way of helping develop a friendly relationship between management and employees.

SHRM-SCP Test 3

(1) Numerous factors including which of the following decide an organization's acumen?

(A) Reasonable comprehension of the business's specialty

(B) Running the business as a dictatorship

(C) Giving more importance to sales strategy rather than financial management

(D) Running the business traditionally

(2) The main reason behind a successful business is:

(A) A good relationship with the stakeholders

(B) A high-profit turnover

(C) Versatile advertising techniques

(D) A well-organized HR team

(3) How can an HR professional acquire the skill of being well versed in the market?

(A) By using the internet to keep up with finance journals, blogs, etc.

(B) By relying on word of mouth from colleagues

(C) By using unreliable news articles on social media

(D) By using outdated books to make future projections

(4) The key to effective internal communication is:

(A) Peer assessment

(B) Updating internal memos more frequently

(C) Having a long-term strategy to deal with internal communication

(D) Writing cordial emails

(5) Face-to-face communication is encouraged in the workplace because:

(A) It is difficult to personalize emails.

(B) Emotions are more effectively shared in person.

(C) Memos/emails can be lost or missed.

(D) All of the above.

(6) What kinds of organizations do major HR consultation firms usually work with?

(A) Small businesses

(B) Established organizations

(C) NGOs

(D) Private limited corporations

(7) Which of the following qualities is not needed in an HR consultant?

(A) Being well versed in the legal aspects of a company

(B) Being able to work independently

(C) Sticking to traditional market trends instead of updating one's knowledge frequently

(D) Having ample knowledge of a business's financial workings

(8) The advantage of picking a specific field of service or specialization for an HR consultant is:

(A) It limits the competition.

(B) The range of clientele is amplified.

(C) It allows for smoother running of the business.

(D) All of the above.

(9) An effective method of making contacts in the consultancy field is:

(A) Advertising your services

(B) Relying on clientele to spread the word

(C) Relying on colleagues to find your clientele

(D) None of the above

(10) Why should an HR professional adhere to the practice of meticulous documentation?

(A) It makes it easier to transition when contract changes are involved.

(B) Chronological documentation makes it easier to refer to previous practices when needed.

(C) It allows leeway in legal matters.

(D) All of the above.

(11) Which of the following definitions best describes ethical practice?

(A) Ethical practice takes place when an organization embeds and upholds its values at all levels in order to maintain and increase trust.

(B) Ethical practice is a kind of self-regulatory practice that aims to contribute to societal goals of a philanthropic, activist, or charitable nature by engaging in or supporting volunteering or ethically oriented practices.

(C) Ethical practice consists of the qualities, experiences, and work styles that make individuals unique (e.g., age, race, religion, disabilities, and ethnicity), as well as how organizations can leverage those qualities in support of business objectives.

(D) None of the above.

(12) Which of the following best describes cultural effectiveness?

(A) Valuing the perspectives and backgrounds of all parties a business interacts with

(B) The process employers use for recruiting, tracking, and interviewing job candidates and onboarding and training new employees

(C) The personnel of a business or organization being regarded as a significant asset in terms of skills and abilities

(D) None of the above

(13) Which of the following practices best boosts employee morale?

(A) Accepting all religious and cultural views within a workplace

(B) Teaching sales employees to be respectful during customer interactions

(C) Distributing code-of-conduct booklets annually

(D) Establishing an eco-friendly company policy

(14) What effect does a reliable company image have on a business?

(A) It promotes an eco-friendly strategy.

(B) It enhances the loyalty of customers and attracts new ones.

(C) It amplifies employee performance.

(D) None of the above.

(15) Which of the following is a technique businesses use to avoid behavioral misconduct in the workplace?

(A) Keeping confidential files under tight security

(B) Encouraging the acceptance of different races, classes, and cultures in the workplace

(C) Ensuring accountability for any misbehavior (e.g., sexual harassment) in the workplace

(D) Encouraging interaction between different age groups

(16) Businesses are run by numerous people working together. In this type of setting, it is crucial for one person among these individuals to take on a commanding role.

What are the two types of leading roles in a business?

(A) Formal and informal

(B) Joint and separate

(C) Primary and secondary

(D) Intermittent and permanent

(17) Which of the following is true about goal-set theory?

(A) The rate of performance is directly proportional to the severity of the set goals.

(B) Individuals following this theory should only loosely adhere to its tenets.

(C) The rate of performance is indirectly proportional to the goals set.

(D) All of the above.

(18) When the HR department is given the task of choosing a leader for a specific team, the department looks for certain traits. However, it has been proven that over time these certain traits do not always result in the best outcome.

Which of the following is one of those traits?

(A) Resilience

(B) Empathy

(C) Vision

(D) Influence

(19) Paul Hersey and Kenneth Blanchard are the theorists of the Situational Leadership Theory® model. Their model states that there is no single quality that contributes to the making of the best leader. Therefore, different situations call for different types of leadership.

What is the first step of leadership in this model?

(A) Participating

(B) Directing

(C) Delegating

(D) None of the above

(20) What are the four utilitarian qualities of transformative leaders?

(A) Charismatic, visionary, invigorating, and considerate

(B) Charismatic, visionary, tech-savvy, and considerate

(C) Charismatic, honest, invigorating, and considerate

(D) Passionate, visionary, invigorating, and considerate

(21) It is a common misconception that conflict only causes negative outcomes.

Which of the following is a positive outcome of conflict?

(A) It makes relationships stronger.

(B) It leads to innovative ideas.

(C) It leads to more frequent discussion.

(D) None of the above.

(22) ___________ occurs when an action done by a certain person within a group is misconstrued by the rest of the people in the group.

(A) Behavioral conflict

(B) Cognitive conflict

(C) Affective conflict

(D) Goal conflict

(23) Conflict can be categorized into different styles. It is crucial that the people in charge are familiar with these different styles so they can solve conflicts properly.

Which style of conflict might cause resentment in one of two parties who are having a dispute?

(A) Avoiding

(B) Competing

(C) Accommodating

(D) Collaborating

(24) Which of the following types of conflicts is the most difficult to resolve?

(A) Interpersonal conflict

(B) Interorganizational conflict

(C) Intergroup conflict

(D) None of the above

(25) Which of the following options should you consider when attempting to resolve a workplace conflict?

(A) The negative impact of the resolution on either of the parties

(B) The possibility of a resolution that satisfies all parties

(C) The repercussions of being stern while resolving the conflict

(D) All of the above

(26) Which of the following factors contributes to the number of people a firm needs to hire?

(A) The recruitment budget

(B) Long-term intentions

(C) Short-term intentions

(D) All of the above

(27) Which of the following factors needs to be considered in a recruitment plan?

(A) A compilation of qualifications and skills needed for a position

(B) A sales strategy for a new product

(C) A new way to make the firm more CSR-friendly

(D) None of the above

(28) Which of the following options is part of a job specification?

(A) The objectives of the job

(B) The tasks to be performed on the job

(C) The skills and qualifications required for the job

(D) The responsibilities assigned to that job

(29) There are many advantages of a workforce that is composed of fresh graduates.

Which types of recruiters are used to hire fresh graduates?

(A) Corporate recruiters

(B) Campus recruiters

(C) Websites

(D) Staffing firms

(30) If prospective employers want to test a candidate's ability to perform a certain task, which kind of test should they ask the candidate to take?

(A) An achievement test

(B) An aptitude test

(C) A personality test

(D) None of the above

(31) Monetary dissatisfaction is not usually the primary reason for employees resigning from their positions.

Which of the following is the primary reason for employee resignation?

(A) Personal disagreements with the managerial staff

(B) Lack of diversity and inclusion in the workplace

(C) Substandard conditions in the work environment

(D) All of the above

(32) Ensuring that the practice of development and training is implemented in the workplace is beneficial for which parties?

(A) The company and its employees

(B) The customer and company employees

(C) Investors and company employees

(D) The company and investors

(33) Job enrichment is defined as skillfully amplifying the number of tasks a certain employee performs in quantity and quality.

Which of the following options falls under the term *job enrichment*?

(A) An increased variety in the tasks assigned to the employees

(B) Giving employees more authority to increase their level of confidence

(C) Giving employees a critical analysis of their performance

(D) All of the above

(34) Which of the following options matches this definition: "Attaching extra but relevant tasks to the existing work"?

(A) Empowerment

(B) Enlargement

(C) None

(D) All

(35) Managerial staff employs a fairness technique when a decrease in employee morale is noticed, which usually happens because of unfair workload and a distinct lack or low level of received benefits.

Which of these theories is used to devise fairness techniques?

(A) Equity theory

(B) Expectancy theory

(C) Reinforcement theory

(D) All of the above

(36) In this new day and age, the demand for a competent HR department has increased. The tasks of an HR employee have been extended to include:

(A) Hiring new employees

(B) Ensuring the extended tenure of new employees

(C) Providing a safe and amicable workplace environment for all staff members

(D) All of the above

(37) The Agile approach to management was created because the ________ approach had become obsolete.

(A) Waterfall

(B) Henson

(C) Richard-Evans

(D) Smith

(38) What is the aim of the Lean management approach, and what do the three Ms stand for?

(A) The aim of the Lean approach is to integrate technology into the managerial system. The three Ms stand for Mira, Muda, Mora.

(B) The aim of the approach is to improve sale tactics and increase sales revenue. The three Ms stand for Mistake, Magic, Money.

(C) The Lean approach aims to amplify the merits of customers and lessen the net waste production of a company. The three Ms stand for Muda, Mura, Muri.

(D) The Lean approach aims to improve employee morale through inclusion and diversity. The three Ms stand for Middling, Mining, Manufacturing.

(39) What is the first step in building a work breakdown structure?

(A) Gauging the extent of the task

(B) Informing the managerial staff of preliminary meetings

(C) Selecting the employees needed to plan the work breakdown structure

(D) None of the above

(40) Which type of work breakdown structure is defined as an "amalgamation of spreadsheet and chronological scheduling"?

(A) A WBS spreadsheet

(B) A WBS list

(C) A Gantt chart

(D) A WBS flowchart

(41) Which part of managerial strategy entails allotting specific duties to qualified employees and designing the hierarchy that is to be followed?

(A) Planning

(B) Organizing

(C) Directing

(D) None of the above

(42) Which management strategy is devised during the revision of rules and regulations in a firm?

(A) Managerial strategy

(B) Advising strategy

(C) Operative strategy

(D) None of the above

(43) When a newly hired employee joins a firm, it is the firm's responsibility to give the person access to training programs and assist them through the initiation process.

This is the definition of which key component of HR practice?

(A) Employee relations

(B) Payroll

(C) Legal compliance

(D) Training and development

(44) Is it possible for a business to simultaneously run its own personal HR department while outsourcing an HR consultancy firm?

(A) Yes

(B) No

(C) Yes, but under certain conditions

(D) None of the above

(45) Which of the following tasks can be taken on only by highly experienced HR personnel?

(A) Organizing interdepartmental meetings

(B) Keeping tabs on the financial aspects of the company

(C) Becoming a part of executive decision-making

(D) None of the above

(46) If the employers in a firm are providing a safe and amicable environment, employees must return the favor by:

(A) Following the code of conduct

(B) Helping with recruitment

(C) Working extra hours

(D) None of the above

(47) How does HR nurture cooperative relationships between a business's employees?

(A) By enforcing minimal wastage of office resources

(B) By providing resolutions to interpersonal/group conflicts

(C) By increasing the wage gap between genders

(D) All of the above

(48) Which two concepts must a company take into consideration when working on improving workplace relationships?

(A) Resilience and perseverance

(B) Honesty and honoring their word

(C) Loyalty and punctuality

(D) Influence and vision

(49) The relationship between union strength and worker signatures on an authorization form is:

(A) Indirectly proportional

(B) Directly proportional

(C) Nonexistent

(D) Equal

(50) Just like large firms, unions also conduct fraudulent practices and violate ethical practices. An example of these fraudulent practices is called *featherbedding*.

What does this term mean?

(A) When a firm hides its malicious intent toward a worker union by using different tactics

(B) When union workers intimidate employers into paying for work that has not been done by employees

(C) When a company's employees and the union form an alliance against the company

(D) None of the above

(51) Which of the following is a principal feature highlighted by organizational development and effectiveness?

(A) An increase in worker quantity

(B) The overall accomplishment of different teams in the firm

(C) Productivity

(D) All of the above

(52) Which of the following is a behavioral intervention mostly used in sales training?

(A) Interpersonal relations

(B) Management by objectives

(C) Developing the grid

(D) Role-playing

(53) Which of the following increases a firm's competitiveness?

(A) Implementing lucrative ways to use given resources

(B) A new business strategy

(C) An innovative sales technique

(D) None of the above

(54) The centralized structure model has a few disadvantages. Which of the following is one of those disadvantages?

(A) A decrease in overall work costs

(B) Bridging communication gaps

(C) Increasing work quality

(D) Lack of autonomy for employees

(55) Which of the following structures boosts employee morale?

(A) Decentralized structure

(B) Centralized structure

(C) Both

(D) Neither

(56) Which of the following departments is a crucial part of technical management?

(A) The research and development department

(B) The sales department

(C) The accounting department

(D) None of the above

(57) What is the IT department's first task during the planning phase of technology planning?

(A) The general priorities regarding all aspects of technology planning

(B) The budget allotted for the entire plan

(C) The resources needed for the completion of the project

(D) None of the above

(58) What is one of the goals of technological planning?

(A) Decreasing waste products

(B) Increasing workforce

(C) Reducing repetition

(D) Maintaining investor interest

(59) Which phase of the SRMS includes the participation of the research and development department?

(A) Technology management

(B) Technology assessment

(C) Technology transfer

(D) Accepting technological change

(60) Prioritizing the ___________ is the best way to ensure the advancement of a new technological system.

(A) Customers

(B) Employees

(C) Managerial staff

(D) CEO

(61) Which of the following is not a workforce management task?

(A) Compiling information to make statistical reports

(B) Financial projections

(C) Hiring a new workforce

(D) Improving sales techniques

(62) What is included in the job of a workforce manager?

(A) Motivating employees

(B) A critical analysis of the company's annual performance

(C) Working out compensation methods in lacking areas

(D) All of the above

(63) When another investor buys a large share of the company, that investor may decide to shuffle some policies. This will lead to organizational restructuring. This is an example of which of the following factors?

(A) A development in current business affairs

(B) Commercial incorporation

(C) Innovation

(D) None of the above

(64) Which type of restructuring takes place when a firm has been downsized due to deficient profit margins?

(A) Merger and acquisitions

(B) Economic restructuring

(C) Financial restructuring

(D) Legal restructuring

(65) Which trait is crucial for getting the best performance out of a firm after organizational restructuring has taken place?

(A) Communication

(B) Diversification

(C) Innovation

(D) All of the above

(66) Which type of corporate social responsibility promotes the sustenance of natural resources on our planet?

(A) Philanthropic

(B) Environmental

(C) Ethical

(D) Economical

(67) Which of the following does not fall under the benefits of corporate social responsibility?

(A) Protecting natural resources

(B) Cutting functional costs

(C) Increasing sales revenue

(D) None of the above

(68) One of the branches of corporate social responsibility is philanthropy. In the event of an earthquake, how can CSR benefit both a firm and the people affected by the earthquake?

(A) Investing in community infrastructure

(B) Educational training for the less fortunate

(C) Funding natural disaster aid

(D) All of the above

(69) Which benefit of corporate social responsibility is more applicable to start-ups and small-scale firms?

(A) Funding opportunities

(B) Amplifying industrial influence

(C) Cutting down on net spending

(D) None of the above

(70) What is a way to combat gender inequality through the ethical branch of corporate social responsibility?

(A) Minimizing the pay gap between coworkers

(B) Diversifying the managerial staff

(C) Creating innovative sales techniques

(D) All of the above

(71) What is the main difference between diversity and inclusion?

(A) Inclusion can be practiced without diversity.

(B) Diversity is only a concept, while inclusion is the practical application of it.

(C) Inclusion requires skilled personnel.

(D) Diversity can be practiced only on a limited number of people.

(72) Which benefit of diversity improves a firm's international relations?

(A) Creativity amplification

(B) Brand enhancement

(C) Increasing reach into the global market

(D) None of the above

(73) Benefits of inclusion include:

(A) Increased productivity

(B) Increased employee retention

(C) Increased firm compliance

(D) All of the above

(74) There are many ways of practicing inclusion in a firm. Which of the following options is an inclusion technique that benefits the older age group more than the others?

(A) Providing health-care packages

(B) Bank loans designed for student debt

(C) Wheelchair-accessible parking

(D) None of the above

(75) It is a well-known fact that when a firm is looking to offer promotions to its employees, multiple biases are uncovered, influencing their decisions.

What is one way to reduce this habit?

(A) Offering a training program on diversity and inclusion to people in managerial positions

(B) Creating an informative portfolio on promotion

(C) Conducting interviews with multiple candidates

(D) All of the above

(76) The art of conflict resolution is an important skill a person in a managerial position should possess. Which of the following set of skills is required to conduct conflict resolution?

(A) An approachable manner and an open mind

(B) Influential thinking and perseverance

(C) Logical reasoning and bargaining

(D) None of the above

(77) Conflicts can be categorized into many types. Which type of conflict is further categorized into vertical and horizontal?

(A) Relationship conflict

(B) Task conflict

(C) Intergroup conflict

(D) Value conflict

(78) The most effective way to resolve a conflict is through:

(A) Constructive talks

(B) Social engagement workshops

(C) Segregation in the workplace

(D) Addressing issues early

(79) Which of the following is a quality of conflict resolution?

(A) Self-confident

(B) Compensatory

(C) Cooperative

(D) All of the above

(80) When resolving a conflict, it is important to have a face-to-face discussion with a neutral party available in the room to mediate. This person needs to be focused on certain things. Which of the following is one of those things?

(A) The possibility of a solution that satisfies both parties

(B) Putting the company's priorities before the individuals' priorities

(C) Being prepared to deal with workers holding grudges

(D) All of the above

(81) What is the Sigma Six technique?

(A) It is a technique used to remove previous errors from a project to make it better.

(B) It is a technique used to increase the efficiency of workers by offering them a raise.

(C) It is a technique used to give managerial staff workshops on management methodology.

(D) None of the above.

(82) Strategic planning is how a company moves forward and grows. Its most important stage is implementation.

This stage will be unsuccessful without which of the following key components?

(A) Communication

(B) Adequate resources

(C) Versatile advertising

(D) An experienced HR team

(83) Which of the following groups of people are not a crucial part of the total rewards system team?

(A) Senior and more experienced members of the firm

(B) The HR department

(C) Intelligent researchers

(D) The sales department

(84) Compliance is an example of a workforce management task. Which of the following factors affects a firm's compliance?

(A) Government rules and regulations

(B) Union policies

(C) Records of employees

(D) All of the above

(85) What is a common reason for the failure of technology management strategies?

(A) Inadequate staffing

(B) Faults in the development phase of the strategy

(C) Improper implementation of the strategy

(D) All of the above

(86) What is the complete definition of risk management in HR?

(A) Dealing with the negative outcome of any undesirable situation

(B) Intercepting workplace problems before they arise

(C) Recognizing the risks that can damage a business and eliminating the chances of their occurrence or reoccurrence

(D) None of the above

(87) What are some of the side effects of not having a risk management plan in a large firm?

(A) Decrease in sales revenue

(B) Unhappy consumers

(C) Waste of company supplies

(D) All of the above

(88) Over time the implementation of a risk management plan is transferred from the executive director to:

(A) All the employees

(B) The CEO

(C) The HR department

(D) The stakeholders

(89) Part of designing a risk management program is assessing the possible risks of a business venture.

What are some important aspects to consider when creating a risk management program?

(A) The monetary burden of said risk

(B) The gravity and prevalence of said risk

(C) The influence of the risk on the employees

(D) All of the above

(90) A risk management plan should be devised during recruitment programs. Which of the following options will help avoid any risks involved during recruitment?

(A) Conducting interviews with a panel instead of one-on-one

(B) Taking referrals from current employees

(C) Creating an extremely detailed job advertisement

(D) All of the above

(91) Besides the obvious benefits of the total rewards system (increasing motivation and keeping morale high), what is an additional bonus of this practice?

(A) It has a positive effect on sales revenue.

(B) It decreases team members' overall workload.

(C) It assures workplace retention.

(D) None of the above.

(92) During the analysis phase in the creation of a total rewards system, it is important to acquire the input of:

(A) Employees who could benefit from the system

(B) Customers of the company

(C) Shareholders

(D) All of the above

(93) Rewards in a total rewards system can be of many types. Which type is the easiest for a firm to give?

(A) Intrinsic rewards

(B) Nonfinancial rewards

(C) Extrinsic rewards

(D) Financial rewards

(94) Which aspect of the total rewards system, usually highlighted by HR staff, might otherwise go unnoticed by managerial staff?

(A) The monetary burden of the system

(B) The number of employees benefiting from the system

(C) The need for variation in the system

(D) All of the above

(95) A reward that has no physical form but is only a concept is a/an _________ reward.

(A) Central

(B) Intrinsic

(C) Extrinsic

(D) None of the above

(96) If you were the head of the HR department in your company, what would be the first step you would take if told about an employee being harassed?

(A) Fire the perpetrator and begin legal action against them

(B) Carry out an investigation into the matter

(C) Fire both parties involved

(D) All of the above

(97) You are the manager of the HR department. You are conducting interviews with candidates your company wishes to hire.

What should be the basis on which you select a candidate to hire?

(A) First come, first served

(B) Choosing the candidate who has the most experience

(C) Choosing the candidate who is best suited for the job in terms of capabilities

(D) All of the above

(98) You are the head of the HR department at a multinational company. Your company wishes to expand its operations to newer avenues. Regarding staffing management, which of the following action(s) are you required to take?

(A) International assignment management

(B) Global relocation

(C) Recruitment and global outsourcing

(D) All of the above

(99) Jim is an employee at a company that recently launched a new initiative known as Leaders of Tomorrow, a business leadership program.

By enrolling in the program, what can Jim hope to learn that will help him with his career in the future?

(A) How to outsource labor to different parts of the world

(B) How to build strong candidates who will manage businesses in other countries

(C) How to deal with labor unions

(D) All of the above

(100) A company wishes to hire a new HR manager. Three candidates have been shortlisted for the job—Henrikh, an excellent manager; José, a legal specialist; and Julian, an HR manager with experience in both the legal and financial aspects of the job.

Who is the likeliest candidate for the job?

(A) Julian

(B) José

(C) Henrikh

(D) None of the above

(101) Gareth is the head of the HR department at FA International. Recently, there has been a clash between two groups at the company that do not see eye to eye on many matters.

As the head of the HR department, what is the best result Gareth should work toward?

(A) A compromise between the two parties

(B) Asking both parties to collaborate

(C) Taking action against both parties for disturbing the office

(D) All of the above

(102) Gareth is hopeful for a compromise between the two parties. Using compromise conflict resolution, what does Gareth hope to achieve other than resolving the matter at hand?

(A) Improving understanding, decision-making, and solution-seeking between the two groups

(B) Avoiding further conflicts between the two groups

(C) Bringing about interdepartmental harmony

(D) Making use of all available resources to improve productivity

(103) Before Gareth undertook the mediation of the matter between the two parties, what outcome(s) did Gareth have in mind?

(A) Improved relations between the two parties

(B) Worsening of the dispute and the argument

(C) Both A and B

(D) None of the above

(104) Manuel is an HR manager in training. One of the first things he learned in his training was to never:

(A) Observe key changes in behavior and attitude

(B) Take hardline steps against those in conflict to prevent further conflicts

(C) Identify the root of a problem

(D) Take necessary steps before a situation gets worse

(105) Jean and Eren are two employees who do not see eye-to-eye on several issues and have totally different personalities. They are tasked by their boss to work together on a project.

As head of the HR department, what type of conflict must you realize exists between these two employees?

(A) Value conflict

(B) Task conflict

(C) Intergroup conflict

(D) Relationship conflict

(106) At Backspace Co., the company heads want to establish a separate, independent HR department. They are convinced that by doing so, they will benefit the organization in which of the following way(s)?

(A) Laying a strong foundation for the organizational structure

(B) Making the organization's goals and objectives clear

(C) Growing the organizational brand

(D) All of the above

(107) Ben is the head of HR at a multinational company. His company has recently expanded its operations to different parts of the world.

As the head of a global HR firm, what factors must Ben take into account when doing business?

(A) All employees working around the globe

(B) The different laws, traditions, and cultures that exist across the globe

(C) Both A and B

(D) None of the above

(108) Nicolo is an HR consultant looking for a smaller company to work at.

Why might he want a smaller work environment?

(A) A smaller company helps formalize long-term relationships.

(B) A smaller company causes less of a workload.

(C) A smaller company lessens the competition in a respective niche.

(D) A smaller company offers employees more chances to succeed and grow independently.

(109) Farlan is an HR consultant who wishes to work independently. What is an important skill that he must possess to ensure his success in the field?

(A) Legal knowledge

(B) Financial knowledge

(C) Both A and B

(D) Neither A nor B

(110) A company's HR department must consider which of the following factors if it wishes to expand its operations into foreign countries?

(A) Legal factors

(B) Cultural and traditional factors

(C) Language factors

(D) All of the above

(111) Kristoff is the head of the HR department at Markup International. He aims to stay ahead of the competition. One way of doing so might be to follow newer trends.

Why is this the case?

(A) To avoid being redundant

(B) To attract customers

(C) To stay ahead of the competition

(D) To work for larger companies and corporations

(112) A growing number of workers at a company have expressed their discontent with their jobs, with some even threatening to leave the company. As the head of the HR department, Jakub is looking for the reasons for these problems.

Which of the following might not be an external factor for these issues?

(A) Flexible working hours

(B) Telecommuting

(C) Health-care costs

(D) Technological advancements

(113) With the advent of the novel coronavirus, businesses across the globe were hit hard financially.

What is the responsibility of the HR department to the employees of a company during such times?

(A) Providing health-care benefits and health insurance

(B) Furloughing staff

(C) Making pay cuts

(D) Ensuring job security

(114) Robert is the head of the HR department at Smile. As a great advocate of face-to-face communication, what does Robert aim to achieve between the company's employees?

(A) Lessening the difficulty of email communication

(B) Better integration of different companies or departments

(C) Allowing customers to voice their opinions

(D) Effective, time-saving decision-making

(115) With the ongoing pandemic, most businesses have had to deal with financial constraints and the loss of revenue. It is the end of the year, and a company has to provide its employees with compensation and benefits.

With a financial cap firmly in place, what should the company do?

(A) Give intrinsic rewards as tokens of appreciation for employee efforts

(B) Give extrinsic rewards such as bonuses and other financial incentives

(C) Do not give any rewards to employees due to financial constraints

(D) None of the above

(116) With recent financial constraints due to COVID-19, organizations have had to downsize and implement some cost-cutting measures. Recently, an HR department was asked to design a new total rewards strategy.

In what order should the HR department carry out the following steps?

(I) Designing (II) Assessing (III) Evaluating (IV) Implementing

(A) II, I, IV, III

(B) IV, I, III, II

(C) III, I, II, IV

(D) None of the above

(117) An organization's finance and sales departments are having a heated argument about the late submission of sales receipts. None of the parties are ready to compromise, and the HR department fears the situation may get out of control.

What would the ideal solution be to this problem?

(A) The HR department should let the two groups battle it out between themselves.

(B) The HR department should hold a meeting and conduct employee-by-employee interviews to filter out any communication gaps and settle the dispute.

(C) The HR department must notify senior management.

(D) None of the above.

(118) Employees of an organization have recently seen a drop in their salaries and are not happy about it. They are discussing going on strike until their pay cuts are reversed.

What should the HR department do?

(A) Agree to the employees' decision to strike and ask them to stay home until senior management reverses the pay cut decision

(B) Set up a meeting between senior management and employees

(C) Ask employees to continue their work while the HR professionals convey their concerns to senior management and look for a solution

(D) None of the above

(119) A firm has hired two employees for the same job role, and they will be working together in the same department. However, the employees have met before outside work and do not get along. The two do not like each other, which could lead to problems within the workplace.

What would be the solution to this dilemma?

(A) Redefine the job roles of one or both of the employees and put them in different departments to avoid any arguments between the two

(B) Do not take any action and wait to see what happens

(C) Do not hire the employees as permanent employees after their probationary period ends

(D) None of the above

(120) Your organization recently hired several employees from different parts of the world. As an HR professional, what actions should you take to help these employees better settle into their new position and country?

(A) Treat them in the same way as you would local employees

(B) Run a cultural diversity program to make the employees feel welcome and build relationships with them

(C) Do nothing and allow the employees to settle in themselves

(D) None of the above

(121) The government has made changes to several rules and regulations involving the textile industry. As an HR professional working in a textile firm, what should be your first course of action?

(A) Take no measures pertaining to change in the rules

(B) Carefully examine the new rules and notify senior management

(C) Both A and B

(D) None of the above

(122) Recently, you have noticed the morale in the workplace has been low. Employees have no energy and get easily agitated.

As a manager, what should you do to take care of this problem?

(A) Organize a party to cheer the employees up

(B) Take no action and hope for the best

(C) Look for the root of the problem by listening to employee concerns

(D) None of the above

(123) As a global HR manager, you encounter several employee performance and motivation challenges.

What should you do to fix this problem?

(A) Fire employees who do not meet the requirements

(B) Introduce an employee assistance program (EAP) to help with culturally diverse issues that stem from working in different parts of the world

(C) Take no actions and hope that the situation resolves itself

(D) None of the above

(124) After a careful assessment of the workforce employed in a firm, you come to the conclusion that the firm has a labor surplus.

As an HR professional, what is the best possible solution to balance out the surplus?

(A) Halt the hiring process

(B) Downsize

(C) Outsource employees

(D) Pay cuts

(125) You were recently hired as an employee relations manager and have identified communication gaps between employees and senior management on several issues.

What should you do to solve this problem?

(A) Urge managers to hold one-on-one meetings with each employee to build trust and communication

(B) Conduct interviews on a frequent basis and gather useful employee feedback

(C) Both A and B

(D) None of the above

(126) There is a dispute between a labor union and a company. As a relationship manager, what should your first course of action be?

(A) Avoid the situation

(B) Support the labor union in its protests

(C) Support the organization and do not listen to any of the labor union's demands

(D) None of the above

(127) As a global HR manager, you recently hired a foreign employee. The employee is having trouble understanding both the local language and his job role.

What arrangements can you make to help the struggling employee?

(A) Seek the help of a company translator to help the employee understand the language better

(B) Make the onboarding process clearer and more understandable

(C) Both A and B

(D) None of the above

(128) As part of a hiring committee, you have been asked to select the best-suited candidate for a job. Due to financial constraints, the firm can hire only one candidate. You are now facing the dilemma of choosing between two potential candidates who are both exceptionally well suited to the job.

How should you appropriately address this situation?

(A) Hire both candidates

(B) Hire only one candidate and apologize to the other

(C) Hire neither candidate

(D) None of the above

(129) You were recently notified by employees that a certain worker is not performing to the level required despite being told to do so repeatedly. As a result, pressure is piling up on other employees and the workload is increasing.

As an HR manager, what steps should you take to resolve the problem?

(A) Ask the employees to deal with the problem themselves

(B) Take no action and simply apologize to the employees for the situation

(C) Set up a meeting with the problematic employee in order to try to solve the situation

(D) None of the above

(130) You have been appointed head of a hiring committee.

What is one thing that you must closely keep an eye on during the hiring process?

(A) The ethnicity of the potential candidates

(B) A check and balance of jobs to avoid any surplus or shortage of employees during hiring

(C) Both A and B

(D) None of the above

(131) A new project has been assigned to a group of employees. However, the employees do not understand how to work as a team or know who should be leading them.

What strategy should you implement as an HR expert?

(A) Ask the employees to work on the project as they see fit

(B) Assign parts of the job relating to the project to different employees and establish a chain of command that all employees must adhere to

(C) Ignore the problem

(D) None of the above

(132) Recently, it has come to the notice of the senior management that a department head has been charged with corruption outside the workplace.

As an HR professional, what suggestion should you make to senior management?

(A) Fire the manager immediately

(B) Bring the manager in for a meeting with the board members

(C) Allow the manager to continue working without asking any questions

(D) None of the above

(133) An employee recently had an argument with his superior and is now refusing to work on one of the projects he was assigned.

What is the best way to deal with this problem?

(A) Let things slide and hope the employee does not act in a similar manner again

(B) Give the employee a pay cut

(C) Fire the employee

(D) Bring the employee in for a face-to-face meeting with the manager and issue a verbal warning.

(134) You were recently made manager of a firm. You now have to manage employees who were once your coworkers.

What changes in relationships must you now make for the sake of professionalism?

(A) Interact with your former coworkers the same way you did before

(B) Be very strict with your former coworkers to make a point

(C) Try to maintain the same friendly relationship with your former coworkers as before, but also show assertiveness so that no employee becomes complacent

(D) None of the above

SHRM-SCP Test 3: Answers and Explanations

(1) (A) Reasonable comprehension of the business's specialty

Understanding a business's specialty helps an organization determine its business acumen. Ample information/experience on the background of the business and its aim makes it more likely all departments of the business can solve future issues quickly. An example of this is when sales representatives are well versed in a store's products and can immediately provide customers with accurate information.

(2) (D) A well-organized HR team

All of the answers provided help make a business successful, but the main reason behind that success is a well-organized HR team. HR team members prioritize the management of employees—they make sure the workplace environment is enjoyable. As a result, employees are satisfied and more productive. In other words, a satisfied employee increases the rate of productivity, which, in turn, increases the company's overall efficiency and makes it successful.

(3) (A) By using the internet to keep up with finance journals, blogs, etc.

The best way for HR professionals to become more well versed in the market is to acquire information unrelated to their field and gather it from a reliable source, such as financial journals and blogs.

(4) (C) Having a long-term strategy to deal with internal communication

Many research articles state that the key to effective internal communication is effectively implementing a long-term strategy. Not only does a long-term strategy reduce conflict, but it also increases employee retention over time.

(5) (D) All of the above

Face-to-face communication between employees and management is encouraged because this type of communication makes it easier to resolve issues and increases overall employee confidence. Additionally, it creates a friendlier environment and makes management more accessible.

(6) (A) Small businesses

The majority of HR consultation firms tend to work with smaller businesses. The reason for this is that smaller businesses have fewer employees—usually less than twenty. Therefore, smaller businesses are always looking for ways to expand. When it comes to needing assistance with this goal, they need an HR consulting firm to plan their strategic expansion.

(7) (C) Sticking to traditional market trends instead of updating one's knowledge frequently

An HR consultant does not need to stick to traditional market trends, as this outdated approach does nothing but stall a business's progress and limit its success. Rather, an HR consultant should be well versed in the latest HR trends and/or business strategies as applicable to a particular company.

(8) (D) All of the above.

It has been statistically proven that HR consultation firms that offer focused service tend to do better than their competitors that offer an all-in-one deal. There are many reasons for this, but one of them is that focused HR consultation provides customers with quality over quantity.

(9) (B) Relying on clientele to spread the word

An effective method of making contacts in the HR consultancy field is relying on clientele for referrals. If satisfied customers spread the word about their positive personal experience with you or your firm, this is helpful to your business.

(10) (D) All of the above.

Meticulous documentation is a core part of an HR professional's daily job. A physical paper trail will allow both clients and HR professionals to navigate their jobs more efficiently. This paper trail can also be used as evidence in any lawsuits. Documentation should include information like deadlines, details about service charges, etc.

(11) (A) Ethical practice takes place when an organization embeds and upholds its values at all levels in order to maintain and increase trust.

Ethical practice is best described as occurring when an organization embeds and upholds its values at all levels to maintain and increase trust. Ethical practice plays an increasingly important role in current businesses. The more an organization upholds and maintains ethical practices, the healthier the workplace will be. The company's reputation will also be that much better, leading to benefits all around.

(12) (A) Valuing the perspectives and backgrounds of all parties a business interacts with

Cultural effectiveness is an integral part of ethical practice. It is best defined as a person or business that has morally correct core values, understands them, and has no problem practicing them.

(13) (A) Accepting all religious and cultural views within a workplace

The simple act of acceptance is the best way to make an employee feel more valued in the workplace, thereby increasing their morale. When employees feel free to express their culture/religion however they want, they feel an increased sense of loyalty to the business they work at.

(14) (B) It enhances the loyalty of customers and attracts new ones.

A reliable company image is extremely important to sustain both a company's success and growth in difficult times. A company can create such an image by maintaining the trust of the current stakeholders—customers, investors, employees, and partner firms. Ethical practice is just one of the ways a company can build and maintain a reliable company image.

(15) (C) Ensuring accountability for any misbehavior (e.g., sexual harassment) in the workplace

This question is specifically asking about techniques that can help avoid behavioral misconduct, which includes topics like sexual harassment. A great way to avoid sexual harassment in the workplace is to ensure the application of a consistent, fair whistleblower policy. This policy states that any victim of a behavioral misconduct event can come forward anonymously and file a complaint against the perpetrator. The complaint can then be addressed by an unbiased board of members, and action can be taken. Therefore, to avoid behavioral misconduct in the workplace, a company should create laws of accountability.

(16) (A) Formal and informal

The two types of leadership roles in a business are formal and informal. Formal leaders are those whom a firm officially appoints. All managerial positions are formal roles. Formal leaders play a more important role outside the group of people they lead. The title of informal leader is given to a leader appointed by the group itself. The basic difference between both types of leadership is the level of formality.

(17) (A) The rate of performance is directly proportional to the severity of the set goals.

The only one of the answer options that correctly describes a key tenet of goal-set theory is Option A, which states that the rate of employees' performance is directly proportional to the severity of the set of goals.

(18) (B) Empathy

It is important to understand that empathy is not always a good quality in a leader. It has been proven that empathy is ineffective in a business setting. Empathy can lead to poor decision-making skills by way of impaired judgment. Additionally, empathy makes it difficult to navigate between a lot of different team member perspectives. This can lead to biased decision-making.

(19) (B) Directing

According to the Situational Leadership Theory® model, being directive is the first step. This entails leaders being precise and consistent with their orders while also maintaining an unwavering faith in themselves. This establishes a solid foundation for future leadership endeavors.

(20) (A) Charismatic, visionary, invigorating, and considerate

The four utilitarian qualities of a transformative leader are charismatic, visionary, invigorating, and considerate. People who take on a leadership role must be charismatic if they are going to affect the people under them. They need vision to tackle serious situations properly. They need to have an invigorating approach to leadership. And lastly, they also need to be considerate toward their subordinates.

(21) (B) It leads to innovative ideas.

While it is true that conflict usually has a negative result, we cannot discount that it sometimes has positive ones too. Conflict is the spark behind many occurrences, movements, and instances of change. It can lead to innovative ideas, which are usually the result of competition between coworkers. New ideas are formed when coworkers try to one-up each other. Another benefit of conflict in the workplace is that it increases employee motivation.

(22) (A) Behavioral conflict

Behavioral conflicts occur when an action taken by a certain person in a group is misconstrued by the rest of the people in the group. Behavioral conflict is one of the most frequent types of conflict occurring in the workplace. A simple example of this is the use of cussing in a formal environment. While this action is normal for certain people, it can be frowned upon by others and is generally viewed to be inappropriate in a formal work setting. However, the person using foul language may not know this, so their behavior may then be misconstrued, leading to misunderstandings and conflict.

(23) (B) Competing

The competing conflict style is characterized by an aggressive and uncooperative approach. One person "wins" at the expense of the other, leading to a possible power imbalance and feelings of resentment by the "losing" party. The other styles (Avoiding, Accommodating, and Collaborating) tend not to cause the same level of resentment. Avoiding sidesteps the conflict, Accommodating emphasizes preserving the relationship over meeting one's own needs, and Collaborating aims to find a win-win solution that satisfies both parties.

(24) (C) Intergroup conflict

Intergroup conflict is the hardest type of conflict to resolve simply because of the number of persons that can potentially be involved. These people tend to pick sides, making it harder to come to neutral terms or a resolution.

(25) (D) All of the above

All of the given answer options are important points to consider during the resolution of workplace conflict. Immediately considering a resolution's negative impact on either party can lead to the minimization of the resulting damage. This then should lead an HR representative to also consider the possibility of a resolution that satisfies all parties, so as to avoid those aforementioned possible negative impacts as much as possible. Finally, an HR rep should always consider the repercussions of being stern while resolving a conflict—come across too stern, and the conflict may be worsened; come across too soft, and the same thing may occur.

(26) (D) All of the above

The recruitment budget and long- and short-term goals are three of the most important deciding factors for choosing the number of people a firm needs to hire in order for it to run its operations smoothly and successfully.

(27) (A) A compilation of qualifications and skills needed for a position

A compilation of qualifications and skills is the first thing that needs to be considered when HR is determining a recruitment plan before beginning the hiring process of new candidates.

(28) (C) The skills and qualifications required for the job

The skills and qualifications required are part of a job's specification. The difference between job descriptions and a job specification is slight, but it should not be overlooked because they do have different key purposes. A job description is a literal description of the job; it describes the aforementioned job's tasks, objectives, and responsibilities. In comparison, a job specification is a list of requirements that must be the candidate for that job must meet. This list includes skills and qualifications and extends to the candidate's required experience and personality traits.

(29) (B) Campus recruiters

Campus recruiters specifically scout fresh college/university graduates for the firms they work for. Campus recruiting is also used to train employees working toward promotions by financing these employees' placement in certain short courses to enhance their knowledge in specific areas that will then be helpful to the company they are working for.

(30) (B) An aptitude test

Testing is a crucial stage of recruitment. It is a chance for candidates to back up the information on their résumés. Aptitude tests are used to test candidates' ability to perform a certain task required by a prospective job they are applying for.

(31) (D) All of the above

Contrary to popular belief, monetary dissatisfaction is not the most common reason for an employee's resignation. Disagreements with the managerial staff can make dissatisfaction personal, causing an employee to take drastic actions, like resigning from a company. Retention is an important concept in HR management. Ensuring the long tenure of employees leads to many fruitful advantages, which is why it is encouraged that businesses avoid as much as possible the factors that may cause employee dissatisfaction.

(32) (A) The company and its employees

Development and training programs contribute to employees' personal growth. This personal growth in employees' careers helps a firm become more efficient and increases revenue. The two groups of people involved in this training transaction are the firm and the employees receiving the special training. Therefore, they are the ones who benefit the most.

(33) (D) All of the above

Job enrichment is a lucrative practice in business. It calls for helping employees feel important. This then has material outcomes that benefit both the firm and the employees, such as contentment in the workplace and an increase in employee self-confidence. There are many ways to ensure job enrichment. An increased variety of work stops a job from becoming mundane. Critical analyses help employees improve in their specialized field, and giving employees a small but substantial amount of authority boosts their confidence.

(34) (B) Enlargement

Enlargement involves attaching extra but relevant tasks to the existing work. This is a tool used to help make employees feel more satisfied in their field of work. Having many tasks keeps employees motivated and working efficiently. This variety of tasks also benefits the company because it increases the employees' shared workload, which decreases the number of people needed for one job. However, this process is known to be a double-edged sword. While it can positively impact certain employees, it can also cause other employees to resent their increased workload. In turn, employees can then start to resent the company itself.

(35) (D) All of the above

Equity theory states that employees are dissatisfied when they realize they have been given an unfair workload. According to expectancy theory, employees expect a greater return from the company if they are willing to put in more effort. Similarly, reinforcement theory says that if employees think that they should be compensated for their efforts, they will be more commonly dissatisfied if they do not receive the compensation they are expecting.

(36) (D) All of the above

In the current world of business, HR plays an increasingly crucial role in a company's growth and survival. Recruitment has become an extremely meticulous process, especially because the HR department has to make sure that it increases employee retention. Another large addition to a modern-day HR department's tasks has been ensuring a safe environment for employees. All of these things, as mentioned in the answer options, have been added to an HR employee's list of daily responsibilities in the modern business world.

(37) (A) Waterfall

The Agile technique replaced the Waterfall technique because Waterfall was not well equipped to face today's technological changes.

(38) (C) The Lean approach aims to amplify the merits of customers and lessen the net waste production of a company. The three Ms stand for Muda, Mura, Muri.

The Lean approach aims to amplify the merits of customers and lessen the net worth production of a company, both of which result in a net increase in revenue. Muda, Mura and Muri are Japanese terms that call for refining office duties and habits to train employees into becoming better versions of themselves.

(39) (A) Gauging the extent of the task

Work breakdown structures exist to make large and complex tasks easier. They essentially divide a larger task into smaller and much more doable tasks, then delegate them to the right personnel. The first step in devising a work breakdown structure is to analyze the limitations and goals of the bigger project.

(40) (C) A Gantt chart

A Gantt chart is an example of a work breakdown structure. It calls for organizing tasks into spreadsheets and then chronologically scheduling them. This makes a project much more manageable and approachable for employees to undertake.

(41) (B) Organizing

Organizing is a management strategy used during the revision of rules and regulations in a firm.

(42) (B) Advising strategy

An advising strategy is devised during the revision of rules and regulations in a firm. The advising strategy addresses problems that occur during changes in leadership, etc. This phase does not always have problematic aspects. Sometimes it just includes explaining the workings of a business to new managerial staff and taking into account the changes they want to make.

(43) (D) Training and development

A key component of HR practice is providing training and development to new employees. When a newly hired employee joins a firm, it is the firm's responsibility to give the person access to training programs and assist them through the initiation process. This helps ensure that they settle well into their new workplace, which helps avoid conflicts and maintains a healthy work environment for all.

(44) (A) Yes

It is a common practice for large firms today to need extra assistance in HR because the tasks of HR have multiplied over the years. Besides needing general assistance, a firm might want specialized help from a specific consultancy firm on certain HR matters.

(45) (C) Becoming a part of executive decision-making

A task that only highly experienced HR personnel can take on is advising managerial staff. The higher up the chain of hierarchy, the greater the decisions weigh. For this reason, only highly skilled employees are allowed to participate in these discussions. They have the temperament for executive decision-making and the experience needed to become assets to the firm.

(46) (A) Following the code of conduct

The relationship between an employer and an employee of a give-and-take nature. Giving is part of an employer's job. It includes things like providing a safe work environment, ensuring employee satisfaction, and assisting with employees' career-oriented growth. When employees receive all these things, it becomes their responsibility to return the favor by following the code of conduct set by the firm. Additionally, meeting deadlines and providing good-quality work are also expected from employees as part of this symbiotic relationship.

(47) (B) By providing resolutions to interpersonal/group conflicts

HR should nurture cooperative relationships between a business's employees. That said, conflict is a part of any office environment; therefore, any conflict resolution must be too. Interpersonal/group conflict usually occurs between employers and employees. The HR department can reduce this occurrence by facilitating proper communication and mediating conflicts. These are only a few of the ways in which HR can nurture this relationship. Another way is providing a safe workplace environment.

(48) (B) Honesty and honoring their word

Certain concepts are mandatory when working on improving workplace relationships. Honesty ensures loyalty between employers and employees, as the assurance of truthful information is essential in strengthening a relationship. Keeping promises is also a part of being honest.

(49) (B) Directly proportional

The relationship between union strength and worker signatures on an authorization form is directly proportional. Union-led directives are usually known by the number of people who are demanding the change. Therefore, it is crucial to have an ample number of signatures in order for action to ensue. The more workers who sign up for the demand for change, the stronger and more popular the union-led directive will be.

(50) (B) When union workers intimidate employers into paying for work that has not been done by employees

The other term for *featherbedding* is *over-manning*. Both *featherbedding* and *over-manning* mean that unions try to provide more workers than necessary for a certain task, then force a company to pay all of the workers equally.

(51) (D) All of the above

Organizational effectiveness and development is a method employed by HR to ensure smooth operations in a firm. OE&D assists in worker productivity and efficiency.

(52) (D) Role-playing

Role-playing is a behavioral intervention mostly used in sales training. It occurs when business employees are given a transcript of a business scenario and then have to role-play it. This practice introduces businesses practices in a risk-free manner to new employees who have not had any training. In a real situation, mistakes might result in dire consequences. Therefore, instead of taking that risk, these scenarios are played out in a controlled environment, where recruits can practice and experienced professionals can advise them on how to improve.

(53) (A) Implementing lucrative ways to use given resources

The more competitive a firm is, the better chance it has to eliminate its rivals and take over the market. When a firm implements lucrative ways to use its given resources, it will get the best possible outcome.

(54) (D) Lack of autonomy for employees

A centralized structure is one in which most of the decision-making power lies at the top of the hierarchy and the formal leadership of the firm. The roles of the other employees are well defined. All employees have a precise job description. There are many advantages to this structure. For example, it produces more efficient results, leads to clear accountability and yields easier communication within the chain of command. However, a disadvantage of this structure is the lack of autonomy that subordinate employees have in the inner workings of the company.

(55) (A) Decentralized structure

A decentralized structure calls for a more relaxed environment where authority is shared between different division managers. Sometimes, managers who have close contact with subordinates also encourage the participation of their subordinates in the decision-making process, which increases employee morale.

(56) (A) The research and development department

The research and development department is a crucial part of technological management. It is important to know the definition of technological management before understanding why. Technological management is a term used for the newfound integration of technology in a firm's administrative aspect. It improves overall efficiency.

(57) (A) The general priorities regarding all aspects of technology planning

The IT department oversees a part of technological management. The department's job is to collect statistical information on the new technology and work on improving it. Therefore, in the planning phase of this task, the department assesses the firm's priorities in order to decide where technology can best be integrated.

(58) (C) Reducing repetition

One of the goals of technological planning is to reduce repetitive tasks that employees must perform. This helps improve worker efficiency, productivity, and morale.

(59) (C) Technology transfer

STMS is divided into six phases, and technology transfer is the fourth one. In this phase, a newly developed technological aspect is shifted from theory to practice. This is why the research and development department is a big part of this fourth STMS phase. The R&D department is responsible for tweaking new technology once it is in the action phase.

(60) (A) Customers

Most business tactics are already centered around customer satisfaction, so it should be no surprise that implementing a new technological system should also prioritize customer satisfaction.

(61) (D) Improving sales techniques

Improving sales techniques is not a workforce management task. Workforce management features include making statistical analyses and financial projections based on the ongoing work in a firm. With this information, HR can dictate the quantity and quality of new job recruits.

(62) (D) All of the above

Workforce managers are an integral part of a company. They are responsible for devising methods to motivate employees so they can do their jobs more efficiently. Additionally, workforce managers come up with plans for improvement in areas where shortcomings are evident.

(63) (B) Commercial incorporation

The example given shows that either a merger is taking place or another shareholder is buying a company. When this happens, a change in business rules and regulations will inevitably ensue. The change is not limited to policies; it can also be physical, such as changing the location of the company headquarters, or it could be a variation in the current number of employees.

(64) (B) Economic restructuring

Economic restructuring is defined by the cut-downs made in every department of a firm. This can happen due to numerous reasons, but it is usually caused by insufficient revenue and poor profit margins.

(65) (A) Communication

Communication is crucial for getting the best performance out of a firm after organizational restructuring has taken place. Organizational restructuring is a massive change, and the people who suffer most from it are the employees. Therefore, it is vital for communication to be clearly established between all hierarchical levels in order to maintain the previous checks and balances that were in place.

(66) (B) Environmental

Environmental CSR aims to reduce a firm's carbon footprint. It uses many different methods to achieve its aim. Some of these methods include reducing paper waste in offices, reducing carbon emissions in factories, and providing shared transport for employees. This is an essential type of CSR not only because it sustains the planet, but also because it benefits employees and enhances the company's image.

(67) (D) None of the above

All of the answer options given are benefits of CSR. The environment is protected through environmental CSR. Functional costs are cut down when fewer resources are wasted. An increase in revenue is seen when a firm markets itself as being CSR-friendly.

(68) (C) Funding natural disaster aid

Philanthropic CSR includes any donation of profits to a cause that does not directly benefit the firm. In the case of something like an earthquake, philanthropic CSR can include providing disaster relief aid. This will benefit both the victims of the natural disaster and the employees of the company, as the firm will gain good press for making the ethical choice to respond philanthropically to such a disaster.

(69) (A) Funding opportunities

A benefit of CSR to start-ups and small-scale firms is increased funding opportunities. It is well known that start-ups and small firms are in almost constant need of monetary help. During the initial stages of a business, it is hard to generate ample revenue reliably. These kinds of new businesses can attract grants and loans by marketing themselves as being CSR friendly. This leads to good press and more market opportunities.

(70) (A) Minimizing the pay gap between coworkers

A way to combat gender equality through the ethical branch of corporate social responsibility is to minimize the pay gap between coworkers.

(71) (B) Diversity is only a concept, while inclusion is the practical application of it.

It is important to note that while both diversity and inclusion are different, they must be applied together in a company to receive optimum gain. Diversity is the concept of acceptance among different races, cultures, and religions. In comparison, inclusivity is the practice of treating everyone equally and fairly.

(72) (C) Increasing reach into the global market

A benefit of practicing diversity is that it improves a firm's international relations and increases its reach into the global market.

(73) (D) All of the above

When inclusion is practiced, it comes with numerous benefits. First and foremost, it amplifies employee satisfaction by making employees feel like they are an equal part of a firm and that they do not need to worry about discrimination. Secondly, inclusion increases employee retention. When employees find a safe work environment, they will be more willing to stay in a job for the long term. And lastly, inclusion causes an increase in a firm's legal compliance.

(74) (A) Providing health-care packages

We have talked at length about making different groups of people in a firm feel equally included. One of these groups is older employees. Contrary to popular belief, these employees are very beneficial to a firm. They have years of experience and are good mentors. Therefore, it is only fair that the firm repay them by making them feel included and valued. A way to do this is to provide health-care packages. Wheelchair-accessible parking can also answer this question, but it is not the best answer choice because it is more specifically oriented toward disabled people, who may not always be older.

(75) (A) Offering a training program on diversity and inclusion to people in managerial positions

Offering a training program on diversity and inclusion to people in managerial positions is one way that a firm can clearly state both to its workforce and the public that it values inclusivity and diversity and is working on eliminating biases in the company.

(76) (C) Logical reasoning and bargaining

Logical reasoning and the ability to bargain are key to conflict resolution. Conflict is a part of any workplace; it is almost unavoidable. Therefore, the solution to this is to find a way to fix the conflict instead of avoiding it. This practice is called conflict resolution. Not everyone has the aptitude for dealing with this properly, but all managerial staff must be equipped to do so.

(77) (C) Intergroup conflict

As the name itself states, intergroup conflict is a conflict caused between any two groups of people but can also be a conflict just among one group in and of itself. These groups usually come from different departments or can be composed of whole departments in different organizations. In horizontal conflict, the two parties are on the same hierarchical level, while vertical conflict exists between different levels of the chain of command.

(78) (A) Constructive talks

Numerous ways exist to resolve conflict, and of course, every conflict is different, so each conflict requires its own personalized approach. However, it has been shown that effective communication is the key to resolving conflict in all cases. Effective communication includes the clear iteration of a point of view and the hearing of the point of view of all parties.

(79) (D) All of the above

A self-confident approach is one in which a member of the conflict decides to take the lead, works on the resolution, and lets others follow their lead. A cooperative approach takes place when parties are willing to compromise to come to a neutral ground. A collaborative approach calls for both parties to work together to find a solution.

(80) (D) All of the above

All of these options are crucial food for thought when a person is given the task of mediating a conflict. They allow for the easiest and fastest method of resolution.

(81) (A) It is a technique used to remove previous errors from a project to make it better.

The Sigma Six technique has a beneficial effect on the quality of a product because it assesses and eliminates errors in the previous product versions. Sigma Six does this by applying the DMADV and DMAIC techniques.

(82) (A) Communication

Communication is especially crucial in situations like the implementation of a new strategic plan. The plan can have been performed meticulously in its analysis and development stage, but it will be a failure overall if its implementation fails. In order for the plan to succeed, employees and employers must have effective communication.

(83) (D) The sales department

The sales department is not a part of the crucial group of people necessary when formulating a total rewards system. When creating a total rewards system, it is necessary to select the most appropriate people for the job. This is because an ample number of resources will go into the formation of the system. Among these people are senior members who will guide the rest of the team with their experience, the HR department that will formulate the plan, and researchers who will provide data needed for the plan.

(84) (D) All of the above

Compliance is how a business is graded in terms of fairness. Consequently, if noncompliance occurs, it can result in detrimental losses for the company in the form of fines. Dealing with firm compliance is one of the more difficult tasks of workforce management, which makes it all the more crucial to achieve.

(85) (C) Improper implementation of strategy

Technology management systems have an ample number of challenges, but by far the most common challenge is implementing a strategy that has gone through rigorous development and analysis. Sometimes, managers emphasize the former stages so that there is no capital left by the time they get to implementation.

(86) (C) Recognizing the risks that can damage a business and eliminating the chances of their occurrence or reoccurrence

Risk management can be defined as recognizing the risks that can damage a business and eliminating the chances of their occurrence or reoccurrence.

Risk management is a crucial part of saving a firm unnecessary expenses and averting possible large problems.

(87) (D) All of the above

A lack of a risk management plan can lead to many dire outcomes for the firm. If a risk is not identified and addressed promptly, problems can spin out of control and cause disasters. For example, problems in the sales department can cause issues with customers, resulting in both unhappy consumers and a negative effect on sales revenue. Additionally, there can be wastage of company supplies.

(88) (A) All the employees

At the beginning of executing a risk management plan, only the person in charge is responsible for its implementation, but later the responsibility of eliminating the risk falls to all the employees. Everyone must then work together to be aware of risks and minimize their occurrence and/or damage.

(89) (B) The gravity and prevalence of said risk

The purpose of risk assessment in a risk management plan is to segregate risks by high and low priority. This must be done according to the information collected about the gravity and prevalence of each risk.

(90) (B) Taking referrals from current employees

Taking referrals from current employees is a good way to avoid risks during recruitment. This is because current employees will know the people they are recommending, as well as what specific needs the company has for the job opening. The employees are unlikely to recommend a candidate unsuitable for the job position.

(91) (C) It assures workplace retention.

Workplace retention is an indirect consequence of the total rewards system. This system mainly addresses employee satisfaction. After this is assured, employees are happier with a company and are far more likely to stay in the long term rather than seek out employment opportunities elsewhere.

(92) (A) Employees that could benefit from the system

During the analysis phase in the creation of a total rewards system, it is important to acquire the input of employees. Since the total rewards system is designed to benefit the employees, their say must be considered in order to ensure the system is maximally effective.

(93) (B) Nonfinancial rewards

Nonfinancial rewards are the easiest for a firm to give out, as they place the least burden on an organization. Examples of this kind of reward include appreciation certificates, free child daycare, free parking spaces, etc. These rewards tend to have a longer life than monetary incentives, as they can be consumed throughout an employee's tenure. On the other hand, financial rewards are short term and can be used up in a couple of months, which could possibly lead to eventual employee dissatisfaction.

(94) (A) The monetary burden of the system

The total rewards system is mainly known for its benefits, but there are also some disadvantages, such as the fact that it can cost a company precious resources. It is important for the HR department to highlight this fact to company managers, as they might not otherwise notice the issue.

(95) (B) Intrinsic

An intrinsic reward is a concept. It does not require physical resources like promotions, titles, etc. These rewards have a psychological effect on receivers. They make receivers feel better about their work environment.

(96) (B) Carry out an investigation into the matter

The correct first step is to launch an investigation into the matter. Firing the perpetrator and beginning legal action without first undertaking a thorough investigation is wrong. Firing both parties involved is also inappropriate because you are also punishing the victim and have still not undertaken the necessary investigation.

(97) (C) Choosing the candidate who is best suited for the job in terms of capabilities

You should always select the candidate best suited for the job. The first-come, first-served rule does not and should not apply here. Experience is vital for smoother HR operations, but it will not make any difference if the candidate is not experienced in the right areas.

(98) (D) All of the above

When expanding operations to foreign countries, the HR department must oversee and implement international assignment management, global relocation and recruitment, and global outsourcing. This is done to ensure that a business is not only set up correctly in terms of a foreign country's laws, but is operated smoothly within the context of a new cultural framework.

(99) (B) How to build strong candidates who will manage businesses in other countries

By enrolling in Leaders of Tomorrow, Jim can hope to learn how to build strong candidates who will manage businesses in other countries. This will be a vital skill for Jim to learn for his future career prospects.

(100) (A) Julian

Julian is the likeliest candidate for the job because he has HR experience in both the legal and financial aspects of the job. An HR manager should be trained to look at a company's finances and the legal requirements in order to make decisions that are in the company's best interests.

(101) (A) A compromise between the two parties

The best result Gareth should work toward is a compromise between the two parties.

(102) (A) Improving understanding, decision-making, and solution-seeking between the two groups

Gareth hopes to improve understanding, decision-making, and solution-seeking between the two groups. These are standard benefits of conflict resolution that is properly executed.

(103) (C) Both A and B

Gareth is aware that multiple outcomes are possible. He is undoubtedly hoping both for improved relations between the two parties while also being aware that there could be a worsening of the dispute during the conflict resolution process. Conflict resolution can be a double-edged sword. It can either improve relationships between parties in disagreement or cause new problems.

(104) (B) Take hardline steps against those in conflict to prevent further conflicts

Manuel would have been advised to avoid taking hardline steps as an HR manager mediating conflicts. That kind of behavior can add to an already troublesome workplace conflict.

(105) (D) Relationship conflict

A relationship conflict occurs between two individuals who may disagree on a multitude of issues. This kind of conflict is a sort of personality clash.

(106) (D) All of the above

Establishing a separate HR department for a company will allow the organization to excel and outperform its competitors. An HR department provides a plethora of benefits for a company, including a strong organizational structure, clearer goals, more transparency, and the ability to promote the brand itself.

(107) (C) Both A and B

As an HR professional, Ben must consider the welfare of the company's workforce and employees both at home and around the globe. Since a company may choose to operate in different parts of the world, it is imperative that HR reps take into account separate traditions, languages, laws, and cultures.

(108) (A) A smaller company helps formalize long-term relationships

HR professionals like Nicolo may stand to benefit at smaller companies, as these companies allow direct access to clients, which helps HR professionals build stronger, longer-lasting business relationships.

(109) (C) Both A and B

An HR consultant such as Farlan, who chooses to work alone, must be well versed in both the legal and financial aspects of the job. This will help ensure his success as an independent consultant.

(110) (D) All of the above

An HR firm must consider the cultural, traditional, and linguistic factors of every region in order for a company to succeed.

(111) (A) To avoid being redundant

An HR department needs to stay abreast of the latest trends. Older ways are both inefficient and less appealing to employees and customers. A company will benefit from an HR rep who is well versed in the most modern HR strategies rather than one stuck in the past.

(112) (D) Technological advancements

Technological advancements are not an external factor related to the HR department. Flexible working hours, commuting, and health care are all important external factors for any HR rep to consider. Technological advancements, however, fall outside the department's direct purview.

(113) (A) Providing health-care benefits and health insurance

It is the responsibility of the HR department to oversee the health-care benefits for its employees and offer them financial aid for medical issues.

(114) (A) Lessening the difficulty of email communication

It is well known that most companies struggle to personalize their emails. As a result, the desired tone and message are often not delivered. Hence, face-to-face communication is largely encouraged for better participation, clarity, and relationships. As the head of HR, Robert will aim to increase this kind of communication among his employees.

(115) (A) Give intrinsic rewards as tokens of appreciation for employee efforts

Rewarding employees for their efforts is always important, but never more so than in a year like the recent one that saw the COVID-19 pandemic hit so many companies hard. Employees who put forth their best efforts in spite of extremely difficult circumstances should be rewarded in some manner so they feel their hard work and dedication are appreciated.

(116) (A) II, I, IV, III

In order to accomplish its total rewards strategy, the HR department should follow the steps in a particular sequence. Once the department assesses its strategy, it can consider designing a layout of the strategy. Next, the department will evaluate said strategy with the help of the assessment and designing team before finally implementing the whole strategy.

(117) (B) The HR department should hold a meeting and conduct employee-by-employee interviews to filter out any communication gaps and settle the dispute.

The HR department should hold a meeting and conduct employee-by-employee interviews to filter out any communication gaps and settle the dispute. This is an ideal solution for the problem because there is a clear miscommunication between the sales and finance departments. Due to this lack of communication, both the parties have ended up blaming each other. The HR department should play a vital and neutral role in this situation by conducting one-on-one interviews to learn both sides of the story and figure out the loopholes in the communication between the two parties that are causing conflict.

(118) (C) Ask employees to continue their work while the HR professionals convey their concerns to senior management and look for a solution

The HR department should ask the employees to continue their work while the HR professionals convey their concerns to senior management and look for a solution. This allows the HR professionals some time during which the employees continue to work, assured that the problem is being addressed. Meanwhile, senior management can be advised of the problem and resolve it before it gets out of control.

(119) (A) Redefine the job roles of one or both of the employees and put them in different departments to avoid any argument between the two

The best solution is to redefine the job roles of one or both of the employees and put them in different departments to avoid any argument between the two. This prevents a clash of personalities and circumvents any conflicts that might occur if the new hires are asked to work together.

(120) (B) Run a cultural diversity program to make the employees feel welcome and build relationships with them

A cultural diversity program will give the employees a sense of belonging in the organization. They will feel that their cultures and backgrounds are accepted and recognized at their workplace.

(121) (B) Carefully examine the new rules and notify senior management

Your first action as an HR professional in this situation should be to carefully examine the new rules and notify senior management of them so you can make sure you remain in compliance with the law, thereby avoiding problems.

(122) (C) Look for the root of the problem by listening to employee concerns

Listening to the employees and gaining their trust will help them feel more comfortable in their workplace and give the HR department access to more information about the employees' mental and emotional stress levels.

(123) (B) Introduce an employee assistance program (EAP) to help with culturally diverse issues that stem from working in different parts of the world

Many foreign employees encounter performance and motivational challenges in their workplace, mostly due to cultural barriers. Introducing an EAP will help a culturally diverse group of employees overcome any hurdles that they are facing in the workplace due to cultural diversity issues.

(124) (B) Downsize

During a labor surplus, downsizing is the best option to balance out the company's resources and help cut down on its excess costs, thereby causing an increase in profits.

(125) (C) Both A and B

You should urge managers to hold one-on-one meetings with employees to build trust and communication. Also, you should conduct interviews on a frequent basis and gather useful employee feedback. This can help smooth communication between management and employees.

(126) (D) None of the above

Avoiding the situation is a terrible idea that will make the problem worse. Similarly, picking one side over the other will only cause greater division between the two parties in dispute. Therefore, none of the answer options are good solutions for the problem.

(127) (C) Both A and B

A translator can help the employee deal with language barriers and minimize the communication gap. Making the employee onboarding process simpler and more understandable will also prove helpful in ensuring the new employee feels welcome in this new environment.

(128) (B) Hire only one candidate and apologize to the other

It is essential for a person on the hiring committee to hire the best possible candidate. It is impractical and financially unwise to hire both candidates, as the job opening is for only one person. A decision must be made about who is the better candidate.

(129) (C) Set up a meeting with the problematic employee in order to try to solve the situation

Having a meeting with the employee will help get to the root of the problem and allow HR to better understand the reason behind the person's poor performance. After that, appropriate steps can be taken to help the employee, thereby avoiding conflict and ensuring improved productivity.

(130) (B) A check and balance of jobs to avoid any surplus or shortage of employees during hiring

While hiring employees, it is vital to keep an eye on any shortages or surpluses. This is important in order to maintain the right balance of resources.

(131) (B) Assign parts of the job relating to the project to different employees and establish a chain of command that all employees must adhere to

Assigning different parts of the job to team members will help employees stay focused on their own work. Establishing a chain of command will establish a certain hierarchy within the team, which will result in systematic performance.

(132) (B) Bring the manager in for a meeting with the board members

You should advise the board members to bring the manager in for a meeting in order to clear up any misconceptions before coming to a final decision. Every aspect of the issue must be carefully looked into before any final verdicts are rendered.

(133) (D) Bring the employee in for a face-to-face meeting with the manager and issue a verbal warning

Bringing the employee in for a face-to-face meeting with the manager and issuing a verbal warning is an appropriate solution to this problem. It is mandatory for employees to follow their superiors' instructions and work with utmost cooperation.

(134) (C) Try to maintain the same friendly relationship with your former coworkers as before, but also show assertiveness so that no employee becomes complacent

The employees might get offended if you stop being friendly with them; however, it is still important to maintain discipline at the workplace and work professionally.

SHRM-SCP Test 4

(1) Albert is acquiring information for an HR audit. What should his main focus be on?

A) HR strategies that fit with the environment

(B) Potential for brain drain

(C) Risk-taking tendencies of the managers

(D) Technology available to the employees

(2) ____________ is related to the coinciding between HR practices and the overall business strategy.

(A) Vertical fit

(B) Horizontal fit

(C) Resource fit

(D) External fit

(3) Which of the following issues is most frequent and important to HR with the rise in the use of technology for telecommuting?

(A) Privacy rights

(B) Monitoring of telecommuters

(C) Monitoring performance and overtime pay

(D) Labor costs

(4) What is a critical and ethical issue that an HR manager will have to deal with when technology is used in the work environment?

(A) Window sitting

(B) Improper use of proprietary data

(C) Increase in authoritarian management

(D) None of the above

(5) How could technology affect a firm's organizational structure?

(A) It could cause a return of the pyramidal structure.

(B) It could cause an increase in authoritarian management.

(C) It could cause a decrease in employees working from home.

(D) It could cause top management to deal directly with first-line managers.

(6) Matching potential employees with the organization and not just the job description is:

(A) Creating dilemmas in today's legal environment

(B) Important but not critical to the firm's success

(C) Getting easier through the use of technology

(D) Important, as competencies can affect company performance

(7) As an HR professional, you are tasked with discussing an employee's appraisal.

What should the context of the discussion be?

(A) The employee's career aspirations

(B) The employee's training

(C) Performance applications

(D) Industry-leading applications

(8) What method should you use as a means of obtaining feedback from employees after training?

(A) A structured interview

(B) Performance after training

(C) Improvement after training

(D) Employee turnover rate

(9) The main goal of empowerment is to:

(A) Reduce employee dependence on senior management

(B) Increase distance between managers and employees

(C) Enable employees to take more responsibility

(D) Both A and C

(10) Human resources can benefit from technology changes in many ways, except for:

(A) Online recruitment to speed up the process

(B) Online learning

(C) Reduction in resistance from employees

(D) All of the above

(11) As an HR professional, it is important that you implement risk management mechanisms for:

(A) HR competencies

(B) HR strategies

(C) Both A and B

(D) None of the above

(12) As a manager, which of the following strategies would you try to implement if the firm's goal is to bring about an entrepreneurial climate within the work environment?

(A) Informal hiring strategies

(B) A strong top-down managerial preference

(C) Discouraging innovation

(D) Ignoring HR strategies

(13) An organization has employed you as an HR professional. What should your key focus be on?

(A) Minding your own business and letting line managers handle the business

(B) Assisting managers with their jobs

(C) Both A and B

(D) None of the above

(14) Which of the following is an important element of an organization's commitment to sustaining a competitive advantage?

(A) Downsizing strategies

(B) Creating distinct capabilities

(C) The ethical code of conduct

(D) Social responsibility

(15) What is the most important issue that affects an organization's competitive advantage?

(A) Inability to control costs

(B) Use of technology

(C) Organizational structure

(D) Joint ventures and collaborations

(16) Decentralization of a firm often leads to:

(A) Inflexibility

(B) Fewer opportunities for employees to move up in the firm's hierarchy

(C) Insecurity and a drop in focus due to communication gaps

(D) None of the above

(17) As an HR professional, you are required to come up with an HR planning process.

What should the first step of the planning process be?

(A) Making an HR inventory

(B) Making a strategic plan

(C) Creating a product evaluation

(D) Analyzing customer demands

(18) A recent HR assessment revealed a surplus of employees. As an HR professional, you should look to reduce the organization's workforce through:

(A) Recruitment

(B) Expansion

(C) Decruitment

(D) Staffing

(19) You have been given the responsibility to head the hiring process for your organization.

What is the best source of potential job candidates?

(A) The company website

(B) The internet

(C) Recruiting organizations

(D) Employee referrals

(20) What learning technique involves a senior employee working with new employees and providing them with information and support?

(A) Experiential exercise

(B) On-the-job training

(C) Mentoring and coaching

(D) All of the above

(21) What system would you implement if you have been tasked with setting certain standards and evaluating employee performance within an organization?

(A) Time-and-motion study

(B) Benchmarking

(C) Legal influence arrangements

(D) Performance management system

(22) To differentiate between effective and ineffective work, an evaluator takes ____________ into account for an accurate judgment.

(A) A simple analysis

(B) A job analysis

(C) Critical incidents

(D) Graphic rating scales

(23) What method or technique would you implement when given the task of appraising managers and professional employees?

(A) Management by objectives

(B) Job analysis

(C) A critical incident

(D) A graphic rating scale

(24) To ease the downsizing process, most companies offer some sort of:

(A) Severance pay

(B) Employee training

(C) Orientation

(D) Family-friendly benefits

(25) As a manager of a firm, to lighten the mood of those who survived the downsizing process, you can:

(A) Offer severance pay

(B) Provide counselors for employees to talk to

(C) Provide job search assistance

(D) None of the above

(26) As a manager, to improve workplace diversity, you should:

(A) Expand the recruiting net

(B) Downsize

(C) Select more employee referrals

(D) Hire more minority candidates

(27) If you have a small-scale business with a very small number of employees and have just started your company, what should you do for the HR management of your company?

(A) Hire a professional to manage your HR department

(B) Seek independent HR consultation providers

(C) Observe the fact that small businesses do not need HR management

(D) None of the above

(28) As an HR manager, you decide to introduce changes in your department that some employees disapprove of. One of those employees files a complaint against you to higher authorities. What should you do now?

(A) Ignore the employee in order to avoid any conflict

(B) Give up on the changes

(C) Have a polite conversation with the employee to remind the person of your authority and explain that a complaint cannot be filed against you simply because someone dislikes a department change

(D) Seek the removal of that employee

(29) You have been working as an HR manager in a company for a very long time and are fully satisfied with your position. Then a new employee is appointed in your department who leaks a rumor that you intend to leave the company soon. How should you respond?

(A) Inform everybody of your real intentions since the rumor might damage your reputation

(B) Ignore the rumors

(C) Discipline the person spreading the rumors

(D) None of the above

(30) On a visit to the office, you overhear three employees expressing their concerns about the boring nature of their work and the unpleasant work environment. What should be your next move?

(A) Call the employees into your office and politely listen to their complaints

(B) Fire those three employees

(C) Discipline the employees in front of the whole office

(D) File a complaint against the employees

(31) You are the head of the HR department. One day, a female employee comes to you with a complaint about a senior employee who is harassing her. She presents video proof and requests that you not bring her name into any action you decide to take. What should you do now?

(A) Name and shame that senior employee in front of the entire office and call for the person's removal

(B) Ask the female employee for more evidence

(C) Ask the female employee to leave the company

(D) Ask the female employee to report her concern elsewhere

(32) The company you work at is mostly composed of a majority of Christian employees. One of your Jewish employees seeks a two-day leave for Hanukkah. As an HR manager, what should your response be to this request?

(A) Grant the leave

(B) Remind the employee that the workplace is a Christian environment

(C) Discipline the employee for being disrespectful

(D) Refuse the request and hold a grudge

(33) If your employees feel unsure about meeting their responsibilities and come to you with their issues, what should your response as a leader be toward them?

(A) Scold the employees for their lack of understanding

(B) Issue warning letters

(C) Take the time to address the employees' concerns

(D) All of the above

(34) To introduce a reward system in a company, it is imperative to distinguish between top achievers and mediocre or bad performers. How can the HR department do that while ensuring that the procedure is reliable?

(A) Through talent calibration

(B) Through performance calibration

(C) Through WBS

(D) None of the above

(35) A company undertook a very comprehensive, complex task that involved many steps. The project was assigned to one individual who failed to submit the work on time. The employee also failed to meet the necessary quality standards and was disciplined accordingly even though it was not the employee's fault. What could have prevented this situation?

(A) The company could have incorporated the WBS technique.

(B) This was a mishap that could not have been avoided.

(C) The company could have requested an extension to the project deadline.

(D) The company should not have taken on such a complex task.

(36) Which of the following is an example of a beneficial conflict?

(A) A conflict that led to the removal of a rude employee

(B) A conflict that led to innovations and new ideas

(C) A conflict that exposed a manipulative employee

(D) No conflicts

(37) When you hope that an issue will disappear on its own, what strategy of the Thomas-Kilmann Model are you intentionally or unintentionally adopting?

(A) Making concessions

(B) Accommodating

(C) Competing

(D) Staying away

(38) During recruitment, you end up recruiting too many people. How can you fix this?

(A) Choose the most talented recruits, then admit your mistake and politely apologize to the rest

(B) Ignore the problem and let higher authorities deal with any issues

(C) Ask the other departments to create more vacancies to accommodate the extra candidates

(D) Blame your colleagues

(39) If there is a vacant position in your firm and an internal candidate matches the job requirements, what is your next move supposed to be as an HR representative?

(A) Encourage the employee to apply for the position

(B) Do not advertise the job outside of the office

(C) Both A and B

(D) None of the above

(40) If you are low on budget, what recruiting techniques should you use to advertise an available job vacancy in your firm?

(A) Social media

(B) Websites

(C) Both A and B

(D) None of the above

(41) You hired an employee based on her responses in an honesty test. It later turned out that her responses were manipulative, so you fired her. But the problem cost you a lot of resources. What does this say about the reliability of an honesty test?

(A) Honesty tests are reliable, and this was just a bad case.

(B) Honesty tests are unreliable and should not be used.

(C) Honesty tests are mildly reliable and should be used occasionally.

(D) None of the above.

(42) According to popular research, 90% of employees leave their jobs due to certain known reasons. What new changes in a system can help an organization retain employees?

(A) Making the job interesting

(B) Encouraging bosses to be friendly with employees

(C) Implementing ethical practices in the company

(D) All of the above

(43) An employee complains to you that he does not feel motivated in his work. As a responsible HR manager, what should you assume about the situation?

(A) The employee wants an increase in his salary.

(B) The employee is overworked.

(C) The employee's work is too repetitive.

(D) Both B and C.

(44) What technique can increase the efficiency of organizational processes and simultaneously lower the number of previous errors?

(A) Six Sigma

(B) Lean

(C) Agile

(D) WBS

(45) You intend to reduce all forms of waste within your company. Which of the following techniques will enable you to do that?

(A) Lean

(B) Agile

(C) Six Sigma

(D) All of the above

(46) In order to bring balance to an organization, what is the role of a workforce manager?

(A) Ensure customer satisfaction

(B) Reduce operational costs

(C) Downsize employees

(D) Only A and B

(47) Two organizations have decided to merge their businesses. Both companies have different ideas for the restructuring of the newly unified business. What is the role of the HR managers in this scenario?

(A) Not intervene in such issues

(B) Ask the parties to sit down and find common ground

(C) Allow the business with the greatest number of sales to decide on the matter

(D) Allow the business that has been on the market for the longest time to make the final decision

(48) Due to organizational restructuring, a lot of employees at a company lose their jobs. This leaves the remaining employees fearing for their jobs, which can affect their performance. What can the HR department do to allay their fears?

(A) Address employees' fears and ask them to stay confident about their jobs

(B) Tell employees that their fears are meaningless when they have not been downsized

(C) Ask employees to focus on their work

(D) None of the above

(49) A company takes on two projects. One is eco-friendly and the other is not. The eco-friendly project does not seem as profitable as the one that might pollute the environment. How should the HR department deal with such a situation?

(A) Choose the project that is more profitable

(B) Choose the eco-friendly project

(C) Take on both projects

(D) Seek other clients

(50) You intend to take your business to other markets in the world. Which of the following can help you do so?

(A) Being inclusive of candidates of different races, religions, and ethnicities

(B) Advertising your business on international websites

(C) Setting up an office in a particular country but hiring only employees from the country of the company's origin

(D) None of the above

(51) After making certain changes, you witness a lower turnover in which employees are not leaving your workplace. What could have caused this huge benefit?

(A) Better salaries

(B) The popularity of the business

(C) Fewer jobs available in the market

(D) The company being more inclusive of people from different backgrounds

(52) To address your company's financial issues, you have proposed a solution, but it is very risky for the company. What should you do to persuade the company?

(A) Apply peer pressure

(B) Share facts, figures, reports, evidence, and logic regarding the advantages of the proposed solution

(C) Make a request

(D) Drop the idea if there are any concerns about it

(53) Your firm recently did a drug test on all its staff. One of the employees who tested positive has been with the firm for a long time and is an important asset.

As an HR professional, how should you deal with this situation?

(A) Terminate the employee's contract immediately

(B) Issue a warning and suspend the employee for a certain period

(C) Take no action

(D) None of the above

(54) What paying system should you implement for individuals who are currently learning the basics of organizational skills?

(A) Paying for knowledge

(B) Skill-based wages

(C) Time-based wages

(D) Both A and B

(55) An employee has a history of failing to meet work deadlines on a regular basis. Until now, no serious action has been taken against him. The manager is starting to grow impatient and has sought the HR expert's help in the matter.

How should the HR expert handle the situation?

(A) Fire the employee

(B) Sit down with the employee and try to understand what's going on

(C) Explain the effect that missing deadlines has on everyone at the company

(D) All of the above

(56) A firm recently hired a dozen employees. However, the employees have not been able to completely understand their job descriptions. As a result, productivity has been affected.

What should the firm do to try to fix this issue?

(A) Give the employees time to learn and settle in

(B) Lay off any new employees who are not able to perform according to their job description

(C) Conduct face-to-face sessions with the new employees while also improving the job description guidelines

(D) None of the above

(57) A firm has recently discussed a potential merger with another firm that would be very profitable. However, a merger also means laying off workers to reduce costs.

What should the firm do?

(A) Accept the merger and lay off as many workers as necessary

(B) Refuse the merger and keep the workers but lose out on a profitable business

(C) Accept the merger but also give out severance pay to workers who are being released

(D) None of the above

(58) The HR department is planning a two-day trip for company employees. However, the location of the trip is undecided and employees have conflicting opinions.

How should the HR department decide on where the trip should be?

(A) Decide on a place without considering employee preferences

(B) Take votes about many locations

(C) Choose two locations and let the employees vote on just those two places

(D) None of the above

(59) Amy has been facing constant bullying at work. This has affected her performance and mental health. She has just notified the HR department of her situation.

Vhat measures should the HR department take?

Take disciplinary action against those bullying Amy

Take no action and expect Amy to deal with the problem on her own

ı an anti-bullying campaign and stress the harmful effects that ay cause to individuals

and C.

(60) Juan has been under a lot of stress lately because of work. He has lost his appetite, and his sleeping pattern has been altered. Juan is seeking help from the HR department and hopes to return to a healthy lifestyle.

What measures can the HR department take to help Juan with his problems?

(A) Motivate Juan to work harder and try to make him understand that his work calls for effort and determination

(B) Send Juan to therapy sessions that will help him both mentally and physically and help him manage his work better

(C) Give Juan some time off work

(D) Make it clear to Juan that if he is not able to perform his job, he will be fired

(61) Steve has come to the HR department with the complaint that he has not been paid his salary despite giving a month's notice before leaving as required.

What should the HR department do in this case?

(A) Ask Steve to speak directly to senior management and sort out the issue

(B) Look into the details as to why Steve has not been paid and take his query to management

(C) Ask senior management to pay Steve

(D) None of the above

(62) Jamal recently faced racial discrimination in his workplace and notified the HR department.

As a member of the HR department, what should you do?

(A) Take no action

(B) Fire those discriminating against Juan and reinforce the company's no-tolerance policy against racial abuse while also reiterating the importance of cultural diversity in the workplace

(C) Ask those who discriminated against Juan to apologize to him and then move on with business as usual

(D) None of the above

(63) An over-50 candidate with a great deal of experience applied to a job opening. A 25-year-old with very little experience but a very strong grasp on technological use also applied to the same job.

Out of the two candidates, whom should the hiring committee choose?

(A) Both

(B) The over-50 candidate, due to her experience

(C) The 25-year-old, due to his grasp of technology

(D) Assess what is more crucial to the job description—experience or the use of technology—and make the decision accordingly

(64) A company is looking to move in another direction by shifting to a different product than what it is manufacturing right now. It asked the HR department to come up with a plan for this transition.

Which of the following should the HR department consider first?

(A) How this transition will affect the HR department and its members

(B) Gather useful data about the industry the company is looking to head into and send it to senior management

(C) Both A and B

(D) None of the above

(65) JB Comm is an up-and-coming business that aims to establish its HR department. Which of the following is not part of establishing business acumen?

(A) Knowing the most profitable aspects of the business

(B) The current market situation

(C) A thorough understanding of a respective niche

(D) A focus on quantitative research and not qualitative research

(66) Core Corp. is looking to hire a new HR professional. Which qualities should it look for before hiring the individual?

(A) Someone who understands the finances of the business

(B) Someone who can make practical decisions

(C) Both A and B

(D) Neither A nor B

(67) In today's world, corporate social responsibility is growing rapidly. At a certain company, the HR department is holding a session on the topic of CSR.

What details about CSR can be relayed to the employees?

(A) Investing in the community

(B) Ethical conduct

(C) Environmental practice

(D) All of the above

(68) You are the head of the HR department at SWOF International, and you aim to establish a fund for charity and the establishment of an NGO that will look after people with special needs.

What part of CSR will you be accomplishing through the establishment of this fund?

(A) Corporate charity

(B) Corporate investment

(C) Donations

(D) Philanthropic responsibility

(69) Kurt and Marco's company has extended working hours. Due to these extended working hours, employee morale has been driven to an all-time low.

What are the necessary steps Kurt and Marco should take to improve this situation?

(A) Approach management and let them know about the situation

(B) Look for newer places to work

(C) Leave for home early despite the extended working hours

(D) Seek methods to improve employees' work-life balance

(70) Krista is a new university graduate. Upon graduation, she is offered a job at a technical company. She accepts the job but struggles to cope with its requirements.

What should Krista do in this situation?

(A) Ask the HR department to enroll her in training programs

(B) Look for jobs elsewhere

(C) Ask her peers and colleagues to help her out

(D) Learn the job over time

(71) Steven, a new hire, is tasked with disposing waste at an industrial company. Prior to Steven's hiring, the waste was discharged into nearby fields and rivers.

What can Steven do to rectify the incorrect practices of the past?

(A) Invest company resources into methods of proper waste disposal

(B) Compensate the locals for the damage done

(C) Look for remote places to dispose of the industrial waste

(D) All of the above

(72) There has been an exponential rise in the levels of worldwide pollution. As head of the HR department, what steps should you take to fight this growing problem?

(A) Educate the public about the dangers of pollution and act more responsibly

(B) Look for ways to curb the level of pollution within permitted amounts

(C) Switch to newer and more ecologically suited business practices

(D) All of the above

(73) Your company is looking to raise awareness about growing pollution problems around the world. What steps should the HR department at your company take to work toward its goal?

(A) Hold educational sessions at various schools

(B) Offer internships and training programs

(C) Promote the issue via various platforms

(D) All of the above

(74) To promote greater participation among the employees of a company and look for fresher and younger faces, what steps should the HR department take to promote fairer competition?

(A) Ensure equal opportunities for all people

(B) Increase training programs, involvement, and transparency

(C) Ensure equal pay for people of the same qualifications and skill levels, regardless of their gender

(D) All of the above

(75) What should the HR department's primary concern be regarding the labor force employed in factories?

(A) Improved working conditions and health benefits

(B) Training programs

(C) Newer technology

(D) Workforce representation for people of all ages

(76) Jamie is an employee who mainly focuses on the digital side of a company's dealings. He has been asked to help out in a matter relating to the financial side.

This is an error on which side of the company?

(A) Planning

(B) Directing

(C) Organizing

D) None of the above

(77) You are the head of the HR department. Recently, there has been a job vacancy at a certain position, and you are looking for someone to fill that vacancy as soon as possible.

What step should you take after acknowledging the job vacancy?

(A) Advertise the job vacancy in public

(B) Advertise the job vacancy to the people in your company

(C) Advertise the job both internally and externally

(D) Ignore the job vacancy

(78) In order to promote healthy competition between the employees at your company, the HR department has decided to distinguish between three groups: excellent, mediocre, and poor.

How will the HR department ensure fair results?

(A) Through talent calibration

(B) Through performance calibration

(C) Through WBS

(D) None of the above

(79) Which of the following best describes the role of HR professionals with strong business acumen in an organization?

(A) They are solely responsible for hiring and firing employees.

(B) They only assist the company in decision-making processes.

(C) They bridge the gap between senior management and the workforce, and aid in strategic decision making.

(D) They solely handle communication within the organization.

(80) What is the impact of treating HR professionals as business partners on a company's decision-making power?

(A) It drastically decreases the decision-making power as it adds another layer of management.

(B) It doesn't have any noticeable impact on the decision-making power.

(C) It improves the decision-making power as HR professionals provide valuable contributions.

(D) It impedes the decision-making power due to potential conflicts with HR policies.

(81) What is one of the crucial financial documents that HR professionals need to understand in order to develop their business acumen and make strategic decisions?

(A) Employee payrolls

(B) Profit-and-loss statements

(C) Employee personal tax returns

(D) None of the above

(82) Why is it important for HR professionals to understand both the external and internal environments of a business?

(A) To navigate the politics within the organization

(B) To be aware of gossip within the industry

(C) To make strategic decisions and stay informed about the market and competitors

(D) To handle the organization's social media presence

(83) Why is it crucial for an organization, regardless of its size, to have a long-term internal communication plan?

(A) It ensures the organization can keep up with its competition.

(B) It guarantees the organization's financial success.

(C) It enables the organization to meet legal requirements.

(D) It helps to secure the organization's intellectual property.

(84) According to Robert House's Path-Goal Theory of Leadership, what is the primary role of a leader?

(A) To provide rewards to team members for achieving their goals

(B) To provide the training necessary for team members to perform their tasks

(C) To increase employees' motivation by clarifying the paths to rewards

(D) To resolve conflicts among team members

(85) Which of the following is NOT one of the leadership styles mentioned in Robert House's Path-Goal Theory of Leadership?

A) Autocratic leadership

B) Directive leadership

C) Supportive leadership

D) Achievement-oriented leadership

(86) According to Robert House's Path-Goal Theory of Leadership, in what scenario is the supportive leadership style most effective?

(A) When tasks are ambiguous or stressful

(B) When tasks are structured and routine

(C) When tasks require individual initiative and creativity

(D) When tasks involve a high level of risk

(87) Performance calibration in an organization primarily refers to:

(A) The act of adjusting the performance levels of employees to a standard scale.

(B) Providing frequent feedback to employees about their performance.

(C) Determining the right compensation for each role within an organization.

(D) The process of identifying the training needs of the employees.

(88) Which of the following is NOT a common goal of performance calibration meetings?

(A) Ensuring consistent performance evaluations across different teams

(B) Identifying high-potential employees for leadership roles

(C) Determining which employees are underperforming and may need to be terminated

(D) Determining the marketing strategy for the next quarter

(89) What is a potential benefit of performance calibration in organizations?

(A) It allows employees to directly compare their performance to their peers.

(B) It reduces the need for ongoing performance management.

(C) It can help increase consistency and fairness in performance evaluations.

(D) It can reduce the workload of HR by simplifying performance reviews.

(90) Cognitive conflict within a team can be best described as:

(A) A disagreement among team members about personal beliefs or values

(B) A clash among team members due to differences in personality or personal styles

(C) A disagreement among team members about task-related issues such as ideas, perspectives, or interpretations

(D) A conflict between an employee's professional responsibilities and personal life

(91) Which of the following statements about cognitive conflict is TRUE according to most organizational behavior theories?

(A) Cognitive conflict always has a negative impact on team performance.

(B) Cognitive conflict should be avoided at all costs to ensure team harmony.

(C) Cognitive conflict, when managed correctly, can stimulate innovation and improve team decision-making.

(D) Cognitive conflict occurs when team members cannot balance their work and personal life.

(92) In a team setting, the role of an HR professional in managing cognitive conflict should ideally be to:

(A) Eliminate all cognitive conflicts as they arise

(B) Promote cognitive conflicts to keep the team on their toes

(C) Encourage team members to suppress cognitive conflicts

(D) Facilitate the constructive resolution of cognitive conflicts

(93) Ethical practice in human resources primarily involves:

(A) Maximizing profits for the organization

(B) Ensuring compliance with all relevant laws and regulations

(C) Ensuring decisions and actions are guided by principles of fairness, respect, and integrity

(D) All of the above

(94) Which of the following scenarios demonstrates a potential ethical dilemma in HR practice?

(A) A hiring manager who knows a job candidate personally and fails to disclose the relationship

(B) An HR professional who is diligent about staying current with labor laws and regulations

(C) An HR manager who implements a new employee wellness program

(D) A payroll specialist who accurately processes payroll each pay period

(95) As an HR professional, how should you respond when you observe unethical behavior in the workplace?

(A) Ignore it, especially if it doesn't directly involve you or your department

(B) Confront the individual involved immediately and demand that they stop

(C) Report it through appropriate channels within your organization

(D) Share what you've observed with other coworkers to see if they've noticed the same behavior

(96) According to goal-setting theory, which of the following is a critical aspect of effective goal setting?

(A) Goals should be ambiguous to allow for flexibility.

(B) Goals should be easy to ensure that they are attainable.

(C) Goals should be specific and challenging to enhance motivation.

(D) Goals should be unrelated to actual job tasks.

(97) What is one way that goal-setting theory suggests to increase employee commitment to their goals?

(A) By making the goals as complex as possible.

(B) By setting the same goals for every employee.

(C) By involving employees in the goal-setting process.

(D) By keeping the goals a secret until the last moment.

(98) According to the goal-setting theory, goals should be:

(A) Impossible to reach to push employees to their limits.

(B) Related to the employee's social life to encourage work-life balance.

(C) Aligned with organizational objectives to ensure relevancy.

(D) Kept private to prevent unnecessary competition among employees.

(99) The Expectancy Theory of motivation suggests that an employee's motivation is highest when:

(A) The employee believes that their effort will lead to high performance.

(B) The employee believes that their performance will lead to valuable outcomes.

(C) The employee believes in both A and B.

(D) The employee is satisfied with their current job role.

(100) According to the Expectancy Theory, which of the following factors influences an employee's motivation to perform a task?

(A) The intrinsic satisfaction derived from performing the task.

(B) The perceived fairness of the reward system.

(C) The belief that performing the task will lead to a desired outcome.

(D) The employee's ability to perform the task without any help.

(101) In the context of the Expectancy Theory, 'Valence' refers to:

(A) The belief that effort will lead to performance.

(B) The value an individual places on the rewards associated with performance.

(C) The belief that performance will lead to desired rewards.

(D) The balance between effort and performance.

(102) Attribution theory primarily helps us understand:

(A) How individuals set and achieve their goals.

(B) How individuals interpret and understand their own and others' behavior.

(C) How individuals are motivated by the expectation of rewards.

(D) How individuals react to stress in the workplace.

(103) According to attribution theory, when an employee attributes their success to their own abilities or effort, this is known as:

(A) An internal attribution.

(B) An external attribution.

(C) A stable attribution.

(D) An unstable attribution.

(104) In the context of attribution theory, what is meant by 'stability'?

(A) The consistency of an individual's performance over time.

(B) The belief that causes of events or behaviors are unchanging or consistent over time.

(C) The internal or external locus of control for an event or behavior.

(D) The degree to which an individual attributes success or failure to their own abilities or effort.

(105) According to Self-Determination Theory, the three basic psychological needs that are central to intrinsic motivation are:

(A) Security, self-esteem, and affiliation.

(B) Autonomy, competence, and relatedness.

(C) Power, achievement, and autonomy.

(D) Esteem, self-actualization, and safety.

(106) Self-Determination Theory proposes that motivation is highest when:

(A) Rewards are tied to performance.

(B) Goals are set by the organization.

(C) Individuals feel they have choice and can self-direct their actions.

(D) Individuals are monitored and directed by supervisors.

(107) According to Self-Determination Theory, which type of motivation is likely to result in high-quality learning and creativity?

(A) Intrinsic motivation

(B) Extrinsic motivation

(C) Amotivation

(D) Achievement motivation

(108) In an Agile HR environment, which of the following best describes how performance management should be approached?

(A) Through annual performance reviews.

(B) Through continuous feedback and iterative performance discussions.

(C) Through bi-annual 360-degree feedback sessions.

(D) Through monthly team performance reviews only.

(109) How does the role of HR change in an Agile project management environment?

(A) HR becomes solely responsible for recruitment.

(B) HR takes on more of a leadership role, guiding managers and teams.

(C) HR becomes more of a facilitator, enabling teams to self-organize and self-manage.

(D) HR's role does not change significantly.

(110) Which of the following is NOT a characteristic of Agile HR?

(A) Focusing on real-time data for decision-making.

(B) Encouraging cross-functional collaboration and open communication.

(C) Using annual performance reviews to evaluate employees.

(D) Empowering teams to be self-organizing and autonomous.

(111) Which of the following best describes the primary purpose of Lean Six Sigma in Human Resources?

(A) To increase the number of employees in an organization.

(B) To identify and eliminate waste and reduce variation in HR processes.

(C) To enforce strict performance metrics for all employees.

(D) To implement a new organizational hierarchy.

(112) What is a common application of Lean Six Sigma in HR?

(A) Creating a strict hierarchy of roles and responsibilities.

(B) Standardizing all job descriptions across the company.

(C) Reducing time and errors in the recruitment and hiring process.

(D) Determining the maximum number of employees a company should hire.

(113) When implementing Lean Six Sigma in HR, which of the following should be a primary focus?

(A) Cutting costs at all costs, including reducing employee benefits.

(B) Improving processes by focusing on the needs and expectations of the internal and external customers.

(C) Hiring more employees to ensure there's no shortage of manpower.

(D) Ensuring every employee has a Six Sigma certification.

(114) Which of the following actions by a union would be considered an Unfair Labor Practice?

(A) Organizing a peaceful strike to protest unfair wages.

(B) Negotiating with an employer on behalf of its members.

(C) Coercing employees to join the union against their will.

(D) Filing a grievance on behalf of an employee.

(115) Which of the following constitutes an unfair labor practice committed by a union?

(A) Causing an employer to discriminate against an employee because of his or her union activity.

(B) Providing representation to workers during collective bargaining.

(C) Requesting the employer to bargain in good faith.

(D) Organizing lawful strikes or protests.

(116) Under the NLRA, it is an unfair labor practice for a union to:

(A) Organize a boycott of an employer's products.

(B) Refuse to bargain collectively with an employer.

(C) Advocate for improved working conditions.

(D) Lobby for increased wages and benefits.

(117) What is the primary role of the National Labor Relations Board (NLRB)?

(A) To enforce federal minimum wage laws.

(B) To ensure the safe and healthful working conditions for working men and women.

(C) To administer and enforce the National Labor Relations Act (NLRA).

(D) To regulate private pension and health plans.

(118) The National Labor Relations Board (NLRB) has jurisdiction over:

(A) All private sector employers.

(B) Only public sector employers.

(C) Both private and public sector employers.

(D) Only private sector employers affecting interstate commerce.

(119) Which of the following is NOT a responsibility of the National Labor Relations Board (NLRB)?

(A) Resolving complaints of unfair labor practices.

(B) Conducting union representation elections.

(C) Enforcing minimum wage laws.

(D) Facilitating settlement of labor disputes.

(120) Which of the following best describes the concept of philanthropic responsibility in a corporate context?

(A) The obligation to pay taxes to the government.

(B) The ethical responsibility to do no harm to stakeholders.

(C) The voluntary actions taken by a company to improve social conditions.

(D) The requirement to meet regulatory standards.

(121) How can a Human Resource department support a company's philanthropic responsibility?

(A) By reducing the company's tax liabilities.

(B) By strictly adhering to labor laws.

(C) By establishing employee volunteer programs and charitable giving policies.

(D) By ensuring that the company makes a profit every quarter.

(122) Which of the following would not typically be considered a philanthropic responsibility of a company?

(A) Donating a portion of profits to charity.

(B) Organizing employee volunteer days in the community.

(C) Complying with environmental regulations.

(D) Providing scholarships for students in need.

(123) Which of the following training methods is most effective for educating employees in managerial positions?

(A) Self-directed online courses

(B) Mentoring and coaching programs

(C) One-time workshops

(D) Detailed handbooks

(124) What is a key competency that should be included in a training program for employees transitioning into managerial positions?

(A) Technical skills related to the product or service the company provides

(B) Understanding of the company's marketing strategies

(C) Ability to effectively communicate and motivate a team

(D) Knowledge of the company's IT systems

(125) Why is ongoing education important for employees in managerial positions?

(A) It ensures they stay informed about industry trends and best practices.

(B) It keeps them busy and prevents boredom.

(C) It guarantees they will get promoted to higher-level positions.

(D) It makes them eligible for higher salaries.

(126) Why is global HR management critical for multinational organizations?

(A) It ensures that the company only hires employees from the home country.

(B) It ensures consistent implementation of policies across different countries.

(C) It ensures that all employees speak the same language.

(D) It ensures that the company only operates in countries with low labor costs.

(127) What is one of the primary challenges of global HR management?

(A) Adjusting HR practices to comply with local labor laws and cultural norms.

(B) Ensuring that all employees speak English.

(C) Limiting employee transfers between countries.

(D) Hiring only expatriates for senior management positions.

(128) Which of the following strategies is most beneficial for managing diverse teams across different countries?

(A) Applying the same management style across all countries.

(B) Treating all employees exactly the same, regardless of their cultural background.

(C) Implementing global policies while considering local cultural, legal, and market differences.

(D) Focusing solely on local practices and ignoring global strategies.

(129) Which of the following best describes a potential risk of non-compliance with labor laws for an organization?

(A) Lower marketing costs

(B) Financial penalties and reputational damage

(C) Increased employee turnover

(D) Decreased competition

(130) How can HR departments contribute to minimizing legal compliance risks?

(A) By focusing solely on hiring and firing decisions

(B) By ensuring that the company's policies and procedures are in compliance with all applicable laws and regulations

(C) By only hiring employees who have a legal background

(D) By ignoring minor instances of non-compliance

(131) What role does employee training play in minimizing an organization's risk of legal non-compliance?

(A) No role, as training is unrelated to compliance

(B) It can help employees understand their roles and responsibilities in maintaining compliance

(C) It should focus on scaring employees about the consequences of non-compliance

(D) It's only necessary for upper management, as they make all the decisions

(132) When a company undergoes legal restructuring, what is one potential impact on HR functions?

(A) HR functions will be eliminated.

(B) HR may need to manage layoffs or workforce reassignments.

(C) HR will be legally required to hire new employees.

(D) HR responsibilities will be transferred to other departments.

(133) Which of the following is a potential legal risk for HR during a restructuring process?

(A) Failure to provide adequate notice of layoffs under the WARN Act

(B) Implementing too many team-building activities

(C) Hiring too many new employees

(D) Assigning new roles to existing employees

(134) What role can HR play in minimizing legal risks during a restructuring process?

(A) HR should focus only on the needs of senior management during restructuring.

(B) HR should focus only on the needs of employees, ignoring the strategic needs of the company.

(C) HR should play a critical role in planning and communicating changes, ensuring compliance with employment laws, and addressing employee concerns.

(D) HR should delegate all restructuring responsibilities to other departments to avoid legal risks.

SHRM-SCP Test 4: Answers and Explanations

(1) (B) Potential for brain drain

If employees stop contributing to the firm and instead have better opportunities elsewhere, they could seriously jeopardize the firm's interests. Thus, the potential for brain drain is something Albert should focus on in his audit.

(2) (A) Vertical fit

A vertical fit happens when a business's strategies coincide with the HR practices and both augment each other.

(3) (C) Monitoring performance and overtime pay

Performance monitoring is vital for a firm so that it knows which department is not performing efficiently and where downsizing is required. Over time, pay analysis acts as a driving force for workers to earn extra rewards. This issue is important to HR with the rise in the use of technology for telecommuting.

(4) (B) Improper use of proprietary data

Maintaining secure documentation ensures a firm's reputation, protects trademarks, and stops leaks from happening—leaks that could harm the firm's interests. Improper use of proprietary data is a critical and ethical issue for HR.

(5) (D) It could cause top management to deal directly with first-line managers.

When top management deals directly with first-line managers as a result of technological advances, the chain of command runs more efficiently. As a result, there is no room for ambiguities anymore.

(6) (D) Important, as competencies can affect company performance.

The organization needs to determine if employees will be a good fit for the organization's long-term vision and if they are flexible enough to adjust to its specific culture.

(7) (A) The employee's career aspirations

An appraisal shows an employee's core competencies, interests, and performance. When meeting with an employee regarding their appraisal, the HR professional should always ask the employee about career aspirations. The resulting feedback will help the HR professional place the employee in a better division.

(8) (A) A structured interview

An interview will allow management and the trainer to learn if the skills they intended to teach the employees have been rightfully acquired, and the one-on-one structured interviews will allow trainees to clarify any confusion.

(9) (D) Both A and C

Empowering employees will allow them to have more authority and help them make decisions on their own without needing to ask their seniors for permission for day-to-day tasks. This will build more trust and confidence among employees, so they will feel more attached to the organization and take more ownership of their work, leading to better results for the organization as a whole.

(10) (C) Reduction in resistance from employees

All of the mentioned benefits are true when working online except for the statement that working online can reduce resistance from employees.

(11) (B) HR strategies

All business decisions can be risky. HR dealings can also be fraught with risk. The only way to limit this risk is to apply risk management strategies to all the processes conducted by HR. For example, the information handled by the HR team should have constant checks on it so nothing can be stolen or accessed by someone who was not allowed to in the first place. The risk for this violation should be calculated, and safety measures should be taken.

(12) (A) Informal hiring strategies

To encourage an entrepreneurial climate within the work environment, the manager should hire people who are visionaries. This can be accomplished only through informal hiring because many visionaries have qualifications that do not match up with recruiters' strict standards.

(13) (B) Assisting managers with their jobs

The HR professional's focus is to build a team that will allow managers to reach their goals and objectives on time.

(14) (B) Creating distinct capabilities

A distinct capability will help the organization survive in the long term, as the company will be able to deliver goods or services in a much better way.

(15) (A) Inability to control costs

An organization's inability to control costs will hamper its ability to provide greater value to its customers in contrast to its competitors.

(16) (C) Insecurity and a drop in focus due to communication gaps

Decentralization leads to longer hierarchical chains in organizations and increases distances among the top and lower-level workers of an organization. The original message is often lost, and a sense of mistrust among employees occurs due to so many entities now being involved in the process.

(17) (A) Making an HR inventory

The first step of the planning process is to come up with an HR inventory that includes information regarding all working employees. This information usually consists of an employee's educational background, skills, salary, and other important data that is vital to the HR planning process.

(18) (C) Decruitment

Decruitment helps HR professionals reduce the size of their company's workforce. This strategy includes options such as firing or temporary terminations of employees that can last for as little as a few days to as long as years. Not filling new job openings on purpose after resignations or retirements is also a part of decruitment. This will help reduce the surplus of employees.

(19) (D) Employee referrals

Existing employees are familiar with the workplace and are already committed to the organization. Thus, a referral from an already hardworking employee could prove beneficial as they would be taking responsibility for the candidate's credibility. A referred employee will feel more engaged, as they will already know someone in the organization.

(20) (C) Mentoring and coaching

Senior employees' coaching and mentoring are learning and development tools that help employees grow in their roles and empower themselves.

(21) (D) Performance management system

The performance management system will allow the person to evaluate an employee's performance by matching their skills or manpower with the company's goals and objectives. This system includes factors such as timely feedback from the employee, setting goals and assessing their completion, rewarding the employee for work well done, and training the person further for improved performance levels.

(22) (C) Critical incidents

The critical incident technique allows management to gather information that contributes to employees' success and helps them work better. Employees are asked to participate in an activity in which a group of workers is observed and evaluated with the help of a recording. Behaviors are also observed and evaluated for effectiveness.

(23) (A) Management by objectives

Management by objectives helps management define the organization's goals systematically. The organization then conveys these goals to the organization members. Each employee has a clearly defined role, and checks and balances are kept in place to regularly evaluate performance levels.

(24) (A) Severance pay

Severance pay helps laid-off employees during the downsizing process, as the payment offers them compensation or benefits for their job loss.

(25) (B) Provide counselors for employees to talk to

Counselors will explain to the workers why the downsizing occurred and help them acknowledge the fact that it is a part of business. They will help employees focus on the future and enable them to be positive.

(26) (A) Expand the recruiting net

Through an expanded recruiting net, the HR manager can focus and advertise the job to new markets and hire talent from different backgrounds, adding to the organization's diversity levels. With strict antidiscriminatory policies, the HR manager can hire people from different religions, ethnicities, and cultures, as well as people with disabilities.

(27) (B) Seek independent HR consultation providers

When there are humans and resources, HR management is essential. But when the number of employees is very limited, such a department is very unlikely to be of any use, so it is not recommended you set up a separate HR department if you have fewer than 10 employees.

(28) (C) Have a polite conversation with the employee to remind the person of your authority and explain that a complaint cannot be filed against you simply because someone dislikes a department change

Employees should be reminded of your authority now and then. You are never required to obey the employees, but neither should you fire them before having a proper conversation about the situation and trying to implement other solutions.

(29) (B) Ignore the rumors

Rumors and false information do not harm you until you acknowledge them. If someone is spreading such rumors in your office, do not lower yourself to their level and go around informing everyone about your true intentions. You do not owe any justification to anyone about your personal decisions so long as they do not impact the workplace.

(30) (A) Call the employees into your office and politely listen to their complaints

It is ethically wrong to fire employees, scold them, or file a complaint against them simply because they are expressing dissatisfaction with the workplace.

(31) (A) Name and shame that senior employee in front of the entire office and call for the person's removal

Making your female employees feel safe in their work environment is your responsibility, so you must take immediate action against anyone who harasses them.

(32) (A) Grant the leave

You are legally and ethically required to be accepting of the needs of different races, religions, and ethnicities in the workplace.

(33) (C) Take the time to address the employees' concerns

You are not just the boss of a company, but also its leader. Issuing warning letters and scolding employees is inappropriate when they are simply seeking help in order to improve their performance. They want sympathy and direction, so be kind and provide the leadership they need.

(34) (B) Through performance calibration

Talent calibration is used to analyze the overall health of a company's talent pool. Work breakdown structure is a technique that can help you break complex tasks down into multiple steps.

(35) (A) The company could have incorporated the WBS technique.

For any complex task that involves multiple steps, a work breakdown structure is the best option. In this situation, it could have prevented the problems the employee encountered when trying to complete the assigned task.

(36) (B) A conflict that led to innovations and new ideas

If a lesson or idea for future improvement can be derived from conflict, then it is a beneficial conflict.

(37) (D) Staying away

The "staying away" strategy of the Thomas-Kilmann Model involves avoiding the problem and waiting for it to resolve itself rather than intervening.

(38) (A) Choose the most talented recruits, then admit your mistake and politely apologize to the rest

It is the responsibility of the HR department to figure out the number of employees required before initiating the recruitment process. Therefore, the department should own up to its mistake rather than ignoring it or putting the blame on other colleagues.

(39) (C) Both A and B

If the internal candidate fits the job requirements, that person should be encouraged to apply for the position. There is no need to advertise the job outside the company if someone within it fits the need.

(40) (C) Both A and B

Social media and websites are the most cost-effective means of advertising an available job vacancy.

(41) (B) Honesty tests are unreliable and should not be used.

Honesty tests can be easily manipulated and should not be used when recruiting job candidates.

(42) (D) All of the above

It is not the salary that makes an employee leave; rather, it is the boring nature of work, bosses with an unfriendly attitude, and unhealthy work environments that cause people to leave their jobs. All of these things need to be addressed in order to improve working conditions and better retain workers.

(43) (D) Both B and C.

Money can be a problem, but the workload and/or repetitive nature of work can make people feel less than motivated to complete their responsibilities and tasks. You should assume the person is unhappy with the workload and nature of his assigned tasks and help him increase his motivation.

(44) (A) Six Sigma

Six Sigma is a project management technique that is used to improve organizational processes by eliminating the errors and mistakes made previously.

(45) (A) Lean

Lean is a project management technique that helps raise customer value and cuts down on any form of waste in a company.

(46) (D) Only A and B

Workforce managers are responsible for ensuring customer satisfaction and reducing operational costs.

(47) (B) Ask the parties to sit down and find common ground

HR managers need to sit both parties down and discuss their various concerns, seeking out a mutually agreeable solution in order to maintain a healthy workplace environment.

(48) (A) Address employees' fears and ask them to stay confident about their jobs

Ignoring employee fears is always unhelpful. The HR department should talk with employees, explain the situation, and help them feel confident about retaining their jobs.

(49) (B) Choose the eco-friendly project

Environmental protection should be given ultimate priority as, without natural resources, no company will be able to stay in business. Furthermore, being eco-friendly is vital for marketing purposes nowadays.

(50) (A) Being inclusive of candidates of different races, religions, and ethnicities

Being inclusive of candidates of different races, religions, and ethnicities is always vital, but never more so than when you are reaching out to a global market.

(51) (D) The company being more inclusive of people from different backgrounds

Even if there were no other jobs on the market or if a business became immensely popular, people could still refuse to work with a firm if required to compromise on their morals. Therefore, the only thing that could cause such a huge benefit would be the company's inclusiveness.

(52) (B) Share facts, figures, reports, evidence, and logic regarding the advantages of the proposed solution

Peer pressure will not work in front of your bosses. Dropping the idea is also not the right thing to do, as the company might lose a fruitful opportunity. Moreover, simply making a request to the company will not work unless you bring the right kind of facts and figures to the table.

(53) (B) Issue a warning and suspend the employee for a certain period.

Issuing a warning and suspending the employee for a certain period will discourage the consumption of drugs among employees. Furthermore, it gives the employee a second chance and prevents the company from having to hire another person, assuming the employee does not make the same mistake again.

(54) (D) Both A and B

Employees learning the basics of organizational skills are eligible for skilled-based pay but are also legally entitled to income while gaining knowledge.

(55) (B) Sit down with the employee and try to understand what's going on

The best possible solution would be for the HR professional to have a chat with the employee and see what is going on. There might be a reason behind the missing deadlines, which the manager and other workers might be unaware of. It would be best to first understand what the employee is dealing with, then act accordingly.

(56) (C) Conduct face-to-face sessions with the new employees while also improving the job description guidelines

The best quick fix to the problem, for now, would be to conduct sessions with the newly hired employees and verbally tutor them about their jobs. To avoid similar problems in the future, it is best that the HR department work on improving the company's job descriptions so that potential employees have a clearer understanding of what their specific jobs require.

(57) (C) Accept the merger but also give out severance pay to workers who are being released

At least one party will be affected by any decision the firm takes. Hence, keeping the firm's interests foremost in mind while also looking out for the employees is a must. Senior management's best option is to go ahead with the merger while also looking out for the employees they will let go by giving them some sort of severance pay.

(58) (B) Take votes about many locations

To avoid any arguments or conflicts, the best possible method for the HR department is to conduct a vote and allow the employees to express their opinions. This is a fair method and one that everyone will accept without showing signs of disapproval or generating potential conflict.

(59) (C) Run an anti-bullying campaign and stress the harmful effects that bullying may cause to individuals

It is important to make clear to the workforce the effects bullying has on people. By running an anti-bullying campaign and making the employees aware of the problem, the HR department will help the workplace become healthier for all employees, including the one who first lodged the complaint.

(60) (B) Send Juan to therapy sessions that will help him both mentally and physically and help him manage his work better

A professional therapist can help Juan talk through his issues and give him advice, such as coping strategies and ways to manage his work-life balance in a healthier manner.

(61) (B) Look into the details as to why Steve has not been paid and take his query to management

Mistakes do happen in organizations. The important thing is to look into what the problem is and why it happened, then rectify it immediately. Take measures to make sure that the mistake does not happen a second time.

(62) (B) Fire those discriminating against Juan and reinforce the company's no-tolerance policy against racial abuse while also reiterating the importance of cultural diversity in the workplace

Maintaining a friendly workplace environment is essential, as it boosts everyone's morale. Incidents of discrimination or abuse will have a very negative impact on everyone's performance. So taking strict action, such as firing those who were discriminating against Juan, will set an example and help deal with such issues permanently. It is important to consistently reinforce the company's no-tolerance policy when it comes to racial abuse and reiterate the importance of diversity in the workplace.

(63) (D) Assess what is more crucial to the job description—experience or the use of technology—and make the decision accordingly

Every job is different due to a multitude of factors. A job vacancy means that anyone can apply, but the candidate with the experience related to the job requirement must be selected. No one should be selected on the basis of technological experience if it is not a basic requirement of the job in question. Similarly, age should never be more than just a number when hiring for an open position.

(64) (B) Gather useful data about the industry the company is looking to head into and send it to senior management

If the company wants to switch products, it must have complete information about the new product it is considering making and marketing. Otherwise, if there is not any prior work done, this could result in many errors.

(65) (D) A focus on quantitative research and not qualitative research

Developing business acumen is essential for a business to operate and function properly. However, stressing quantitative research while foregoing qualitative research is not at all a part of developing successful business acumen.

(66) (C) Both A and B

An HR professional should understand the finances of the business. They should also be well versed in making practical decisions. Both of these skills are key for any HR professional and must be something a company looks for.

(67) (D) All of the above

The employees should be told CSR is now becoming an essential part of modern-day businesses' goals. Explain to employees all the good done when a company invests in the community, the importance of being more ethically sound, and why it is vital to look after the environment.

(68) (D) Philanthropic responsibility

Looking after people with special needs and nurturing NGOs can all be considered a part of corporate social responsibility that the company will address when establishing this fund.

(69) (A) Approach management and let them know about the situation

Approaching management should be the first step Kurt and Marco take before filing a complaint. It is always better to be clear and transparent so that no confusion occurs and clearer communication takes place.

(70) (A) Ask the HR department to enroll her in training programs

If Krista is finding it hard to complete tasks and responsibilities, she should approach the HR department and ask them to register her for training programs that will help her improve her skill set. This promotes honesty, loyalty, and productivity in an organization. It will allow Krista to become a better employee, benefiting both her and the company.

(71) (A) Invest company resources into methods of proper waste disposal

Although compensation is also important in this situation, the first step that needs to be taken in this case is engineering a proper waste disposal system that can prevent any future issues. Looking for remote places to dispose of waste is not the ethical step to take. It is also very possibly illegal.

(72) (D) All of the above

A company should always look for ways to curb its pollution levels. It is important for an organization to adopt more eco-friendly means. Educating the public is also crucial, as this will benefit the world in the future.

(73) (D) All of the above

Awareness in regard to the growing amount of pollution needs to be spread via every available means, be it educational sessions at schools, internships or promotions on various platforms.

(74) (D) All of the above

A company should always look to offer equal salaries to people regardless of their gender if they have the same qualifications. There should also be equal opportunities for all and an increase in the number of training programs offered to employees and the labor force in order to promote healthy and fairer competition.

(75) (A) Improved working conditions and health benefits

Training programs are always necessary for increasing workers' skill levels and productivity. But the more pressing matter that should be addressed first in this situation is an improvement in working conditions and access to better health facilities and health benefits. The introduction of newer technology is also important, but less so than health and working conditions. However, representation of people of all ages is incorrect as an answer given that child labor is strictly forbidden, illegal, and unethical.

(76) (C) Organizing

There are three components of the managerial strategy: planning, organizing, and directing. When you are organizing, you are assigning people in a company the tasks and responsibilities they are supposed to carry out. Hence, this error was on the part of the company's organizing committee.

(77) (B) Advertise the job vacancy to the people in your company

The first step to take after acknowledging the vacancy is advertising the job vacancy to the people in the company. If a suitable candidate is found, they should be given the post; however, if a suitable candidate is not found, the post should be advertised to the public.

(78) (B) Through performance calibration

Performance calibration will show you the level and quality of work performed by each individual. On the other hand, talent calibration is carried out to analyze the overall health of a company's talent pool. Work breakdown structure is a technique that helps break down complex tasks into multiple and achievable steps.

(79) (C) They bridge the gap between senior management and the workforce, and aid in strategic decision making.

HR professionals with business acumen serve multiple roles within an organization. Not only do they bridge the gap between senior management and the workforce by effectively communicating messages to employees, but they also aid the company in its strategic decision-making processes. While hiring and communication are part of their roles, these tasks don't fully encapsulate their responsibilities.

(80) (C) It improves the decision-making power as HR professionals provide valuable contributions.

When HR professionals are treated as business partners, a company's decision-making power improves. Their involvement in strategic decisions—owing to their understanding of the business and its challenges—adds unique insights and valuable contributions to the decision-making process.

(81) (B) Profit-and-loss statements

To develop business acumen, HR professionals need to understand various financial documents of a business, including financial statements, cash flow, balance sheets, and importantly, profit-and-loss statements. Employee personal tax returns are typically private and not directly relevant to a company's financial standing.

(82) (C) To make strategic decisions and stay informed about the market and competitors

HR professionals need to be familiar with both the external and internal environments of a business. This includes keeping up with news, social media, industry publications, and business competitors. They should also stay in touch with business leaders. This understanding enables them to make strategic decisions that align with the business's goals and objectives and respond effectively to market changes and competition.

(83) (A) It ensures the organization can keep up with its competition.

Irrespective of an organization's size, having a long-term internal communication plan is vital for survival and competitiveness. While the communication plan might have indirect effects on financial success or the management of intellectual property, the primary purpose is maintaining a competitive edge.

(84) (C) To increase employees' motivation by clarifying the paths to rewards

The Path-Goal Theory of Leadership, developed by Robert House, suggests that a leader's main job is to help their team members achieve their personal and professional goals by clarifying the paths to these rewards and removing obstacles along the way.

(85) (A) Autocratic leadership

Robert House's Path-Goal Theory of Leadership mentions four primary leadership styles: directive leadership, supportive leadership, participative leadership, and achievement-oriented leadership.

(86) (A) When tasks are ambiguous or stressful

The supportive leadership style, as per the Path-Goal Theory, is most effective in situations where tasks are ambiguous, complex or stressful. In these scenarios, a supportive leader can alleviate job-related stress by showing concern for their followers' psychological well-being. For routine or high-risk tasks, or tasks requiring creativity, other leadership styles may be more appropriate.

(87) (A) The act of adjusting the performance levels of employees to a standard scale.

Performance calibration in an HR context usually refers to the process of adjusting or aligning the evaluation of employee performance to ensure a consistent standard across the organization. It helps ensure that all managers have the same understanding of what constitutes a particular level of performance.

(88) (D) Determining the marketing strategy for the next quarter

Performance calibration meetings typically focus on matters related to employee performance, including ensuring consistency in performance evaluations, identifying high-potential employees, and discussing underperformance. They usually do not involve strategic planning outside of the HR scope, such as marketing strategies.

(89) (C) It can help increase consistency and fairness in performance evaluations.

One of the main benefits of performance calibration is its potential to increase consistency and fairness in performance evaluations. It does this by standardizing the understanding and application of performance criteria across different managers or departments

(90) (C) A disagreement among team members about task-related issues such as ideas, perspectives, or interpretations

Cognitive conflict refers to task-oriented, issue-related disagreement among members of a group or team. It is often related to differences in perspectives, ideas, and interpretations about a task, and it can be constructive if managed properly as it can enhance problem-solving and decision-making.

(91) (C) Cognitive conflict, when managed correctly, can stimulate innovation and improve team decision-making.

Cognitive conflict, which pertains to task-related disagreements, can be constructive for teams if managed appropriately. It can lead to better problem-solving and decision-making as it encourages diverse thinking and stimulates innovative ideas. Cognitive conflict is not about work-life balance issues or always detrimental to team performance, nor is it something to be entirely avoided.

(92) (D) Facilitate the constructive resolution of cognitive conflicts

As cognitive conflicts can lead to innovative ideas and improved decision-making when managed well, an HR professional should ideally aim to facilitate their constructive resolution rather than eliminate or suppress them. This can involve creating a safe space for open dialogue, providing conflict resolution tools, or mediating disagreements when necessary.

(93) (C) Ensuring decisions and actions are guided by principles of fairness, respect, and integrity

Ethical practice in HR primarily involves making decisions and taking actions that are aligned with ethical principles such as fairness, respect, honesty, and integrity.

(94) (A) A hiring manager who knows a job candidate personally and fails to disclose the relationship

A potential ethical dilemma occurs when there's a conflict of interest or a situation that could compromise the principles of fairness and integrity. In this case, the hiring manager knowing a job candidate personally and failing to disclose the relationship could lead to favoritism or perceived bias in the hiring process, which would be an ethical issue.

(95) (C) Report it through appropriate channels within your organization

When observing unethical behavior, an HR professional should report it through the appropriate channels within the organization. This might include speaking to a supervisor, contacting a designated ethics hotline, or following a specified procedure outlined in the company's code of conduct.

(96) (C) Goals should be specific and challenging to enhance motivation.

Goal-setting theory posits that setting specific and challenging goals can enhance people's motivation and performance. Goals that are vague or too easy might not provide a sufficient challenge to engage people's efforts. Similarly, goals unrelated to actual job tasks may not lead to improved performance in meaningful work tasks.

(97) (C) By involving employees in the goal-setting process.

According to goal-setting theory, involving employees in the goal-setting process can increase their commitment to these goals. When employees have a say in setting their own goals, they are more likely to be committed to these goals and work towards achieving them.

(98) (C) Aligned with organizational objectives to ensure relevancy.

According to the goal-setting theory, goals that are aligned with organizational objectives are more likely to result in relevant and beneficial outcomes for the organization. This alignment helps ensure that employees' efforts contribute to the overarching objectives of the organization, which increases the overall effectiveness and efficiency of the organization.

(99) (C) The employee believes in both A and B.

According to the Expectancy Theory, an individual is motivated to perform when they believe that their effort will lead to high performance (expectancy), and that this high performance will lead to valuable outcomes or rewards (instrumentality).

(100) (C) The belief that performing the task will lead to a desired outcome.

Expectancy Theory states that an employee's motivation is influenced by the belief that their effort will lead to performance, and that this performance will result in a desired outcome or reward (valence). While other factors like intrinsic satisfaction and perceived fairness can influence motivation, they are not specifically part of the Expectancy Theory.

(101) (B) The value an individual places on the rewards associated with performance.

In Expectancy Theory, 'Valence' refers to the value or importance that an individual places on the potential rewards or outcomes that may result from their performance. If an individual values the rewards highly, it can enhance their motivation to perform.

(102) (B) How individuals interpret and understand their own and others' behavior.

Attribution theory is a psychological theory that helps to explain how individuals interpret events and how this relates to their thinking and behavior. It involves how individuals understand and attribute causes to events, including their own and others' behavior.

(103) (A) An internal attribution.

According to attribution theory, if an individual attributes their success or failure to factors within their control, such as their own abilities or effort, this is considered an internal attribution. If they attribute their performance to factors outside their control, such as luck or difficulty of the task, this is considered an external attribution.

(104) (B) The belief that causes of events or behaviors are unchanging or consistent over time.

In attribution theory, 'stability' refers to whether individuals perceive the causes of events or behaviors as stable (unchanging over time) or unstable (changing over time). For example, if an employee believes they failed a task because they lack a stable trait, like intelligence, they are making a stable attribution. If they believe they failed due to lack of effort, which can change from moment to moment, they are making an unstable attribution.

(105) (B) Autonomy, competence, and relatedness.

According to Self-Determination Theory, the three basic psychological needs that influence intrinsic motivation are autonomy (the need to have control over one's actions), competence (the need to be effective in dealing with the environment), and relatedness (the need to have close, affectionate relationships with others).

(106) (C) Individuals feel they have choice and can self-direct their actions.

Self-Determination Theory suggests that individuals are most motivated when they feel that they are in control of their own behavior and can make choices freely (autonomy). The theory proposes that intrinsic motivation is highest when people feel autonomous, competent, and related to others.

(107) (A) Intrinsic motivation

According to Self-Determination Theory, intrinsic motivation, where individuals engage in an activity because they find it inherently interesting and enjoyable, is most likely to result in high-quality learning and creativity. This type of motivation promotes greater engagement, effort, and enjoyment compared to extrinsic motivation, where individuals engage in an activity for external rewards or outcomes.

(108) (B) Through continuous feedback and iterative performance discussions.

Agile HR promotes the idea of ongoing and continuous feedback, rather than relying on traditional, infrequent performance reviews. The aim is to have regular, meaningful conversations about performance throughout the year, allowing for real-time adjustments and improvements.

(109) (C) HR becomes more of a facilitator, enabling teams to self-organize and self-manage.

In an Agile environment, the HR department shifts from a controlling role to more of a facilitator role, enabling teams to self-organize and self-manage. They guide the organization in becoming more adaptive, innovative, and resilient, and assist in creating the right conditions for Agile teams to thrive.

(110) (C) Using annual performance reviews to evaluate employees.

One of the key aspects of Agile HR is the shift away from traditional annual performance reviews. Instead, Agile HR focuses on frequent and iterative feedback and development discussions. This helps organizations to be more responsive and adaptive, which is critical in today's fast-paced business environment.

(111) (B) To identify and eliminate waste and reduce variation in HR processes.

The Lean Six Sigma methodology is about eliminating waste (Lean) and reducing process variation (Six Sigma). In the context of HR, it can be used to streamline processes, such as recruitment, onboarding, and benefits administration, thereby increasing efficiency and effectiveness.

(112) (C) Reducing time and errors in the recruitment and hiring process.

Lean Six Sigma can be applied in HR to streamline and improve various processes. One common application is in recruitment and hiring, where Lean Six Sigma can be used to reduce the time taken to fill vacancies and to minimize errors in the process.

(113) (B) Improving processes by focusing on the needs and expectations of the internal and external customers.

A key principle of Lean Six Sigma is to focus on customer value. In HR, this means improving processes based on the needs and expectations of the internal (employees) and external (applicants, regulatory agencies, etc.) customers. This customer-centric focus helps organizations increase efficiency and improve overall quality.

(114) (C) Coercing employees to join the union against their will.

Unions are prohibited from coercing employees to join against their will, which is considered an unfair labor practice under the National Labor Relations Act (NLRA). The right to join a union is a personal decision and should be made voluntarily by employees.

(115) (A) Causing an employer to discriminate against an employee because of his or her union activity.

It is an unfair labor practice for a union to cause or attempt to cause an employer to discriminate against an employee because of his or her union or non-union activity. This includes both pro-union and anti-union activities.

(116) (B) Refuse to bargain collectively with an employer.

Refusing to bargain in good faith with an employer is considered an unfair labor practice committed by a union under the NLRA. The Act requires both employers and unions to bargain in good faith over wages, hours, and other employment conditions.

(117) (C) To administer and enforce the National Labor Relations Act (NLRA).

The National Labor Relations Board (NLRB) is an independent agency of the United States government charged with conducting elections for labor union representation and with investigating and remedying unfair labor practices.

(118) (D) Only private sector employers affecting interstate commerce.

The NLRB has jurisdiction over private sector employers who affect interstate commerce. It does not have jurisdiction over agricultural laborers, those who are employed by a parent or spouse, independent contractors, workers employed by a person who is not an employer, and employees of air and rail carriers covered by the Railway Labor Act.

(119) (C) Enforcing minimum wage laws.

The NLRB's primary responsibilities are to resolve complaints of unfair labor practices, conduct union representation elections, and facilitate settlement of labor disputes. However, enforcing minimum wage laws is outside of its mandate and is the responsibility of the Wage and Hour Division of the Department of Labor.

(120) (C) The voluntary actions taken by a company to improve social conditions.

Philanthropic responsibility refers to corporate actions that are in response to society's expectation that businesses should contribute to improving the quality of life of people and their communities. This is often accomplished through charitable donations, community volunteering, and similar initiatives.

(121) (C) By establishing employee volunteer programs and charitable giving policies.

HR departments can support a company's philanthropic responsibilities by creating and managing programs that encourage and facilitate employee participation in charitable activities. This could include setting up volunteer programs, matching gift programs, and guidelines for charitable activities.

(122) (C) Complying with environmental regulations.

Environmental regulations is an important aspect of corporate responsibility but it falls under the category of legal responsibility rather than philanthropic responsibility. Philanthropic responsibilities are voluntary activities undertaken to improve social conditions, and typically go above and beyond what is legally required.

(123) (B) Mentoring and coaching programs

Mentoring and coaching programs are often the most effective tool for managers. They provide individualized attention, offer immediate feedback, and allow managers to learn in a real-world context from experienced leaders.

(124) (C) Ability to effectively communicate and motivate a team

The ability to effectively communicate and motivate a team is essential for those in managerial positions. Technical skills, marketing strategies, and IT systems knowledge are often important but these can vary greatly by role. On the other hand, strong communication and motivation skills are universally valuable in management.

(125) (A) It ensures they stay informed about industry trends and best practices.

The primary goal of ongoing education for managers is to keep them updated on industry trends, new management techniques, changes in labor laws, and other relevant topics. Ongoing education may also contribute to career advancement and potential salary increases but these are not guaranteed outcomes.

(126) (B) It ensures consistent implementation of policies across different countries.

One of the key roles of global HR management is to ensure the consistency of HR policies and practices across various geographical locations. Having some level of consistency helps maintain company culture, standards, and strategic objectives.

(127) (A) Adjusting HR practices to comply with local labor laws and cultural norms.

One of the main challenges of global HR management is adjusting HR practices to fit within the boundaries of local labor laws and cultural norms while maintaining alignment with global HR strategies. This often requires a deep understanding of different cultures, employment practices, and legal environments.

(128) (C) Implementing global policies while considering local cultural, legal, and market differences.

It is crucial to consider local differences in culture, law, and market conditions. Ignoring these differences can lead to misunderstandings, demotivation, and even legal issues. A balanced approach that respects local differences while maintaining global standards is often most effective.

(129) (B) Financial penalties and reputational damage

Failure to comply with labor laws can lead to financial penalties if the organization is fined by regulatory bodies. Additionally, it can lead to reputational damage if the non-compliance is publicized, which could lead to a loss of customers or difficulty in recruiting quality employees.

(130) (B) By ensuring that the company's policies and procedures are in compliance with all applicable laws and regulations

An important role of HR is to ensure the organization's policies and procedures are in line with all applicable laws and regulations, thereby minimizing the risk of legal non-compliance. This involves staying current with changes in the legal landscape, developing and implementing appropriate policies, and educating managers and employees about these policies.

(131) (B) It can help employees understand their roles and responsibilities in maintaining compliance

One of the most effective ways to ensure compliance is through regular and thorough employee training. Employees need to understand what compliance looks like in their specific roles, the importance of compliance for the organization, and the potential consequences of non-compliance. This helps create a culture of compliance throughout the organization.

(132) (B) HR may need to manage layoffs or workforce reassignments.

During legal restructuring, organizations often need to adjust their workforce. This can involve layoffs, reassignments, and sometimes hiring. HR plays a central role in managing these changes in a way that minimizes legal risks and maintains employee morale.

(133) (A) Failure to provide adequate notice of layoffs under the WARN Act

The Worker Adjustment and Retraining Notification (WARN) Act requires that employers provide 60 days' notice in case of mass layoffs or plant closures. If a company undergoing restructuring fails to provide this notice, it could face legal penalties.

(134) (C) HR should play a critical role in planning and communicating changes, ensuring compliance with employment laws, and addressing employee concerns.

During restructuring, HR can help balance the strategic needs of the company with the rights and concerns of employees. This involves careful planning, clear and compassionate communication, and diligent attention to compliance with all relevant employment laws.

Access the Bonus Audiobook and Flash Cards!

Scan the QR code below with your phone and you will be given a link where you can download the audiobook and flash cards.

If the QR code does not work for you, please contact us at Newstonetestprep.com

Made in the USA
Columbia, SC
15 September 2023

22905571R00280